SOFTIMAGE°|XSI° 5
for a Future Animation Studio Boss

The Official Guide to Career Skills with XSI

George Avgerakis

Tutorials by Tony Johnson

THOMSON

COURSE TECHNOLOGY

Professional ■ Technical ■ Reference

ISBN: 1-59200-846-1
Library of Congress Catalog Card Number: 2005922186
Printed in the United States of America

06 07 08 09 10 PH 10 9 8 7 6 5 4 3 2 1

THOMSON

COURSE TECHNOLOGY

Professional ■ Technical ■ Reference

Thomson Course Technology PTR,
a division of Thomson Course Technology
25 Thomson Place
Boston, MA 02210
http://www.courseptr.com

Publisher and General Manager, Thomson Course Technology PTR:
Stacy L. Hiquet

Associate Director of Marketing:
Sarah O'Donnell

Manager of Editorial Services:
Heather Talbot

Marketing Manager:
Heather Hurley

Executive Editor:
Kevin Harreld

Senior Editor:
Mark Garvey

Marketing Coordinator:
Heather Hurley

Project Editor:
Kezia Endsley

Thomson Course Technology PTR Editorial Services Coordinator:
Elizabeth Furbish

Copy Editor:
Sean Medlock

Interior Layout Tech:
Marian Hartsough

Front Cover Image:
Bryan Eppihimer

Indexer:
Sharon Hilgenberg

Proofreader:
Sara Gullion

To all our sons and daughters
who risk life, limb, and peace of mind
in the defense of our nation,
particularly my daughter, Stephanie,
who will graduate from West Point this spring.

Acknowledgments

This book began at a National Association of Broadcasters convention press party, where my special guest was the most elegant and fetching model and producer, Preeti Shrivastava. Preeti succeeded in capturing the attention of the current honcho of Softimage and telling him that I'd written a book about other animation programs, but not Softimage.

The honcho, considerably distracted by Preeti, then succumbed to my pitch for a Softimage book, but after the party, he reneged on his interest and shortly thereafter, probably by coincidence, departed Softimage.

Jennifer Goldfinch from Softimage's public relations staff responded to my periodic emails attempting to resurrect the NAB deal and eventually, Jennifer introduced me to Kevin Harreld, my indefatigable and incredibly patient editor at Course Technology PTR.

Jennifer also held my hand through the many months of learning Softimage and writing this book. During that time, she secured the dedicated assistance of many Softimage employees (Christine Charette, Genevieve Laberge, and Ron Mannic, most frequently), who kept me equipped with the latest beta versions, tutored me in person and over the phone in many fine points of the software, and answered my hundreds of off-the-wall, often stupid, questions.

This is my first book for Course Technology PTR and I am deeply indebted to and very fond of the staff there who made this book possible. I should admit here and now that Kezia Endsley and Sean Medlock were the two text editors who kept my mother from kvetching for eternity about my never having learned to write a decent English sentence.

One person who worked tirelessly to make this book appealing to every reader who picks it up is Bryan Eppihimer. Bryan designed the cover art for the book, taking patient input from our editors and me, and always producing extraordinary work. Even after a major, last-minute redesign dictated by "powers beyond our control," Bryan kept his cool, took the criticisms (more professionally than I, I might add), and turned in the required revisions in record time.

Although the cover art looks very organic, as if executed in oils or water color, Bryan does all of his work using 3D animation programs. He builds the scene, populates it with creatures both human and inhuman, and props it with the skill of a magazine cover photographer or fine artist.

If you would like to see more from this talented young man, I suggest you visit his Web site, bryaneppihimer.com. Pay particular attention to his work, "Temptation of Eve," which, for obvious reasons, is my favorite piece in this gallery.

And then there's the acknowledgment that begins with, "This book would not have been possible without . . ." That honor belongs to Tony Johnson, about whom more follows.

About the Author

GEORGE AVGERAKIS is VP Creative Director and co-founder of Avetka Productions Inc. (www.avekta.com) in New York City, a company that produces video, CD, DVD, Web site content, and print in English and all foreign languages. Educated at the University of Maryland and London Film School, Mr. Avgerakis produced the first co-production between Public Television and a corporate entity, the first Russian infomercial and the first pilot for an American-made sitcom for the ex-Soviet states. His clients include AOL Time Warner, Bristol-Myers Squibb, JVC, Forbes, HP, Brink's, Microsoft, Avid, IBM, and Pfizer.

George began producing animation for clients in 1982, beginning with the domestic and international broadcast logos for his client, Bristol Myers. Until 1991 he supervised many animation assignments for such clients as Dracket, Texaco, Ricoh, DEC, and Sandoz using the Dubner and Bosch FGS 4000 rigs. After purchasing the first NewTek Video Toaster in New York in 1991, George became a beta tester for that product's LightWave software. Later, he wrote the animation documentation for Touchvision's D-Vision system. Since the mid-1990s, George has supervised animation, using virtually all of the leading animation programs, often using more than one program to complete an assignment.

George has served as Contributing Editor to *Videography, Studio Monthly*, and *Digital Cinema* magazines. He also writes occasionally for *Forza*, the magazine about Ferrari. George has lectured at the University of Maryland, London University, CUNY, Iona College, and DVExpos East and West. He is the chairperson of the Business Track lectures at the National Association of Broadcasters (NAB) conventions in Las Vegas and New York. He is author of *Desktop Video Studio Bible—Producing Video, DVD, and Web Sites for Profit* and *Digital Animation Bible: Creating Professional Animation with 3ds Max, LightWave, and Maya*, from McGraw-Hill. More information on George's books with chapter excerpts and helpful links may be found at www.spectra-ny.com.

George lives in Westchester County, New York, with his wife, Maria, and an ever growing collection of classic automobiles. In their spare time, George and Maria restore and manage residential real estate.

About Your Tutor, Hamilton "Tony" Johnson

Tony wrote the up-to-date tutorials you find throughout this book. He was originally trained in traditional theater as a lighting, sound, and technical director. In the mid-80s, while attending the Yale School of Drama, he discovered that there were students in the Architecture school next door using computers to create three-dimensional wire-frame buildings. The seed was planted! In the early '90s, he opened his first computer graphics company with a massive workstation containing the unheard of amount of 8 MB of RAM; he was off to the races. Since then, he has been the president of two animation studios on Long Island—*Hamiltoonz*, which closed its doors in 2001 and the newly opened *Searight Studios*. He has been a certified Softimage instructor since 1996 and currently teaches classes at Future Media Concepts and the Fashion Institute of Technology in New York City.

If you like Tony's tutorials in this book, you can find more at www.softimage.com or www.XSIbase.com. Another site for which Tony contributes, www.edharriss.com, is dedicated to providing useful tutorials to Softimage animators. This site is sponsored by Ed Harriss, a major animation producer, from whom you can also learn a great deal.

But just in case you haven't met Tony or seen him lecture, here's a photo of him. If you see him for real, ask him to autograph the book!

Contents

Chapter 6 **Just In Time: Adding the Aspects of a Timeline, Keyframes, and Motion to Your Animation Project** **155**

Chapter 7 **Bowling for Dollars** **187**

Chapter 8   **Bones and Skeletons:
Imparting Objects with the Ability
to Move and Deform** **227**

Chapter 9   **Showtime! Presentations to Employers
and Clients** **247**

Introduction

What You'll Find in This Book

I sat down and thought about what specific skills you would need to get your first job as an animator. This task was similar to planning for a shipwreck, where one decides what essential survival tools one will take on the life raft and what, for not overloading the raft, one will have to sacrifice. What animation skills would you need, given that I couldn't offer you them all?

First, you have to learn the interface of Softimage. Then you have to learn the basic tools. Then, most important, you have to make a *showreel*—a video presentation of what you can do—so that a potential employer can see it and determine your probability of being a billable worker. Eventually, you will need some advanced skills, both to polish up your showreel, and to apply yourself to advanced animation duties, like building and applying choreographic attributes to a character.

This book is like the fingers of two hands, interlaced. The left hand's fingers are tutorials, dedicated to starting you off as an animator in SOFTIMAGE|XSI. The right hand's fingers are the business aspects of what you must learn to get an internship, build a showreel, get a real paying job, and then start and manage your own animation studio.

All of the tutorials are very easy and can be executed using the free downloadable version of Softimage Foundation. We even show you how to download the free version!

Eventually, you will need to purchase Softimage, but if you work fast, you may finish the tutorials before you accomplish the odd chapters' destiny of making yourself a professional. That's okay. We understand you are probably more interested in learning the software than getting a job. We're the same way. (Well, Tony is— I love making cold calls!)

Who This Book Is For

This book is intended for beginners. If you look forward to being a great animation artist *and* a business owner, this book is for you.

There are many books about Softimage, and virtually every other leading animation program. There are very few, perhaps no books on Softimage for a novice.

There are very few books to teach animators how to get a job as an animator. *How to Get a Job in Computer Animation* by Ed Harriss is very, very good.

So this book's goal is to introduce you, the novice reader, to Softimage and then to coach you through the process of getting your first job all the way to starting your own animation studio. I think that this book, therefore, is unique. If you are just graduating from high school or college, and wondering if animation is for you, this is just the book to test yourself. It is my hope you will own it for many years, and refer to it as you climb the ladder that leads to success in our mystic circle.

Although I lecture at colleges and universities, I am not an academician. I write like I speak, coloring my text with snide remarks, witless humor, and thinly veiled social commentary. At work, Tony Johnson and I always have an intern or two working through their early stages of learning. It is from them whom we learn what needed to go into this book.

No one in today's business world can afford the time to oversee interns and beginners. Such people, therefore, are given an envelope of responsibility and expected to make many mistakes. By staying within the envelope, the mistakes remain harmless to the business and educational to the intern.

So one could say this book was created by interns for interns. We hope you enjoy it.

How This Book Is Organized

I know an animator from Peru, Renzo Signori, who frequently uses the Spanish word, "maniaco" (maniacal) to describe the mindset of the average animator. I can walk into Renzo's studio at 8AM and find him, bleary eyed, a three-day growth of whiskers on his face, empty bottles of Inca Cola rolling around his bare feet, his girlfriend and animation partner Sophie, asleep, her face plastered to the monitor screen with "baba." Renzo will notice me after a few moments and as if in explanation for all of the mess, simply say, "Maniaco, eh?"

Maniaco is a state of mind and soul. Animators have truly maniaco personalities. It is not uncommon to see an animator burning through Costco sized bags of Doritos at 4 in the morning, desperately trying to capture a certain kind of reflection, like an arcade video game freak with a trunk full of quarters.

The secret of this book actually, is that it is cleverly designed for the maniaco mentality. We give you a taste of Softimage—a tutorial—and then make you work through a chapter of business tutorials (dedicated to making sure you start making a living), before giving you the next XSI taste.

You'll soon notice, then, that the even number chapters of this book are mostly Softimage tutorials. The odd chapters are mostly business.

Because you are most probably going to want to dive into the software and try to learn everything in one, sleepless binge, the business chapters are to throw a little cold water in your face, and wake you up to reality.

We also added in some humorous tweaks, like our Mom and Dad sidebars, that goad you along as if your folks were actually nagging you. Who knows, maybe they really are! And of course, there are Tony's Tips—clever workarounds and solutions that you can apply in XSI to give yourself that extra professional's edge that is hard to find outside of a live class.

That's our hope, really; that you experience this book as if it was a live class being run by Tony and I, tag-teaming you in a relentless pursuit of fun and profit.

We hope you enjoy this unique layout and since you are probably the first person on your block to have this book, we'd appreciate it if you told your friends.

Icons Used in This Book

Throughout the book, you'll see special elements and icons we've developed to indicate tips, sidebars, and other elements outside of the norm of the regular text.

KEY POINT

A key point is an important tip or a piece of information that you really want to remember—perhaps the basic idea to walk away with as you are reading this particular section.

Sometimes you'll see humorous banter from "your" Dad, Mom, and spouse throughout the book. It's just placed to help break the mood a bit, so you can relax, laugh, and ground yourself.

TONY'S TIP

A Tony's Tip sidebar includes special helpful tips from the venerable Tony Johnson, who wrote the tutorials in this book. In these tips, you can benefit from Tony's considerable experience in the industry.

Note from the Author

Hello. My name is George Avgerakis and I am an addict. I have been "clean" now for about 10 years, so you can trust me—sort of—not to steal the money in your wallet or hijack your car. I will, however, gladly accept my humble share of the price of this book, even though there is a good chance you are an addict too, and maybe you stole it.

This world is full of addictive behaviors and addicts who misbehave. This book is dedicated to one such group of addicts known as *computer animators*. Just like coke or heroin addicts, computer animators get their start with that famous "free taste." In schoolyards all across the country, our kids are innocently approached by their teachers: "Hey, Jimmy, have a look at this computer screen! It's just like a Game Boy." And wham, before they know it, Mom is screaming at them, "James! You've been at that screen for 18 straight hours and your dog has crapped all over the living room!"

As I said, I've been clean for 10 years. I am no longer a full-time animator. In fact, I don't really animate much at all anymore. What I do is *produce* animation. I am an Animation Producer, and I make a very good living and have a lot of fun doing it.

Producing animation means that I find people who want to *buy* animation, and then I *sell* it to them. In-between finding the buyer and selling the animation, I have to *listen* to what the buyer desires, *interpret* those desires in terms of animation, *present* my interpretation of those desires creatively and economically, *close the deal* by way of a contract, *allocate* the labor into various tasks, *hire* competent animators and other craftspeople, *manage* the various tasks and craftspeople to execute the project within the budget, *direct* the project to its conclusion, *pay* the craftspeople their wages so that none go away dissatisfied, *deliver* the project to the buyer, and *collect* payment for the project from the buyer. Whew! Being a recovered addict is no easy job.

Obviously, this is a lot more work than simply creating an animation with SOFTIMAGE|XSI! And yet, this complicated process is completely explained in this book, with the explicit intention of teaching you how to become an Animation Producer. You see, if I'm going to be responsible for getting you addicted to animation, I believe it is my responsibility to show you the whole life—that is, the road to recovery. Then, years later when you're strung out on Cheetos and reheated frijoles burritos, and your dog's morning messages have ossified into white pebbles across the living room carpet, you'll have a way out of your sorry mess.

So take heed now. You needn't spend your entire life as an enslaved computer geek. The shivering meniscus between your eyeballs and the computer screen can be severed, and you can learn how to actually make a living as an animator! That's what makes this book unique.

There are many, many books available on the market to teach you how to animate. There are even quite a few that teach you how to animate in Softimage. There is only one book, however, that can teach you how to animate in Softimage *and* how to make a living as an animator in Softimage. And you are holding that book.

This book is intended for the novice animator. You could be a brilliant high school student searching for the perfect combination of fun and work—kind of like playing a video game and getting paid for it. You could be a college student, searching for the perfect course that will carry you from academia into the business world with hardly a burp of transition—kind of like graduating from West Point with a five-year contract with the U.S. Army as a Second Lieutenant (but a lot safer). Or you could be out of school entirely, maybe even suffering a midlife crisis, and wondering what else you can do in life that will allow you to be creatively employed.

If you're any of these three types of people and you're not already an animator, this book is for you. If you're already an animator . . . hmmm . . . there might still be something here for you.

So, you are holding a book that offers you the opportunity to be a *professional* animator. Does that mean you already *are* a professional Softimage animator? No, of course not.

Many people will pick up this book. Some of them will read it—cover to cover! Some will even start out doing the exercises. But only a small percentage of those who buy this book will read it *and* do all the exercises. I don't know why this is. Maybe their desire to be successful professional animators is completely satisfied somewhere before the process is complete. Maybe these people will read the book, try one exercise, and then say, "Well, that was great. I'm happy."

Good. I enjoy making people happy. But I enjoy making professional animators happy even more. That's why I took time away from being an Animation Producer to teach you about it in this book. It makes me really, really happy to meet a professional animator with a huge showreel full of really cool animations and an investment portfolio full of valuable commodities, and for that animator to tell me, "I read your book. It helped me be what I am today."

Therefore, I urge you to read the whole book and do all the exercises, especially the ones that seem stupid or the ones you hate doing, like making phone calls to promote yourself. Selling animation is clearly the hardest part of your future job. But really, it only takes one good sale to put you on an endless road of greater and greater successes. I know this to be true, and you must believe me. After all, as I write this, I am 56 years old and have been happily selling my creative animated visions since 1984 (long before Softimage existed), enjoying every minute of the job, and intending to keep on doing this until "worms play pinochle on my snout." Wouldn't you like to be able to say that in the future? And you, lucky dude (or dudette), won't have to bungle with primitive 1984 animation systems costing upwards of $250,000 (and those are 1984 dollars). You'll have the most powerful software on the planet, which you can buy for under a thousand dollars, and the most powerful computers necessary, which you can buy for under two thousand dollars. Boy, that makes me want to go out there and start all over again!

George Avgerakis, New York, NY
November 2005

P.S. Years of experience have taught me that every addict needs a co-dependent. No doubt, if you're getting into this business, someone is going to be your co-dependent. (You might even have two!) Maybe it's your dad or mom, or your spouse. Just to make things interesting, I've added some imaginary comments from these people into the text of this book. Occasionally, you hear some plaintive pleas from your spouse, your dad, or — bless her caustic little heart—your mom. Don't be too worried about what they say. Hey, if you were worried about them, you wouldn't be getting into this business!

Chapter 1

A Typical Day in the Life of an Animator

Let's visualize the life you will lead. Hey, this is an easy one. Fantasize about your life as a professional animator. Let's start off like this: You're in a car—a racy, two-seater sports model. You pull up to the studio door and step into your work environment. What do you picture?

Right now, before you read another paragraph, make two columns on a sheet of paper. At the top of the left column, write "Things I like about my job." In the right column, write "Things I hate about my job." Now, pretending you are already a professional Softimage animator, fill in at least five things under each column.

Continue reading after you've done the exercise.

I made a list like this once. I was stuck, trying to decide if I wanted to give up my job and take the risk of starting my own company, or stay in my job and enjoy a predictable, secure life. To become, as they say, a "lifer." My wife was pregnant with our first kid. I had just bought a dilapidated Brooklyn brownstone rooming house with the intention of renovating it into a four-apartment condominium.

My love/hate list was my attempt to graphically outline my state of mind and what I was going to do, sooner or later, to straighten it out. I wrote the list on the wall of my bathroom, just before I covered it with sheetrock and covered that with tile. At the time, I was a full-time employee of Nabisco, running their in-house video department. It was 1982 and I was fed up. So under the "Things I hate" column, I wrote:

1. Mickey Mouse work. (I had to do everything from schlepping projectors to meetings to making PBS documentaries.)
2. Low pay. (Even then, $26,000 a year with benefits was low pay—now it's what I spend in a month.)
3. Driving 45 minutes to work and back every day. (If I had the Ferrari then, things might have been different.)
4. Putting up with incompetent associates. (I was cocky then. I didn't realize these people were the best I would ever get.)
5. Working for The Man every night and day. (It's a Credence Clearwater, '70s kind of thing.)

Under the "Things I like" column, I wrote:

1. Regular paycheck. Kid on the way.
2. Expressing my creativity every day.
3. Regular paycheck. Kid on the way.

And then I stared at the list for about an hour. I had lunch there, munching my sandwich and staring at the list. And then, I tossed the Tropicana carton across the room and circled the item "Mickey Mouse work." That was the thing that tipped the balance. I covered up the wall with sheetrock, and as I pounded each nail in place, I resolved to form my own company and never work at a full-time job again. That list is still there behind the second floor bathroom wall at 386 State Street, and I'm still running my own company. Now let's look at your list and see if we can't straighten out your life.

Okay. I'm not concerned with the things you like. I know what those are already. After all, fantasies are make-believe. They are full of things you like and rarely include things you don't. Reality is different. Years from now, I hope you still have the list you just made. It will be interesting to see if, after you have fulfilled your fantasy, there are any things about the job you hate, and if those things are the same things you wrote down today.

But for now, let's look at what you wrote in the "hate" column. Your goal, over the next few months, is to tackle that list honestly. If you wrote "looking for a job," for instance, I want you to make "looking for a job" one of your top priorities. You should start thinking about all the things you need to do before you go looking for a job: writing a resume, making a list of possible employers, making calls, etc.

If you wrote "reading books about animating," you should spend some extra time reading such books.

The reason I am asking you to concentrate first on the "hated" parts of your fantasy is that at this moment, those are the things that will keep you from making the first step toward success. After all, those were the things you imagined even before you had your first real experience as an animator! Later, you will come up against *real* issues that you will hate. What will you do then? Sit down and cry? No! You will remember the silly things that scared you on your first day and say, "Damn. This is nothing! I can lick this!" And you will.

Now let me tell you how it really is. Sit back and relax while I mix about six or seven real people's career stories together into a sort of a "Day in the Life of a Real Animation Production Studio."

You hang your car keys on the bracket that holds up your bookshelf, wondering for a moment if the weight will finally break the back of whole office cubicle and bury you in a pile of software documentation and plastic action figures. It's 10:30 in the morning. Only one other animator is working—Andy, who always wears fresh clothes to work, arrives at 9 a.m. sharp, and leaves at 6 p.m. with all his work done. Andy is the new guy.

Your computer is already on, in sleep mode. It never gets shut off. You nudge the mouse to activate the monitor and see that 7,200 frames of your animation were rendered during the night. A command prompt system window message from BatchRender says "Render Completed." With a satisfied grunt, you lean over the keyboard and tap out the code that will send the frames to your Technical Director (TD) for review. Then, it's off to the coffee room for your first morning brew.

In the coffee room, Suzy, the TD, is writing with a dry marker on a large whiteboard, which is divided up like a calendar. "You got my foreground sequence?" she asks.

"Yeah, done," you reply.

What you were doing up until this morning was creating and animating a short five-minute scene for an upcoming movie about a popular children's doll that has started a suburban dance club. The doll has gathered some friends in her backyard to teach them some dance steps.

For the past four months, you've been copying hand drawings of characters into your computer system. This process is creative, but a bit tedious. Your job isn't to impart your own creativity into the computer model of the doll character; your job is to precisely impart the creativity of the sketch artist (who happens to be your boss) into the computer. *Your* creativity is to make the doll look as good in 3D as the boss made it look in 2D. That means "good" from every possible camera angle and every possible pose. This is called *modeling*.

If you were in business for yourself, son, you'd be doing the sketches *and* the modeling. Then you'd be making double money. That's why you should have spent more time in those live sketch classes I paid for at Pratt!

Your next job, which takes about a week for each doll, is adding devices to each doll (called bones and control objects) that constrain the shapes of the doll's body and movement of the doll's joints to allow it to move like a human. This is called *rigging* the character.

Last week you showed your rigged models to your boss and his clients.

"They dance a little weird," said the client. Indeed, the little stuffed bear was breaking a mean funk that had been captured from a drunk Fly Girl wannabe who the guys at the MIT media lab had kidnapped from a Roxbury strip club.

Your boss moved up to cover for you. "It's swiped code, Josh. We have to do our own mocap yet."

"Oh yeah," said Josh, chewing on his big capitalist cigar as you, remembering what your spouse said that morning, kept judiciously silent.

Remember, dear, you're just the senior animator, not the studio boss or technical director. Keep your mouth shut and listen, listen, listen. And don't forget to take notes, dear. You always forget what they tell you, right?

With the models and rigging approved, two weeks ago you met some dancers in a large room of your company's studio, serving as a stage. You know nothing about dance, so a choreographer was there to show the dancers the moves. Your job was to run a motion capture system, known as *mocap*.

Before you came on the stage, one of your assistants dressed the dancers in black Spandex leotards and attached small white ping-pong balls to all the dancers' joints. These balls assisted the eight special cameras mounted around the room's walls, which would capture the motion of the dancers and translate that motion into computer code.

By the end of the day, you had all the mocap code you needed to animate the six dolls in your scene. By applying the code from each dancer, you gave the dolls the dance moves of the human dancers. It's like in *The Matrix*, when Trinity learned how to fly a B-212 helicopter.

Soon, you had the dolls dancing in a kind of cute way, with just a little bit of soul. There was no problem getting enthusiastic support from your managers and the client to finish the scene. A few weeks of tweaking the motion, lighting, and textures, and you were ready for the render that began at sundown last night.

Now, Big Suzy is examining your frame sequence on her terminal in the corner office. If she likes what she sees, your frames will be scheduled for transfer to Mitch, the *composite* guy. Mitch's job is to take your dancing dolls, which were rendered with a blank background (what we call an *alpha channel*), and paste them over the background scenes of the playground. On top of these scenes, Mitch will paste foreground elements, like a passing firetruck, that other animators were responsible for creating. This is called *compositing*.

You are the master of character modeling and rigging. You are da man. You make big bucks and get to put your feet on Big Suzy's desk and—"Hey!" It's Big Suzy leaning precariously on the wobbly side of your cubicle. "Yank up Frame 785. Ya got a hole in your main character's kneecap."

"Bugger," you reply, bringing up the frame in question. Sure enough, there's a small black triangle in your main character's knee, a mistake you must correct before compositing. Is it a small bug or a big bug? You don't want to ask Big Suzy, but she knows.

"How many frames?", you ask her.

"Sixty. In three sequences. Here's the list." Suzy is maniacal in her precision. She has little Bug Reports sheets printed up with the logo of a RAID can on top, on which she's printed a report listing your bad frames. (Jeez, what makes that woman tick?) This is called *tweaking the render*. Cynically, you call it *tweaking the TD*.

This bug will take most of your morning to fix and re-render. The coffee is already cold. You head back to nuke it and start your work. It's just another day at the image factory. Animation is a consuming profession. As one Los Angeles veteran says, "It eats you up alive."

The Passion

Every day it gets easier and easier to get hooked on animation. The computer software that is used to create the most sophisticated effects and character scenes gets easier to learn and cheaper to buy. As early as high school, you might get a chance to play with a "light" version of a program, or even the real, full-blown release. Or maybe you'll get to visit an animation studio during a vacation tour in Orlando or New York.

Let's say some mentor sits you down at a workstation, called a *seat*, and shows you how to pull a sphere into the shape of a funny rabbit. Simple. You probably remember this stuff from geometry class, except it wasn't as easy to understand as this animation stuff. Then, the mentor adds the dimension of time by placing the object in one place onscreen at Frame 1 and another place onscreen at Frame 30. For fun, the mentor selects Frame 30 and asks you to make a change to the way the rabbit sits. Thinking that you can fool the system, you screw around with the controls, and the rabbit ends up like Dennis Quaid in the movie *Inner Space,* all twisted and jumping around.

Nonplussed, the mentor smiles and hits a button. Instantly, the computer makes 28 new frames between Frames 1 and 30, responding exactly as your outrageous precocity dictated. Miracle of miracles! Automatically, the computer starts playing the frames in a continuous loop. This is so cool.

Is the machine goofing on you? It's like those video games that eat your quarters and precious self-esteem as you try to prove that wetware is superior to hardware. Yes! Yes, it is like that, but better. This is free. No quarters. Better yet, they say if you're good enough, you can get paid to do this.

"Once more," you plead, taking the mouse in your hand. But the mentor is pressed for time. You have to move on. The tour proceeds. But you are hooked.

The endorphins that flooded your cerebral cortex wrote a note to be read later, when you were faced with a decision between computer camp and basketball camp, or when your Mom offered to let you spend the weekend with an uncle in the animation business (unlike that other uncle she won't let you visit, no way, no how), or when you had a hole in your curriculum and needed to fill it with an easy elective course. The note says, "Pay attention, Bucko. If anyone ever says the words 'computer animation' and offers you a chance to make that funny rabbit bounce around again—take it."

The Pay

Working as an animator—or in practically any other creative enterprise—can be a joyful experience. The pure satisfaction of working at a job that you really enjoy is the best thing in life. Very, very few people get to do this. After my dad retired, for instance, he often commented that during the last 22 years of his job, he hated every day he went to work. Imagine the horror of that. Well, that's what most people do. You, you lucky dog, you're getting into a job where after a decade, you'll still be able to count on one hand the number of days you didn't want to go to work.

Sounds like a free lunch, doesn't it? And you know what they say about a free lunch, right? There's no such thing. So where do you end up paying for your lunch?

The scene I sketched earlier, where you worked on the doll animation project, was taken from real life. What I failed to illustrate, however, was the other half. I just showed you the glamorous half, where everyone works long hours doing really interesting stuff, having creative, challenging fun. These people—and you too, I would bet—could easily be convinced to do this work for free. Well, maybe not free, but say if I covered your rent, paid your grocery bill, and threw in a few bucks for movie tickets and an occasional checkup at the doc, you'd probably say, "Hell, yes. Gimme that."

Well, the bosses in the animation profession know this. They know you'll come begging for a job as soon as you finish your showreel. They know you don't mind working all night long to perfect a scene. They know you have nothing else to do when you're addicted to this animation thing. And, well, even though the bosses may not be mean or exploitive, you can't blame them for taking advantage of a good thing. They get the contracts—you do the work. They get the money—you get a share.

How much of a share? Well, that's hard to say. Nobody wants you to know. You could be making $20–$50 an hour as an animator and feeling really content. Would you be angry to know that every hour you work on the terminal, your boss is making double, triple, quadruple what you are making? No? It doesn't bother you? Okay, fine. You can come work for me. I pay the animators exactly one half what I bill for their work—and that's a pretty fair deal. After all, I go out and find the clients, close the deals, and do the basic creative work. I feel I deserve the other half. *But you could get that half too*, and still have a great time at work.

If you're happy with just half (or less) of what you could be making, save yourself the time. Don't read the parts of this book that show you how to become a studio boss.

Young people don't concern themselves too much with material things (probably because most come from families that have taken care of them for many years). But once you get into your 30s, get a mate, and maybe start thinking about buying a house or having a kid, you suddenly look up from the computer screen and say, "Hey, damn. I'm still broke."

Older folks, changing careers in midlife, usually change because they are fed up with chasing the almighty buck and now want to do something for pleasure. They, too, often don't think about the money angle as they dive into the joys of a creative profession. They get onto a fun new career path, and then one day, they wake up and find the repo man taking away the SUV, or their spouse packing bags and talking to a lawyer on the cell phone.

Whether you're younger or older, you would be cheating yourself big-time if you didn't explore both the *creative* and the *business* aspects of the animation profession. I just couldn't let you make that mistake. So please, please, keep one eye on the animation console and the other on the phone, because *at the phone* is where you are going to make sure that every hour you spend *on the computer* is going to put the maximum number of dollars in your pocket.

So, with that in mind, you can see that the fantasy scene I sketched for you earlier is not quite complete. It has you doing all the cool creative stuff, but it doesn't show you making any money.

Now, I know you may not be convinced about the reality of what I am going to show you, so let's look at two versions. Version 1 is what happens more often.

It's now the end of the day, and, aren't you lucky, it's payday. Annette, the perky young assistant to the bookkeeper, drops by your desk on her way out for a fun weekend of surfing and raves. You are still noodling with the hole in the doll's knee, and it will be way past midnight before you're done. You don't mind, though. And hey, what's this? A pay envelope! Goody. Rent's due.

You tear open the envelope and look at the check. There it is—a whopping 65 hours in two weeks. Ouch! And yep, there's your hourly rate, $50! Yummy. And there's the total gross bi-weekly pay, $3,250. Wow!

But what's this? FICA deduction? That's social security, mate. For when you are a fat old geezer. Minus $201.50 for FICA. And what's this? Federal withholding tax, no dependents? Of *course* you don't have dependents; you aren't even dating anyone because you're working so late. Minus $678.26. In the next box there's another minus for Medicare—healthcare for when you're over 65? Minus $47.13 (a bargain). And oh yes, state (minus $188.98 for New York State), and city (New York City) withholding tax (minus $110.86). And now you see the final amount of money you're actually going to put in your checking account: $2,023[1]. Bummer. Oh well, back to the hole in the knee. Shucks. *Mucho trabajo, poco dinero.*

But as you work, in the back of your mind, further deductions are going on. Rent on your apartment: $750 for the last two weeks. Health insurance: $800 for the last two weeks (you've got food allergies—you need that health insurance). Electric, phone, and home DSL: $300. By the time you pay all the bills, you'll have a net of $173 and change for rest and relaxation. But your Dad was telling you something last week at Thanksgiving . . .

---

[1]These figures were kindly calculated by my own accountant, Eli Levine of Eli Levine & Co., New York, NY, based on current withholding tax guidelines for a non-married, salaried individual working in New York City. The total bi-weekly "tax hit" is a whopping $1,226.73! And you say you're apolitical and don't vote?

Son, you're making some serious money now, and I'm proud of you. But you should be thinking about building a nest egg. You know, some money set aside for buying a house . . . or . . . well, you know, when you're too old to work. Social Security ain't going to be paying you squat when you turn 65.

Dad has a point. Every Joe Schmoe over 30 out there in the workplace is socking a little away for those sunset years. And every Suzy Schmoe is doing the same to buy that little cottage with the white picket fence. Heck, she can't count on her boyfriend having that kind of cash.

So what are you going to do with that $173 remaining out of your 65-hour paycheck?

Man, this is depressing. Let's switch to Version 2 before you throw this book across the room.

Version 2 takes us around the corner and behind the tightly closed doors of your studio boss.

If you want, you can imagine the Hollywood version—a fat guy in a suit, cigar chomped in his jaw, fat fingers with pinky rings. But hey, Hollywood's image of capitalism is way out of date. This isn't *Little Orphan Annie* here.

I want you to imagine the studio boss as a guy or gal just like you. Okay, put a few years on yourself, but still dressed in an Ecko sweatshirt. The Mets baseball hat is turned sideways. The jeans have holes in the knees (but they're tailored holes). Bare feet (neatly pedicured, by the way) are on the desk. A Plantronics phone device dangles from one ear. Get the picture? This is a person *just like you*. The only difference is that the boss already owns the Z Car free and clear, as well as a condo in the city and a country house. Vacations in Belize and Zermat.

Do you want to be like the boss? Do you want to know how the boss's day goes? Here's a taste. You're the boss, and at the moment, you're on the phone talking to your banker. There's this problem. You've got a contract from a major studio to crank out 20 scenes for a new feature film. The contract is like money in the bank, but not exactly. Like all good production contracts, it pays a third of the total price up front, but the second third comes in after your studio delivers 3D motion samples—in other words, three-quarters of the way through the job. You don't have enough money to pay your staff for the time it's going to take to get to the second payment. And even it you did, you'd have no cash left in the bank to cover contingency expenses, like the cost of another project if it comes in, or even the heat if oil prices go up (and as you know, they just did).

So right now, you're trying to "sell your paper." This means you give the banker your contract, and in return you get all the money up front, immediately. Nice. The only catch is, the bank wants to take out something like 12% for their cut. In other words, the bank waits until you finish the job and then collects from your client when the job is done. This isn't such a bad deal. The percentage being offered is reasonable. The problem is, you bid the job so tight that a 12% fee leaves you with very little profit. So as you try to trim the fee to 10% or 11%, you are doodling on your computer screen, trying to see if Big Suzy can also trim some detail from the 3D models so that it won't take your staff so long to create the final result.

The banker doesn't budget on the percentage, but you figure out some cool routine for cutting 20% of the cost of rigging the characters. You close the deal with the banker and slip on your shoes. Out in the bullpen, your animators type a bit faster, knowing you're on the prowl. You come up to Big Suzy and show her your notes.

"Look, Suze," you say, "Can we employ some VBScript or JScript to cut down on our rigging time?"

"This is for that new feature contract we just closed?", asks Big Suzy, demonstrating the uncanny wisdom you hired her for. *With brains like this*, you wonder, *how long will it be before she's running Big Suzy Animations, Inc?* You make a mental note to raise her profit sharing in the new year. You can't lose Big Suzy now.

"Yeah," you reply, and gaze into Suzy's face as she scans your code. Is she suitably impressed? Suzy whistles through her teeth, and you know you still have the chops to out-animate anybody in the bullpen. But you're getting old. Next March, you turn 30. It'll take more than brilliant code to impress Suzy, and you wonder how the hell you're going to keep up with the creative stuff when you have to do the sales, financing, and run the company at the same time.

"This will work," says Suzy, smiling. "We can trim about 15% from the rigging schedule." *Good*, you think, *I just made back the 12% banker's fee.*

"I gotta get on the sales machine until 2," you tell Suzy. "I'm yours after that."

"Yours" means that after 2, you become one of Big Suzy's rank-and-file animators. Suzy manages labor, and you plug in under Suzy's lead whenever you can to save money. It also keeps you sharp, and while you still have the chops, it impresses the hell out of the brilliant youngsters you've hired to keep your shop cutting-edge. One day, you know you'll no longer have the time to "plug in under Suzy," nor will it serve any economic advantage. But for now, it's a jolt and you love it.

You leave Suzy to her devices and head back to your office. It's 10:30, and you've got an hour and half until all your clients go to lunch. You fire up the ACT! program on your computer and minimize Softimage. Clicking the daily schedule, you see you've got 22 calls scheduled for yesterday, 10 from the day before, and 20 more for today. You'll never get to them all, so you focus on the hot leads.

"Hi!", you chirp into some suit's voicemail, "This is Mimi Slang from Slang Studios. I'm calling you personally to offer our services as CGI specialists on your new feature film, *Go to Hell in a Handbag*. We just finished six sequences for *Life Bandits* that *Hollywood Reporter* called 'The best effects for an independent feature we've seen this year.' To put it short and sweet, Bill, I want your CGI contract, and I'll do whatever it takes to make you scream 'Yes, yes, yes!' Call me."

One down, 42 to go. By noon, you've made 23 calls and spoken to four people. One asked for your reel. One made an appointment to meet you. Two said they already had a favorite studio lined up, thank you very much. Not bad. One appointment a week is your average. It's all you need.

Feeling satisfied, you head out for lunch. On the way, you notice that Juan in the editing room is looking depressed. His girlfriend left him because he spends too much time at work. Although you planned to have lunch with your mother, you stop to call her and push that lunch to the weekend. You take Juan to Chez Blatzah. He's so impressed, he hits on the waitress—and scores. Hell, they both work weird hours. It might work.

Back at the office, you open Softimage again and start creating a new monster. This one has been invading your dreams for the last two weeks. The monster is called Go For Broke. Although your studio grossed $2.3 million dollars last year, your take-home pay, after taxes, was $252,000. Your college roommate, who took a job as a studio boss, is earning twice that much in her bonus alone. Life is good, but it could be better. How could it be better? If you could sell a concept of your own to the networks and be a show creator. Kids like monsters. They like video games. Go For Broke is a monster that never has enough energy to kill—so he's always just barely dangerous and always hungry. The concept is urban and edgy. The game value is good. A feature film or Saturday morning serial will kick it all off. What kind of skin should this guy have? Slimy and dripping pus, or dry and flaky, like psoriasis?

By 9 p.m., you're beat and hungry for dinner. Things are just getting warmed up in the bullpen. Most of the late risers are just getting their lunch glucose fits.

"Hey, everybody," you yell through your open office door, "Is it pizza or Chinese?"

End of fantasy. Now I ask you, which lifestyle suits your self image? The worker bee or the queen bee? The hourly slave or the banker's slave? As Dylan says, "You gotta serve *somebody*." Hell, man, it doesn't matter right now. What matters is that you've actually read this far and both lifestyles appeal to you. If so, that's good. You're just starting out. You have no choice but to enter this profession—this craft—at the bottom. (Unless you're from a rich family, but even then it's best to start at the bottom.) Little by little, you'll learn the tricks of the trade as fancifully described in Version 1. But don't forget Version 2. Life doesn't end at 25, when you're working 18 hours a day for big bucks and noodling away at Softimage in a Benedictine monk's delirious rapture.

I'm here to take you from the basics of Version 1 to the operating manual of Version 2 in 12 chapters. Along the way, you're going to have some exercises to do. I'm going to help you build your resume and your showreel. I'm going to send you out on your first job interview. I'm going to show you what to write, how to talk, and what to do to make a successful career in animation—if you really want it. If you like, you can follow the schedule in the Appendix and actually see your career form before your eyes as if by magic. But it won't be magic. It'll just be common sense, applied diligently and lubricated by your unique talent (which, in reality, is the least important element of all—sorry to say).

Truth be told, there are a lot of bosses out there with no talent whatsoever as animators. (Sometimes, I am sure I am one of them.) It's the talent of *presenting yourself as a talent* that counts most in attaining material success, and if this book teaches you nothing but that, you will have added seven zeroes to your investment. Incidentally, spiritual success is not going to be left by the curb in this book. I've seen what happens when the spiritual precedes the material. It's not a pretty sight. So let's try to give you a house of your own, a nice car in the garage, a happy spouse, educated kids, and a white picket fence around a well-trimmed lawn, and *then* we'll talk about inner joy, bliss, and how that fuzz gets in your belly button.

A Note About Common Sense

This is my third book. I've carefully read the Internet reviews of my first two to see what I could learn to make this book better. Every criticism but one will be dealt with here, to make this book the best so far. However, except for this note, I will ignore one of the criticisms I've received repeatedly: a lot of my writing is "nothing more than common sense."

You see, I noticed that the people making this criticism already had a lot of common sense themselves. That's probably why they discounted the value of *my* common sense. I plainly admit, much of what I write and teach is common sense. Old guys like me (and many of my critics) could read a book like this and say, "This is dumb. Everybody knows this stuff." Not so.

I've tested the concepts in my two previous books in numerous lectures at such venues as the National Association of Broadcasters convention in Las Vegas (the biggest tradeshow in the U.S.), at several Showbusiness and DVExpos, and at several colleges and universities in the U.S. and abroad.

Invariably, the professors say my material is mostly just common sense, but when I ask the students if this material is new to them, 90% raise their hands. They enthusiastically support my effort in explaining such simple necessities as making sales calls, keeping a daily log of activities, and other "common sense" techniques that I believe are the real key to success in any job search or independent business venture.

So why the criticism? Try this: Call a local university or college and ask the registrar if there is a course offered in resume writing or cold call salesmanship. My guess is that the answer will be vague, if not a flat-out "No." Why is this? My only logical assumption is that institutes of higher learning want to perpetuate *their* craft at the expense of yours. If you actually go out and apply what you've learned, you won't need to come back to learn more. You'll be out applying your learning and making money doing it.

So is this a conscious conspiracy to inculcate economic stupidity in an otherwise highly educated student population? I don't think so. Like a force of nature, it just works out that way. At least I hope so. Because when the students raise their hands, the professors seem genuinely and delightedly surprised. Do they then go to their department chairs and say, "Hey, let's offer a basic sales course to our students so they can go out and sell their craft!" If so, you might get a registrar who says, "Yes, we offer such courses."

But if the registrar says that these common sense courses are not offered, ask him or her why. If this knowledge is so common, like English composition or basic mathematics, how come it isn't commonly taught? Maybe the registrar will tell you something you don't know yet. If so, let me know.

As for my other critics of common sense books, those who don't teach but are out there doing it, I ask the same question. If this information is so common, how come my recent lectures at the Washington, D.C. Government Video exposition (October 6–7, 2004), where such "common" topics as Adobe After Effects and Final Cut Pro classes were offered, were the most attended of the event? I'm not particularly good-looking, and my jokes always fall flat. Can't be the entertainment value. Maybe the stuff you are about to read *isn't* so common after all. Maybe it's actually the best-kept secret of all. So I'll continue to report. You decide.

So much for the first business chapter. Now let's get down to the operation of Softimage and have some fun animating!

Chapter 2

The Softimage Interface

This is always the most dangerous chapter. After opening up the book with some previews of what your life might be like as an animator and studio boss, and warming you up with concrete examples of what you might be picturing already in your fantasies, this chapter now brings you into the first stage of reality—dealing with the actual program that will transform your images into something you can watch and sell.

This chapter breaks down into two parts—the hardware and the software. Obviously, you are going to need some hardware on which to run Softimage. Namely, a computer. Next you're going to need to acquire a running version of Softimage, install it on the computer, and then learn how the software works. So this chapter is divided into "The Equipment You Will Need" and "The Softimage Interface."

The Equipment You Will Need

Years ago, when I first got into the animation business, the cost of a computer was a major obstacle. My first animation computer cost $46,000. That's a lot of money even today, but this was back in 1983! Back then, you could by a nice house for $46,000.

Today, you are the lucky beneficiary of something called *Moore's Law*. In 1965, Gordon Moore, co-founder of Intel, established a theory based on the number of transistors per square inch on integrated circuit (IC) boards. He noted that the density doubled every year since the IC's invention, and concluded that the trend would continue for the foreseeable future. The formula has recently settled down to doubling about every 18 months. In other words, the current state-of-the-art computer is twice as powerful as a state-of-the-art computer 18 months ago.

In my last book, I proposed a corollary to Moore's Law, based on the tendency of computer owners to always want the fastest computers. This corollary suggests that as each new, doubly powerful computer model enters the marketplace, the preceding model's price will drop by half. Stated quite simply, Moore's Law means that almost every two years, it becomes twice as easy for you to buy a powerful computer, the central piece of equipment around which you can establish and run your own animation studio!

Chances are, you already have a computer that has more than enough capability to run SOFTIMAGE|XSI. It might be your office computer, an old laptop, your parents' computer, whatever. The good news is that you probably don't have to go out right now and buy a new computer. A little later in this chapter, I'll tell you how to get a free copy of SOFTIMAGE|XSI so you can just load it into your computer and see how it works. If your computer can fly with Softimage, keep flying, and save yourself the money of buying a new computer right now. If the program clunks out or you want to gear up right away for professional work, it's likely you'll have to shell out for a better computer. But before you go and spend big bucks for something you may not need for another month or so, take a moment to read through this chapter and get a heads-up.

As of this writing, one of the most common configurations for a high-end workstation is a dual Pentium IV processor with each processor running at a max speed of 3 *gigahertz* (or *GHz)*. The prefix "gig" means 1 billion, so these chips clock at 3 billion cycles per second. It must be installed with up to 4GB of SDRAM (512MB minimum). If you're willing to sacrifice dual processor capability and opt for the fastest single processor (known as a *uniprocessor* configuration), you can acquire up to 3.06GHz of processing speed (that's 3 billion, 60 million cycles per second), employing the latest Pentium IV (which does not yet support dual processor installation). For uniprocessor applications, many animators swear by the AMD Athlon MP processor, which is comparable to the Intel Xeon processor and sells for considerably less.

For the writing of this book, I have been the fortunate owner of three excellent examples of the kind of computer you can afford for your own studio. Each runs Microsoft Windows XP Professional in the 32-bit mode. Softimage can run in Windows or Linux, but I have yet to experience the Linux environment. As a novice animator, if you are not already familiar with Linux, I would caution you to put off that education until you are more familiar with XSI.

In this section, I will total up some of the costs of these computers. Since these are the latest models, the costs may seem high to you. In addition to the computer itself, the costs of the optional equipment could be more than 75% of the total cost of your studio. Let's consider these computers as top-of-the-line, the kind you'll buy if you have a large bankroll to start your studio, or a generous investor.

Currently, you can purchase a computer with either 32-bit or 64-bit processing. These numbers refer to the size of the instructions your computer can process in each clock cycle. Both the Advanced and Essentials licenses for SOFTIMAGE|XSI support the installation of the 32-bit or 64-bit version. You must install the XSI version that matches your computer's processor. Obviously, purchasing the newer 64-bit processors will make your animations run exponentially faster.

The first of the computers used in creating this book is a Hewlett-Packard XW8200 equipped with two 3.6GHz Intel Xeon processors, 1GB of DDR RAM, a 3Dlabs Wildcat III 6110 AGP Pro video card with 384MB of online memory, a 36GB Seagate Cheetah system drive, a pair of 146GB Seagate Cheetah drives for redundantly storing media and sequences, and a Compaq TFT1825 flat-panel monitor.

I particularly suggest the Seagate brand of hard drives, which I've used under mission-critical pressure for over 10 years, because of their consistent reliability and long life. In all that time, only three of their drives have failed, and this was after thousands of hours of continuous operation in room environments that were often warmer than the manufacturer recommends.

In addition to the warmth of the room, I later learned that two of these drives were connected to substandard power supplies. A faulty or insufficient power supply can easily kill a hard drive. Today's computers have been designed to lower specifications than their megabuck ancestors. Newer circuitry requires less power. Consequently, the power supplies in today's servers and workstations may not be suitable for long-term hard drive support.

I recommend consulting a computer engineer with specific hard drive experience to recommend a suitable outboard hard drive enclosure and redundant HDD power supply, or at least to provide a redundant HDD power supply inside your computer.

While we're on the topic of making drives last longer, I would also suggest that you invest in good temperature control for your hardware that allows you to maintain ambient temperatures at or below 70 degrees Fahrenheit. This configuration retails for about $10,000. You can easily price your own system over the phone with HP by dialing 1-800-888-0262.

The second model is an IBM IntelliStation Z Pro equipped with two Intel Xeon 2.8GHz processors, 1GB of DDR RAM, an Nvidia Quadro FX3400 video card with 128MB of RAM, an 18GB IBM Ultra 160 SCSI hard drive for programs, and a 73GB IBM Ultra160 SCSI for media, all feeding to an IBM P77 17" flat-screen monitor. Package price: approximately $8,000.

Figure 2.1 shows the author's IBM IntelliStation Z-Pro ensemble amidst the usual mess of a busy studio. Notice the topless hard drive array to the left of the IBM, and the cheap house fan to keep the drives as cool as possible in the awfully hot New York summer of 2005. Dual flat-panel monitors ease the eyes. To the right, multiple video recorders (a Sony BVW2800 and a JVC Digital-S machine) allow for high-resolution input and output of analog (Sony) and digital (JVC) video. The 3-pound SCUBA weight on the desk is for frequent arm and hand exercises that help alleviate carpal tunnel syndrome. Yes, it's messy, but it's home. The third computer is, oddly enough, a laptop! I am a very mobile person. During the week, I might be traveling out of town to a video shoot location. Nearly every weekend, I am either heading off to the country, to the beach, or to visit friends and relatives. My wife likes to drive at least 50% of the time, so during her times at the wheel, and whenever I'm bored (which is often), I whip out the laptop.

Most of this book was written and edited on a laptop running Microsoft Word, Adobe Photoshop, and XSI simultaneously. I would test a configuration in XSI, grab a screen capture and modify it in Photoshop, and then write about it in Word. A laptop that's powerful enough to run SOFTIMAGE|XSI is not rare. A laptop that runs XSI quickly enough to be of any use costs a bit more.

The laptop I used was a Dell Precision M70. This model is a little bit heavier than your common notebook, but it sports an Intel Pentium M 770 running at 2.13GHz, with 512MB RAM, a Toshiba 60GB hard drive, and an Nvidia

Figure 2.1 *The author's IBM IntelliStation.*

Quadro FX Go1400 video card. The cost of this laptop was just under $2,500, with a three-year warranty.

If you only have enough money for one computer and you need mobility, this is the one to get. It has enough power, RAM, and storage to handle the needs of almost any beginner or intermediate Softimage animator, and you can always network it to your boss's computer. Then you can dump the really intensive scenes to that and work on them when you can.

As a magazine reviewer, I keep these three computers constantly filled with all the latest software sent to me for evaluation by the manufacturers. These computers have held NewTek's Lightwave ($3,495), Alias|Wavefront's Maya 5 Complete

($1,999), Discreet's 3ds Max 8 ($3,495), and a wide assortment of Digimation plug-in bundles for 3ds Max, including Particle ($700), Character Animation ($1,000), Materials ($700), Nature ($950), and Special Effects ($900).

On each of these systems, I also installed several other software tools that are indispensable in animation work. Programs for compositing, rotoscoping, illustration, photo manipulation, font management, standards conversion (referring both to video formats and frame or aspect ratios), and picture compression are all necessary tools in the animation process.

Compositing is the process by which various layers of animation within a frame are combined to form a complex finished result. As you will learn later in your career, as your compositions become more and more complicated, it is often faster to develop a complex animation by building it in layers (clouds, ground, houses, people) and rendering separate *passes* or subfiles for each layer. Later, when each layer is approved, the layers are combined in a compositing program. The program also allows the various layers to be tuned individually before they're combined into a final scene. The two most common compositing software products for PCs are Adobe's After Effects and eyeon's Digital Fusion.

Rotoscoping is a form of compositing where animation and live action are combined. For instance, when a digital explosion is composited into a scene in an action movie, or when a computer-animated character is shown interacting with live actors (such as the robots in *I Robot*), this is rotoscoping. The term refers back to the days of cel animation, when the animated elements were painstakingly painted on each frame of film. The tool used for this, a rotoscope, was a rotating glass surface with a bright light under it. The artist could view the film and one or more acetate sheets on which the animation was painted.

Illustration refers to creating art from scratch using a program like Adobe Illustrator. *Photo manipulation* refers to the now-common practice of cutting, pasting, and redrawing original and/or scanned art with a product like Adobe Photoshop. *Font management* is most often addressed directly in the animation program or with both Adobe Illustrator and Photoshop. It's the simple use and manipulation of fonts (or the original creation of new fonts) to support the text necessities of an animation, such as a corporate logo presentation.

Standards conversion refers primarily to *standard definition (SD)* television, which employs four video formats: *NTSC*, which is used in the U.S., Japan, and much of South America; *SECAM* and *PAL*, which are used Europe and the Middle East;

and *PAL-M*, which is used in Brazil. For instance, you cannot watch a PAL video-tape from France on a typical NTSC videocassette recorder or television in the U.S. Animations must be either rendered for or converted to their respective geographical targets. The most economical way to execute standards conversion may be to create various versions of the original animation. A somewhat more expensive method is to re-create the animation in different formats by using the same scenes and models as the original. The most costly conversion method, in terms of quality if not money, is to use hardware devices or software programs. The growing popularity of *high definition television (HDTV)* further complicates the issue of standards conversion. When specifying contracts with your clients, take care to discuss where your work will be employed.

The *aspect ratio* is the relationship between the width of the rendered frame (horizontal) to the height (vertical), expressed either in the lowest common denominator (such as the SD ratio of 4:3 and the HD ratio of 16:9) or the actual number of pixels (such as the SD ratio of 720 x 486 and the HD ratio of 1920 x 1080). Like standards, aspect ratios complicate the process of specifying work for a client. They must be addressed as early in the creative process as possible, preferably before contracting the work.

Picture compression is the process of reducing (or sometimes increasing) the data density of animations so they can run on systems with narrower (or wider) bandwidths than your original creation. The most common example of picture compression is the conversion of an SD video file into a *streaming video* file, suitable for transmission over narrowband Internet connections, such as the dialup modems used by many consumers. Other examples are *downrezzing*, or taking an HD animation from its very high resolution to the lower resolution of SD, and *uprezzing* an SD video up to HD level without degrading the picture. There is an entire subindustry opportunity for this work alone. Common software for picture compression include Sonic's Scenarist (www.sonic.com), which is a complete DVD authoring package, and discreet's Inferno and Flame (www.discreet.com), which are principally high-end compositing suites.

In addition to the animation software, plug-ins, and compositing software, I also employed various types of render software or render engines. *Render engines* take your finished scene data and produce individual frames that form the finished sequences of animation. Render engines are like factories that allow you to put information in one end and see final frames come out the other end. This is done automatically, usually overnight. (Often over many nights!)

In addition to simply making the frames, rendering engines also allow you to add complex effects to each frame. These effects usually determine the behavior of lighting and surfaces that bounce, absorb, or emanate light during the rendering process.

Most animation programs employ their own rendering engine within their basic package. Some of these engines are quite elaborate. However, many animators prefer augmenting their favorite animation program's rendering engine with one or more third-party engines. The reason for this is that some third-party developers are making significant advances in this limited field. Many of their products are outpacing the efforts of the manufacturers who produce complete animation programs. For instance, some rendering engines take over the entire aspect of a scene's lighting, automating and improving the process to such an extent that the lighting is not addressed within the animation program at all!

In addition to render engines, a new device that's also employed at the rendering stage is the *custom display engine*. The most notable custom display engine, Massive, was developed by WETA Studios in New Zealand to create vast armies in the first of the *Lord of the Rings* films. Using a custom display engine, the animators from WETA created one warrior and then replicated that warrior thousands of times across a varied landscape. In addition to the replication, which itself was rather simple, each replicated warrior was enhanced with its own rules of behavior. For instance, a warrior marched forward until it encountered an object or another warrior. If it encountered an object, it attempted to go around it. If it encountered another warrior, it determined if the warrior was a friend or foe. If friend, it continued marching beside it. If foe, it employed one of several random attacks, such as an axe chop. The result of the attack (and the defense or counter-attack of the opposing warrior) was calculated by Massive, and the result was enacted by each warrior, such as losing a limb, falling, dying, or marching onward triumphantly!

Behavior, the custom display engine in SOFTIMAGE|XSI Advanced, has many of the same capabilities as Massive (and a few new ones). It can produce vast armies and any randomized behaviors you can imagine. You are certainly in for some exciting times!

Even better, Mental Ray, the rendering engine supplied in all versions of SOFTIMAGE|XSI, is one of the most robust products of its kind, and certainly the most time-tested. It will take a long time before you exhaust its capabilities.

If you plan to get into the field of gaming animation, you will be happy to know that SOFTIMAGE|XSI supports *multiple render hosts*. This feature allows you to use third-party real time plug-in render engines and custom display engines without the hassles of installation and conforming to Softimage's specifications. This feature will keep you up to date with the very quickly changing realm of game design.

Of course, the more features you build into your render process, the slower your computer will churn out the frames. Or to put it another way, the more computer power you will need to achieve fast processing, or *throughput*.

But don't worry. If you have additional computers, you can use the *distributed rendering* feature of Softimage, which sends various parts of each frame to any number of different computers and then assembles the results on your master hard drive. You can also use distributed rendering interactively within XSI, using the Render Region tool. This allows you to quickly render selected areas of your frame in order to check a recent revision. *BatchServe* is another rendering management program that sends complete frames to different computers on your local network. You might use this tool to batch process a completed job.

Finally, you may wish to consider purchasing an Avid Mojo unit. This piece of hardware allows you to examine any view, render region, or animation directly on an external monitor, using a direct render and output system that displays your results instantly.

SOFTIMAGE|XSI may prove to be an economical choice when you're determining how to equip your studio, either for the basics of creating your first showreel or doing contract work for a major feature film studio.

Although your choices of platforms and software may vary considerably from mine, I want you to note that none of these systems, which are ready to put to work and earn you money, cost more than $10,000. Adding on the required and optional peripheral gear, such as a scanner, VCR and video monitors, should run you no more than another $5,000-8,000, depending on your needs. Your complete investment for a top-of-the-line system should therefore be under $15,000. This is about a third of what it cost to start a computer animation company just five years ago, and a tenth of what I spent back in the 1980s.

Keep in mind, however, that these prices reflect the current state-of-the-art models. Models equipped with lesser configurations and older computers available on the used market will certainly cost a lot less, perhaps less than 50% of these prices.

You should also consider refurbished or B-stock computers, which are available directly from computer manufacturers.

Refurbished computers have been returned to the manufacturer for any number of reasons. (Some reasons have little to do with the way the computer works.) Federal law prohibits a manufacturer from selling such returned equipment as new. Consequently, the manufacturer must sell it at a reduced cost, usually about 30-50% off. Such equipment has been completely checked out and repaired to new specifications, and usually carries a significant warranty.

B-stock equipment has not been sold to anyone, but may have been used in such venues as manufacturers' trade shows, demos, window displays, and so on. Again, this equipment cannot be sold as new, but is often sold with a complete warranty for considerably less money than a new machine. The places to find good B-stock are large tradeshows like Comdex, where savvy buyers speak with manufacturers' representatives and buy the equipment right off the tradeshow floor.

Many people ask me what they should pay for used computers. By Moore's Law, you shouldn't offer more than half the retail price for a computer that is more than 18 months old. (That is, 18 months from its original issue date—not the date it was originally purchased, which in most cases is a few months after the issue date.)

You can acquire used computers at low cost, and then, if necessary, upgrade them as your business grows. If that's your plan, consider a basic, single-processor workstation with one monitor, a utility-grade video card, and two small hard drives. This can reduce the HP EVO W8000 from $10,000 to less than $2,000 and still provide you with plenty of computer power to get started in animation production.

Incidentally, I like to work in a wide variety of places. I get a lot of work done, for instance, on the commuter train between my home in the suburbs and my office in New York City. Right this moment, I'm on vacation in Florida, sitting by a pool. At times like these, I use a simple laptop computer. In this case, I'm using two laptops, because I'm testing each for compatibility—an old IBM T-21 Thinkpad and the new Dell Precision M70.

On both the IBM Thinkpad and the Del M70, I installed *two* versions of Softimage: Softimage Advanced and Softimage Foundation. I wanted to compare the two versions side-by-side. Even on the laptops, I can launch both versions at the same time.

The point here, and it is probably the most important point in this chapter, is not to spend a dime more than necessary to get to the next step on your path to success. I call this *just-in-time purchasing*. Computer manufacturers have a similar term, *just-in-time manufacturing*. With computers becoming obsolete so quickly, it's risky to make a lot of them and put them in warehouses waiting to be sold. This inventory is getting obsolesced minute by minute. The ideal situation is to make the computer exactly when a customer wants to buy it. (Maybe a little *after* the customer buys it—so you can make a few pennies of interest on the purchase price!)

Dell Computers, for instance, brilliantly came up with the idea of building their computers to the buyer's specifications. That's cool. Until your order comes in, there's no need to make the computer. That's just-in-time manufacturing.

But you don't need a computer until—when? The day after you get a contract to do an animation that requires a new computer, right? That's just-in-time purchasing! Resist the urge to go out and buy a computer just to learn Softimage. Try to get by with the computer you already have, or one you can borrow. Once you get your chops, build a showreel, go out and get some work—*that's* when you should see if you can still do the job with the old computer.

Wait until you are really up against the wall before you go out and spend money on hardware. Use a school computer. Barter your labor for free time on a production company's computer. (More on this in Chapter 3, "Getting Your First Job in an Animation Studio.") Get a night porter's job and use the hotel's computer. Do whatever you have to, but don't go out and spend money until you really need a computer or else the job just won't get done. Get the first third of your payment for the job (more about this in Chapter 7, "Bowling for Dollars"), and make sure the check clears the bank before you actually spend money. Then buy the best computer you can afford! You're probably going to need it—and by then, you'll know exactly what you need.

One other item I like to have around my shop is a USB memory device. Although I rely on my shop's network of over 12 computers to shuttle around scenes, models, sequences, and other data, a memory device is a good, portable way of backing up essential files. For this, you can use a small USB drive, or even a personal music player like the Apple iPod.

Minimal Computer Requirements for SOFTIMAGE|XSI

So how do you know if your old computer will cut the mustard? Okay, here are the minimum requirements for SOFTIMAGE|XSI Foundation:

First of all, SOFTIMAGE|XSI was designed for computers running Windows or Linux. So far, there is no way to run it on a Mac. Sorry, Apple fans. If you want to animate on an Apple, I suggest Alias|Wavefront's Maya. However, I cannot vouch for its suitability or stability on Apple equipment, since Apple never responded to my requests for a test machine. I've heard good things, though, if that means anything to you.

Of the various versions of Windows, Avid, the manufacturer of SOFTIMAGE|XSI, recommends Windows 2000 installed with Service Pack 2 (SP2), SP3, or SP4. Windows XP Professional (including SP1 and SP1a) is also suitable, but in some cases it may require a special software package, downloaded for free, known as a *hotfix*. More information on this hotfix may be found at http://support.microsoft.com/default.aspx?scid=kb;[LN];Q328979.

Next, when it comes to hardware, SOFTIMAGE|XSI prefers workstations equipped with the AMD K7 (or higher) processor, or the Intel Pentium III processor or higher. You can use any brand of computer, even home-built clones.

Since 3D animation requires a means of displaying complex graphics on your monitor, you should have what is known as an *OpenGL* accelerated graphics card with at least 64MB of RAM. (Having more RAM will produce quicker updates and eliminate a lot of wasted time as your monitor redisplays each change you make to the animation.) The minimum monitor resolution to run SOFTIMAGE|XSI is 1280×1024. You can find a continually updated list of recommended cards and drivers at www.softimage.com/hardware-certification.

The Softimage Web site recommends that your computer have at least 512MB of RAM for a typical installation, but you will need a lot more during setup for decompressing files, and even more for storing the results of your rendered animations. Consider that the typical video frame is composed of about 350KB of data, which means it's about 10MB for every second of animation. I would plan on having an extra 30GB on your system just to store animated media.

Softimage, like many memory-hungry programs, employs a technique of swapping data from the random access memory (RAM) of your computer to unused hard drive space. This process is known as *swapping*, and it would be wise to consider between 200MB and 300MB of swap space when evaluating your hard drive requirements.

The minimum amount of RAM is 256MB, although you'll find the computer grinding a bit with anything less than 512MB.

In order to obtain service and other online data from Softimage, you'll need an Internet connection with Internet Explorer 5.5 or later. If you are not already experienced with setting up in-house networks or LANs, you should become familiar with TCP/IP service protocol. Eventually, when the need for multi-machine rendering arises, you might need to hook up your in-house computer to one or more computers on a LAN network.

And finally, a CD-ROM drive and a three-button mouse round out the hardware requirements. Not too much to ask for, is it?

Most computers manufactured in the last few years offer all of the above as standard equipment. There is nothing exotic here. I might add that in order to get data into and out of your computer, you may need at least a CD-ROM writer, if not some kind of backup device, such as a spare hard drive, DAT, 1/4" tape drive, DVD-ROM, or, bless your heart for asking, a videotape recorder or DVD writer to make your showreels.

Free Version of SOFTIMAGE|XSI!

In order to introduce you to SOFTIMAGE|XSI, Avid provides a free 30-day trial of Foundation, the most basic version of the software. During those 30 days, you don't need a hardware or software key to run XSI Foundation. A *software key* is a simple bit of code, like a password. A *hardware key* (also known as a *dongal*, named after its inventor, Don Gall) is a device about the size of a lipstick that plugs into your computer.

Each time you start the free version of Foundation, the number of days remaining is displayed, along with buttons that allow you to purchase the program, download a software key, and install the key in the program. Once you purchase the software, of course, it is yours to run forever. As long as you have days left on the startup window, you just click the Continue Evaluation button and the program starts.

All legal, functional, purchased versions of SOFTIMAGE|XSI, with the exception of the free trial version, will require you to install some form of key to run the program. The key will be installed either on the serial port or the USB port of each machine on which you wish to run the software. You can run the software on any number of machines, one at a time, by moving the dongal from machine to machine.

If you obtain a copy of SOFTIMAGE|XSI that does not require such a key, it is most likely an illegally copied version. Serious penalties apply to anyone who installs and uses such software on their computer. Obviously, someone who has obtained an illegal copy of Softimage could use this book to learn Softimage without the manufacturer's documentation that comes with the legal product. I don't recommend this for many reasons ($$$).

An interesting anecdote: Several animation programs have been designed to display a visible marker on animation that is produced on pirated versions of the software. At a recent convention attended by many professional animators (and employers of animators), an animation was displayed in a major screening that featured this marker. To say the least, the reaction of the audience was not kind to the exhibitor.

If you intend to install and run XSI on someone else's computer, you will need Administrator status on that computer to install the license software that allows XSI to function. Once XSI is installed, most of its functions will work for a *restricted* or *standard* user login.

This wraps up the minimal requirements for any computer running XSI, but be warned: These requirements might change anytime after I publish this book. For the most up-to-date information on system requirements for XSI, visit softimage.com and click Support.

The Persistence of a Vision: Softimage and Avid

During the 20 or so years I've been in the business of selling 3D animation, I've seen times of feast and famine. I've seen many programs and computer systems come and go. Nothing is certain in life, and things are even more precarious in the world of computer graphics technology. Only a few animation products have withstood the test of time.

Softimage is the oldest continually functioning 3D animation software on the market. It came before 3ds max, Lightwave, and all the others. It has been through several owners. (Once, it was owned by Bill Gates!) It has been through many revisions. I won't belabor you with a history lesson. You can find some of that in my last book, and since no one has written me with any praise for the work I put into the history chapter, I'll save you the trouble of reading one here.

Let it stand, however, that when you sit down to learn a complex software program, you are investing a lot more than even the $6,999 that SOFTIMAGE|XSI Advanced will cost you. A hell of a lot more. You don't want that learning time to be wasted if your favorite program's manufacturer goes bankrupt or the software becomes totally obsolete. Believe me, that's a real squat in the cactus. I can't tell you how many long-dead software programs still inhabit cells of my brain, to no practical use (except to write history chapters). Therefore, you want to find out how long a program has been successful, and what the risk is that your learning time might go wasted.

Learning Softimage has several advantages over learning any other animation program. First, as I've already implied, it is time-tested. Second, it is designed to employ the common work routines of Windows, such as drag-and-drop and the cut, copy, and paste tools. Third, it is extensively supported by an ever-growing array of free tutorials, tools, and upgrades available on the Internet. Fourth, it is now owned by Avid, the oldest continually functioning nonlinear video editing software manufacturer—and has been optimized so that it's the only 3D animation program that is coded for nonlinear production and interlinked with a well-established video finishing suite. Finally, SOFTIMAGE|XSI attempts to incorporate all of the ancillary tools an animator might need (and some might say it succeeds).

Consider this: Of the 60 significant features offered by the top-of-the-line XSI Advanced, only 17 are missing in Foundation, the "light" version, and only *four* are missing in the mid-priced Essentials. These four are additional batch rendering, Syflex advanced cloth, hair & fur, and the Softimage Behavior Animation System.

Figure 2.2 is a comparison of the three levels of SOFTIMAGE|XSI—Foundation, Essentials, and Advanced—with indications as to which of 60 different features is contained in each. For more information, see http://www.softimage.com/products/Xsi/v5/comparison/default.asp. Compliments of Avid.

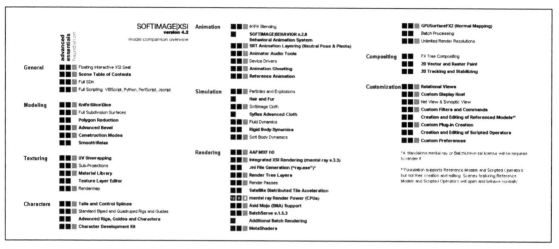

Figure 2.2 *SOFTIMAGE\XSI's three levels.*

The Typical Animation Workflow

Obviously, there are many ways to produce animation. Generally speaking, there are about nine principal steps that are required, regardless of the type of animation or its complexity, audience, deadline, or budget:

- Pitching the project (see Chapters 7 and 9)
- Contracting and billing (see Chapter 11)
- Storyboard or previsualization (see Chapter 4)
- Creating objects, models, scenes, and characters (see Chapters 4 and 8)
- Lighting (see Chapter 10)
- Motion (see Chapter 6)
- Testing (see Chapter 12)
- Rendering and finishing (see Chapter 12)

More information about each step is in the chapter given, but how about a brief description of each step to give you a perspective on what you'll be doing for the rest of your life?

Pitching the Project

Unless you are creating the animation for yourself, you will have to explain your animation to someone else. Eventually, this explanation will conclude with an agreement with your client, which should be addressed in the form of a written contract. Any work done for the client as part of the pitch, but before the contract, is usually done for free and is called *speculative* or *spec work*.

Contracting and Billing

A contract is your agreement with the client to supply a certain product, composed of work and materials, for a certain fee, usually paid in thirds. You get one-third before you start, one-third when you show the working models or a low-resolution (low-res) test, and the final third when you deliver the work. There is nothing frightening about a contract. Every good client expects one, and the more information contained therein (oops, there I go sounding like a contract!), the better.

Billing is the act of asking for your payment in a formal, written way. There is a proper form for the bill, just as there is a form for the contract. Before you begin a project, you must propose a contract, get it signed, and issue a bill for the first third of the payment. After you get the payment (some say after the check clears the bank), you begin the job. *Not a moment sooner.* More on this later.

Storyboard or Previsualization

A storyboard is a pencil-drawn or computer-sketched representation of the animation, with descriptions of the action, dialogue, and sound effects noted for each panel, usually as printed text below each frame. A storyboard resembles an elaborate comic book. This is probably why so many comics are being made into animated feature films—the storyboards are done already!

You'll need to produce a storyboard for nearly every animation you produce, and for many on which you will work as an employee. If you never thought drawing skills would be important when you went through art school, think again. "Life class—don't fail me now!"

Another tool, similar to a storyboard, is a *previsualization* or *previz*. Over the years, many software programs (and a few inventive animators working on their own) have enabled the user to design low-res storyboards in 3D space. Eventually, these programs incorporated rudimentary action and motion scripting. Although they are not full-blown animation systems, they work on a simpler level to produce something that a client and crew can see, agree upon, and use as a tool for further development. Because this is exactly what a storyboard does, previz is a good step after the storyboard. Or, if you have a big budget, you can use it in *place* of the storyboard. In fact, previz is becoming a tool on many feature films that do not use 3D animation or computer generated imagery (CGI) at all. Hey, here's a completely new career path!

Create Objects, Scenes, Lights, and Motion

Once you are contracted and have a blueprint for production (as expressed in a storyboard and/or previz video), you are ready to start creating the animation. Traditionally, an animation includes four basic elements: objects, scenes, lights, and motion.

Objects are any 3D forms within the scene that have shape, surface and position, and sometimes mass. Softimage introduces the term *models*, which are a higher order of object. A model defines a complex object, such as a boat, train, or human character, implying a collection of simpler objects that are linked together into a sometimes vastly complicated hierarchy of elements.

It is important to understand the concept of hierarchy in animation. Let's say we have a humanoid character, like Shrek. The primary object, or model, is Shrek himself. His head, however, would be a subordinate element of the model—a subset. Within the head, you have eyes, which are sub-subsets. Within the eyes, you have irises—sub-sub-subsets. Because Shrek is an expressive individual, his irises can expand and contract. (Scientists have found that real humans' irises contract when they see something unfavorable and expand when they see something attractive. They also contract under bright light.)

Obviously, there are limits to how much you want Shrek's irises to contract and expand. You don't want them going down to pinpoints (what ugliness would cause such an effect?), and you don't want them expanding beyond his eyeballs. These limits are called *constraints*. Yep! Iris motion constraints are sub-sub-sub-subsets of the character Shrek. All of these collected elements make up the hierarchy of the model. (And let's not even consider the arms and legs yet!)

Obviously, the best way to organize an hierarchy is with a text outline. Roman numeral I, capital letter A, Arabic numeral 1, and so on. Glad we got that out of the way. Don't forget this—I'm going to test you on it later.

Getting back to the four basic elements of an animation (five, if we include models), we have yet to describe scenes. A *scene* is the "stage" where the objects (and models) play their parts. (In fact, at least one animation program actually calls the viewport a "stage.") It's where we place our characters and move them around. Clearly, there can be little difference between the complexity of a building—its walls, windows, doors, chimneys, and so on can certainly classify as a model—and that of a character as complex as Shrek. Why is one classified as part of a scene (which is how I will classify the building) and one is classified an object or model? Simple. If an object moves around and takes over the narrative of the story, it is an object or model. If it sits there like a lox—as we in the film business customarily refer to an object that doesn't move—it's part of the scenery. Same goes for live theater, as anyone who has played the "tree" in the ChristmasKwanzaHanukkah RamadanPaganSacrifice play can attest. As my son's third grade teacher said one cold December, "You don't move—you be the object."

Another kind of scenery is easier to define: the *backdrop plane*. Instead of working for days to create, say, a pretty painted scene of mountains, behind a grove of trees, through which a herd of buffaloes are posing, you can use a photograph, or a frame of video. It looks like the animator did a lot of work, but it's just a two-dimensional surface on which you project an image electronically. Blam! It's there. So what. Obviously scenery.

Lighting

Traditionally, computer-generated lighting has imitated the science and art of cinematic lighting. Computer-animated lights are still named for their cinematic equivalents, such as *spotlight* (narrow, intense beam), *fill light* (soft, wide-angled beam), or *ambient light* (no specific source, but affecting the entire scene).

But computer programs like Softimage can do things that would be impractical or impossible for a cinematographer to do in real life. In some software products, an object can be given internal lighting (luminosity) by virtue of its surface attributes or by installing a light within the object.

Lights have attributes, such as color, brightness, and direction, and these attributes can vary during your animation. In order to vary with time, these attributes must be keyframable. That means you must be able to take a specific keyframe, assign a light attribute to that frame, move ahead (or back) in time, change the attribute, and assign it to another keyframe. This creates the varying glow of a faulty light bulb, for instance.

Motion

The addition of motion to an animation implies the application of the fourth dimension, time. Without the passage of time, animation could not exist, because every scene would be an indefinitely long still frame. Hey, that's not animation, that's an art museum.

Animation is created by displaying a *sequence* of individual frames, within a specific span of time, such that each frame remains onscreen for a specific fraction of a second. What fraction? That's interesting. The illusion of motion is actually caused by a fault in the design of our eyes, called *persistence of vision*. If you show a sequence of frames to a typical viewer for, say, 30 seconds each, there will be little or no perception of movement. On the other hand, if we show each frame for a second, there is a greater perception of movement, but the movement appears jerky. As the interval of each frame's presentation becomes less, the perception of movement becomes finer. At some point, the movement is fine enough, and no greater expense (because it costs more money to make more frames) need be wasted to further shorten the interval.

Cut the time down to 1/10th of a second, add a lot of frames, and presto, persistence of vision creates motion. Show the frames at 24 per second (the typical speed of feature film) or 30 per second (the typical speed of television), and the motion seems quite smooth and realistic.

Your job as an animator is to impart motion on your creations. You will pose your objects and models in 3D space (your scene), assign a keyframe, and then move them somewhere else, where you'll assign another keyframe. From this, the computer will make motion! If you move the objects too little between keyframes, the motion will not be apparent. Move them too much, and the motion will seem jerky and unrealistic. Here is where your artistry will flourish—where the semblance of reality is your individual creation.

Testing

Once you have created something in an animation program, you will want to render it out to a sequence of 30 or more pictures to create an animation. After the first two or three renders you do, you will learn that it takes some time. Usually, you sit around and wait. (Some animators like to munch while we wait, which is why many of us are a bit gravity-challenged.) Eventually, you will learn that it is wise to test your animation in some fashion that's less than a full render. There are several ways you can do this in Softimage. For instance, you can render a region or cropping of the audience's view, containing all the layers and nodes. You can render a *layer*, which is the full-screen view of one layer or a limited number of layers. You can also render in less than full resolution. All of these techniques allow you to evaluate your work and check for mistakes that would otherwise waste your time during a full render.

Rendering and Finishing

Once you have tested an animation's elements and corrected all apparent mistakes, you are ready to render. Rendering is the creation of each individual frame, complete with all the objects, props, lights, special effects, and motions that the animator intends. The animator initiates the rendering process by setting an array of controls. These controls establish values for such parameters as the resolution and dimensions of each frame, the names and storage locations of the frame sequence, and, if the operation is taking place on a network, the computers on which the sequence will be rendered.

Getting Paid

Although I did not list this essential step in my workflow chart, a good part of the work of an animation studio boss is spent in collecting moneys owed. Although the overwhelming majority of clients will pay their bills on time and thank you warmly for your efforts on their behalf, you will find that a few clients can cause you extreme duress by delaying your payment or not paying you at all.

Getting paid is called *collections*. Sounds a bit like what happens in your local place of worship, doesn't it? Maybe we use the word *collections* because there is a certain prayerful aspect to attempting to get paid! Not really. In fact, if you follow some very careful guidelines, which begin at the contracting stage and end with a clear, logical, and well-substantiated invoice, you may never have to worry about getting paid at all.

And then—there are those clients who believe you are their bank (because they keep your money and invest it during the time they keep you waiting) or their sugar daddy (because they keep your money and use it to buy something sweet). These two kinds of clients must be dealt with firmly. If all else fails, you may have to resort to tactics that will end the client relationship. In such cases, I always remember an axiom that a wise record producer told me: "There is only one thing sure about a client. One day you will lose it." Better for a good reason—demanding what is due you—than a bad one, like unnecessarily blowing a deadline.

Now let's get down to the creative work you can do with Softimage. We'll tackle the interface or working screen before we call this chapter quits, and then we'll get back to furthering the money side of your career in Chapter 3.

Watch out, kid! This is where they're going to get you to go out and buy one of those newfangled, $10,000 software packages. That's why I bought you this book—so you could learn *before* you buy. Then you'll know if you really like this stuff, or if it's another drum set. You *remember* the drum set I bought you in junior high, don't you?

Let's Get a Free Copy of Softimage

How's that for good Dad-news? Softimage makes it easy for you to learn their software without going out and spending a bundle first. You simply download the basic version, and you have 30 days before the software self-destructs. Here's how you do it:

1. Go to www.softimage.com.
2. In the left column, under Current Updates & Downloads, find the latest version of Softimage. This is currently XSI Foundation Trial. Click it.

3. Scroll down the page and fill out all the information. The red text indicates the information you must include. The rest is optional, except for the state, which is not red but needs to be filled out.

4. When you submit this information, in a matter of minutes the Web site automatically emails you a confirmation and instructions for downloading XSI Foundation.

5. There is a hyperlink line of text in the email. Click on it. This takes you to a login page. Since you have never been here before, click on Click Here to create an account.

6. Again, you have to fill out some information, but this is pretty standard stuff. The account you establish will be useful later, if you actually decide to buy SOFTIMAGE|XSI. Click Go! when you are done.

Hey, kid, nothing's for free in this life. Remember *I* told you that.

7. Once your account is recognized (if there are any problems, the Softimage site may send you another email link—oh, bother), you're given a choice of free software to download. Choose the version of SOFTIMAGE|XSI Foundation that matches your operating system, and download the file setup_XSIFND_4.2_MSWin32 (if you're using Windows—it's different for Linux).

8. Choose the Typical install, which includes the Online Library. You can eliminate this from the installation if you are short on space. The total space needed for all options is 915MB.

9. From the hard drive and subdirectory where you stored the setup file, double-click on it to launch Softimage. If you don't have enough HDD space, the installation program warns you. You can go back and change the installation options or cancel the install.

Figure 2.3 shows what you see when Softimage launches on your system.

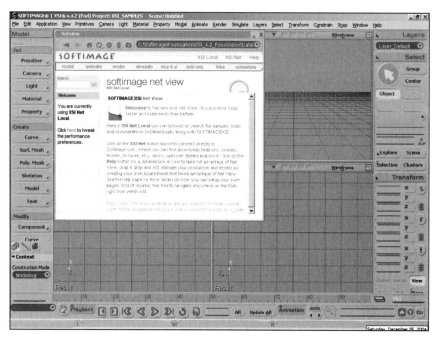

Figure 2.3 *Initial launch of Softimage.*

First off, notice that the Softimage Net View overlays your Softimage interface. This is kind of a rude way of introducing you to Net View, but once you explore it, you'll find the rudeness justified. To get rid of Net View, just click the X in the upper-right corner (we'll call this *X-out-of* from now on). If you want to get Net View back without rebooting, go to the Main menu bar at the top of the screen and choose Application > Views > Net View.

Net View is a powerful tool for accessing the Internet from within Softimage. If you have several computers spread out over your home, office, town, or anywhere else, you can customize Net View into your own personal Softimage intranet. There are two valuable places to go in Net View: XSI Local and XSI Net. Use the buttons at the top right of the Net View interface.

XSI Local is an Internet-style database stored in the Softimage subdirectory on your computer. Here you will find many useful tools and animation elements, but of course, these do not change frequently without an online download or disk update.

XSI Net is a vast portion of the Softimage corporate site where similar goodies can be found, except this resource is much larger than the one on your computer, and it changes almost daily.

I encourage you to thoroughly explore Net View and learn its powerful features. Where appropriate, I may ask you to use it later in this book to obtain necessary files. For now, let's X-out-of Net View and have a look at the Softimage interface.

Figure 2.4 shows the main interface screen of Softimage XSI 4.2, featuring four viewports and associated menu screens.

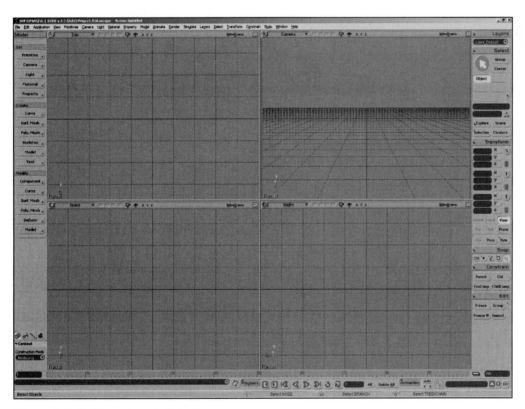

Figure 2.4 *Softimage's main interface screen.*

It's Like Driving a Car

It has long been my desire to see all computer programs become as easy to use and ubiquitous as cars. If you own a Ford, you don't have to read the documentation to drive a Chevy. The same should be true of computer animation programs. Well, we're almost there. Most animation programs have the same elements in their interfaces: control panels, four or more viewports, and a timeline. Softimage is no different.

What differentiates Softimage from many other animation programs is that it incorporates many of the functions of an animation artist into one suite. In addition to the most common functions, such as modeling and animation, Softimage includes texturing, rendering, compositing, simulating, and scripting into its seamlessly integrated environment. The interface is one complicated puppy!

Viewports

The most dominant area of the interface, smack dab in the center, is the Viewport array. The default view shows four viewports, which include three orthographic views (top, front, and right) and a perspective view, in this case the Camera view.

The orthographic views employ the Cartesian Plane, a grid of lines. (They don't actually render into final frames—they're just shown as references.) These lines represent x, y, and z coordinates. Depending on the view selected in the viewport, the lines represent any two of the three coordinates. For instance, the Top View shows the x and z coordinates, while the Right View shows the y and z. Orthographic views are devoid of perspective. Think of them as blueprint drawings. They are useful when you're creating objects or accurately positioning them in the scene.

In the perspective view, the illusion of 3D space is created by converging the z-axis lines (or whatever lines currently run from front to back) at some distant vanishing point in the center of the horizon.

The perspective view allows the contents of the viewport to be seen as the human eye might see it. You can rotate the object(s) or point of view around all three axes. Softimage offers perspective views from one or more cameras (as shown in Figure 2.4), from the render engine (which may be one of the cameras), from any light source in the scene, or from an omniscient point of view, known as User.

Okay, enough theory. Let's load an object and start fooling around with these viewports.

Exercise 2.1: Mapping and Noting the Softimage Interface

Sometimes I feel a bit weird writing this book, because I'm sitting here pretending to teach a class to you, but you aren't really here. I figure you probably feel something similar, because as you're reading, I'm not there. So let's do something to emulate a real classroom, okay? This may seem silly at first, but bear with me, because it's going to help build your memory of the vast universe of the Softimage interface. And at the same time, it will make this a valuable reference book that you will use for many years.

So, go get yourself a lined white notebook. The spring bound $8^{1}/_{2}$ x 11 size is just perfect. As you start to explore the Softimage interface, either as you read this book or as you explore on your own (which I highly encourage you to do, and don't worry, you can't break anything), I want you to build an outline of all the elements of the interface. Use a sharp pencil with a new eraser—you're going to need it. I warn you, this is a very daunting task, but I want you to start.

For instance, in a minute we're going to load an object into the viewports. I'm going to ask you to explore all the buttons that control the viewports. When you open up a menu of buttons or commands, I want you to write down the list in your notebook. Leave some space after each name, because you never know, each name may include levels upon levels of submenus. Noting them may require you to erase and rewrite a few times to make enough space for the names and your notes. That might be frustrating, but it's a good exercise. The frustration will yield way to understanding, and as you gather understanding, your brain will remember each function better. You may never have to look them up again. But if you do, you'll have your notebook as a reference. Eventually, your notebook will be the best map of Softimage you'll ever find. It will be the map *you've* used to explore this fascinating world.

Okay, let's find ourselves an object to load:

1. In the main menu at the top of the screen, all the way to the left, click on File > Import > Model.

2. Navigate to the HDD that has the subdirectory Softimage. If that directory is C, the path is C:\Softimage\XSI_4.2_Foundation\Data\ XSI_SAMPLES\Models\Digimation. Be sure you have the File Types window at the bottom of the panel set to All Files, or you will see nothing in the subdirectory.

3. In that directory, load the model Man_Character.emdl.

4. With the model selected, click Okay. Depending on your computer, it may take several minutes to load this model, which is a pretty nice (if emasculated) model of a man's body. By the way, this model comes from Digimation, a superb company that maintains a vast library of 3D models that you can purchase online (www.digimation.com).

Now that you've got the man loaded in your viewports, we're ready to explore. By the way, if you're like me, once in a while you want to depart from the book and go off on your own. Kind of like leaving the tour and getting to know the natives! That's going to get you into a little trouble. Nothing serious—no barroom brawls or knife attacks—but you may wind up with something on your screen that doesn't make sense, and you won't know how to get back to the tour.

If this happens, first try the Ctrl+Z keyboard combination. This is the Undo command, and you can click it over and over to undo your previous commands. If this fails to get you home, just click your heels together . . . er, just restart Softimage and follow the appropriate tutorial's steps back to where you left the tour.

Go to the top-right viewport, known as Viewport B (as designated by the letter in the upper-left corner). It's set to display a perspective view of the camera.

Notice the top edge of the viewport. As shown in Figure 2.5, the top edge of the viewport contains an array of menus and tools for controlling the view and some of the aspects of its contents.

The square icon in the upper-right corner is a switch that toggles the viewport up to full-screen view and back down to the quad view (you can also use the F12 but-

Figure 2.5 *The top edge of the viewport.*

ton on the keyboard). In your notebook, you might want to start a fresh page and call it Viewport. On the first line, perhaps write, "Leftmost square icon: Toggles full and quad view—also use F12."

The next control to the left of this button, which currently says Wireframe, opens a drop-down menu. This menu mostly deals with how the viewport displays its contents. You're welcome to explore here on your own, filling out your notebook. (I'll warn you in advance about the bottom two Options choices. They're going to eat up a few pages of your notebook!) For the moment, however, let's concentrate on the nine choices that begin with Bounding Box, just above the check mark next to Wireframe.

Start by clicking Bounding Box. Notice that the display in Viewport B has changed. The wireframe of the man has disappeared and a portion of a box is now shown. Let's zoom the view back to see what we've got.

Press the Z key on your keyboard. This changes the cursor from an arrow, known as the Select icon, to the Pan and Zoom icon. Left-click and hold the cursor in Viewport B. Now you can drag the contents of the viewport up, down, left, and right. If you left-click, the view quickly zooms back. Ooops! It's not hard to zoom back so far that the box completely disappears! Be careful. If you middle-click, the view zooms in. You might use the middle-click to bring that vanished box back up to full size. Once you explore the attributes of this new cursor tool, you can switch back to the Select arrow by clicking the large arrow in the circle in the upper-left corner of the interface. (See Figure 2.6.)

Figure 2.6 *Select arrow.*

The box, called a *bounding box*, is the simplest method of displaying any object or model in Softimage. We use bounding boxes to reduce a scene to really simple contents. For instance, you might have a squadron of space fighters, replete with laser cannons, engine pods, antennae, and so on. You want to move up just one of these fighters to lead the pack. But every time you adjust the one fighter, the computer has to rewrite the scene, sometimes taking up valuable minutes. If you convert the entire view to bounding boxes, each fighter is just a simple box. You can move the boxes around really fast, with no delays as the computer recalculates the display.

Sometimes, however, a bounding box is too simple. That's when we use a wire-frame. You've already seen that, so let's skip down to Depth Cue. This feature emphasizes the distance between the viewer and the horizon, which now fades away behind the man. Depth Cue mode is used when you want to place models into various positions in the scene, and you need some means of judging relative distance. Of course, you could also reference the Top View in the A viewport.

Another display type that offers a simplified display is Constant. This fills the outline of the model with a single display color. Like Bounding Box, Constant takes very little time to display, yet offers a more realistic view of the model. If, in your space fighter scene, you wanted to interlace the wings of the fighters so they overlapped, you might use the Constant display mode to avoid colliding the wings, which would not be displayed in the bounding box.

The Shaded display type begins to make the display look really interesting. This type of display sprays a one-color shade over the surface of the object. It's a mode that is really useful in character animation to verify that your character's joints and surfaces are working as you expect.

This is where I'll leave you to explore for a while. Try out the other buttons in this drop-down list, making notes as you go along. When you're ready to continue the interface tour, leave the view in wireframe and come back here.

Views Menu

Welcome back. Let's move now to the top-right corner of the viewport, where the Views menu is located. Right now it says Camera (unless you messed with it, you little devil). This means you are looking through a camera at your scene. There are three basic types of views in Softimage: perspective (such as this camera view), orthographic (such as what's shown by the other three viewports), and data (an alphanumeric representation of the scene or other information useful to the animator).

Notice that each viewport's Views menu features a different entry pertaining to the mode of view. At this time, certain views are not appropriate for your use. These are Custom Displays, Render Tree, Animation Editor, Dopesheet, Animation Mixer, Texture Editor, Image Clip Viewer, Texture Layer Editor, Weight Editor, and the three FX views at the bottom of the list. Sure, you can open them up and explore them, but at this point, they won't be much help to you.

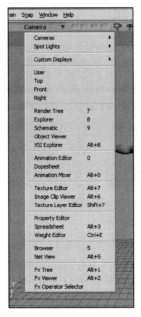

Figure 2.7 *The Camera Views menu.*

Let's mess around with the other controls in the Views menu of Viewport B. Right- or left-click on the word Camera to open the Views menu, as shown in Figure 2.7.

If you roll your cursor over the word Cameras in the menu, you see a secondary window display the word Camera with a check beside it. This indicates that the viewport is showing that particular camera. Of course, you only have one camera in the scene at the moment, but if you had several, the check would correspond to the currently active camera, and here you could switch cameras.

Also note the listing Render Pass. The *Render Pass* view shows the view from the camera that is linked to the Render command. When you are ready to render your animation scene to individual frames, this view will allow you to verify the results.

Spotlights allows you to view your scene from the perspective and angle of a lighting instrument. As you load lights into your scene, you will see choices displayed here.

User is an easier form of custom display, which you can set up to show either orthographic, perspective, or data. Figure 2.8 shows the views available in XSI.

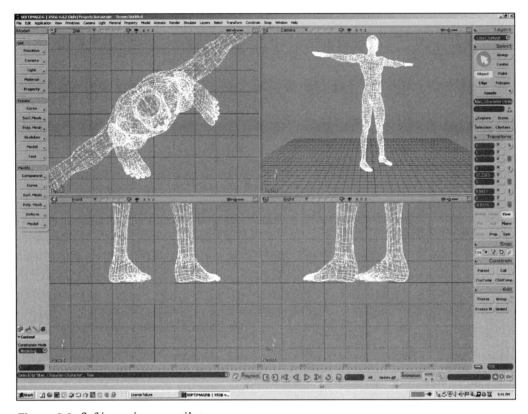

Figure 2.8 *Softimage is a versatile program.*

The next three choices, Top, Front, and Right, are the orthographic views already displayed by the other three viewports.

The next five choices produce data displays that present the animator with valuable alphanumeric information and allow the animator to adjust the settings. Notice that to the right of each title, there is a keyboard equivalent that you can use instead of opening this menu. When opened by keystroke, these windows appear in a floating view over your display, instead of being embedded in the viewport.

Explorer is a tool you will use from your first day of working in XSI. The Explorer displays all of the contents of your animation in text form, arranged in an outline style called a *hierarchy*. Open this view now, and notice how the major element of your scene is shown as text. Click on the + signs to open submenus. You can drill pretty deep, opening up a vast list of elements called *nodes*. Click on any node and a property editor opens up, allowing you to execute certain commands. This is just one of the ways to modify your scene elements. You can open Explorer in any window your cursor covers by pressing the 8 key.

Figure 2.9 shows the Explorer view with a vast array of elements in the present scene, arranged in an outline that reflects the hierarchical relationships between elements.

Object Viewer is another 3D viewer, similar to the Camera view, but it displays only the objects that are currently selected.

XSI Explorer expands on the Explorer view by providing you with a two-window view of your scene. The left window features the Explorer view described previously, while the right window shows the selected element. You can set the right one to also show any of the other view options.

Property Editor, when used from the View menu, docks the property editor of any selected object into the viewport. You can also open a floating property editor by pressing the Enter key. Property editors allow you to change any of the parameters of the selected object, such as size, position, color, and many more. In one of the orthographic views, click on the man character so the wireframe is bright white.

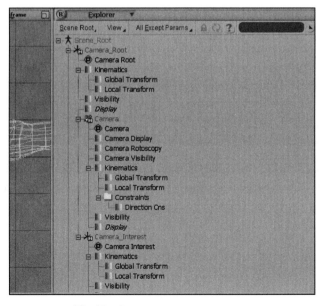

Figure 2.9 *The Explorer.*

This means the man character is selected. Then open a property editor and start changing things. This is a fun way to learn some of the powers available in this essential tool.

Animation Editor, *Dopesheet*, and *Animation Mixer* are view tools you will use when you start animating. They display the frames of your animation and the keyframes that store significant changes in the scene.

Schematic displays the contents of the viewport in a block diagram or schematic. Later, you will learn to create or change the links between these elements. The display also makes it easier to find and select elements within a very complex scene. Double-click the boxes, representing nodes, to open their property editors.

Spreadsheet is yet another graphic representation of the scene. The contents of the spreadsheet are determined by queries. You can find some predefined queries in Query > Open. This tool is useful if you have to make one change to a large group of elements. You specify a query with all the elements you want to change, and the spreadsheet lists them in one place for you to execute the change.

Browser opens up XSI's version of the standard Windows browser. Use this view to search for files you may need on your HDDs. This view supports drag-and-drop capabilities to the other views of your interface.

Object Transformation

The tool set for affecting objects is called *transformers* (not to be confused with Lionel). In Softimage, you can manipulate cameras, lights, bones, and objects, in any axis or plane. These manipulations are called *transformations*. Normally, we think of a transformation as being a change in shape or size, such as a morph effect. In Softimage, the word *transform* is a bit confusing, so listen up. *Transform* refers to both the full set of manipulators and one of those types of manipulators.

The three types of transforms are scale, rotation, and—get this—transform! Sure, it would have been better to call one of these transforms a different name, but that's the way it is. All of the transform controls are in the lower third of the left vertical column.

The first transform is scale, which allows changes in size on the x, y, or z axes. Or, if you click the box with horizontal stripes, all three axes can change identically at the same time.

The second transform is rotation, which allows changes in the rotation on any axis. Or, if you click the box with horizontal stripes, all three axes can change identically at the same time.

The third transform is—oh, bother—transform, which could easily be called position. This control set moves the object along any axis. Or—you guessed it—all axes can move identically at the same time, if you click the horizontal striped box.

The radio button selections at the bottom of the transform controls, Global, Local, and View, refer to the effect of each transform, and whether the transformation will affect the selected object(s) in relation to the entire world, each other, or only your view of them. Be careful to select the right one to get the right result. For instance, you could make a lot of transformations while in View mode (which does not affect the object itself), and then see nothing happen when you go to render the animation!

Each transformation may be assigned to a specific keyframe in the timeline, allowing you to execute transformations from one state to another *over time*. This, of course, is the basis of animation.

When each of the transformers is selected, an appropriate symbol appears in relation to the selected object(s). The scale symbol is usually composed of a box outline with three colored vector lines emanating from it, with arrowheads at the ends representing the three axes (red x, green y, blue z). In addition to selecting the axis buttons in the transform panel, you can scale the selected object freely on all axes if you click the central symbol, or you can isolate one axis by clicking one arrowhead at the end of that axis.

The rotate symbol is composed of three intersecting rings (red for rotations on the x axis, green for rotations on the y axis, and blue for rotations on the z axis) around a central point, which represents the pivot point of the object. Again, clicking on the center of the symbol allows free manipulation of all axes at once, while clicking on any one of the colored rings selects a single axis.

The transform symbol is similar to the scale symbol, but the center symbol and the ends of the vector lines are cubes instead of arrows. The colors of the vector lines and end symbols are the same as those for the scale tool, and they refer to the same axes as the scale transformer symbol. When you click the center symbol, the mouse affects all three axes simultaneously.

Layers and Histories

Animation, particularly the modeling phase, is an *iterative* process. This means that you tend to try something, evaluate it, and then back up or go forward. Each revision is a new iteration. In the process of modeling an object, you might execute hundreds, perhaps thousands of iterations. Softimage offers a sophisticated tool for assisting this odd behavior, the Explorer.

Histories

Every decision made in a Softimage project is recorded by the program and logged in an outline format that can be examined by the artist at any time. By opening this outline, you can go back over many decisions and find a place where perhaps you went off on an unproductive tangent or made a mistake. But clicking on that entry in the outline, you can restore the state of the design back to that point, and then begin again from there. Of course, this new tangent is also recorded and entered into the outline, so you can go back up the chain of decisions without ever destroying your history. This can become awesomely complicated.

Layers

Another useful tool is *layers*. Layers are useful in building and maintaining complex objects and sets. For instance, if you were building a somewhat symmetrical apple, you might create the left half of the shape in one layer, duplicate it to another layer, and mirror it into a circular shape. In another layer, you might design the stem, and in yet another layer, a leaf for the stem. Each layer allows for other layers to be superimposed, so the various elements can be aligned with one another. At some point, you may save all the layers separately to form a file collection that represents the entire object, or you may combine any two or more layers to weld all the elements together into one object.

On more complex objects, such as a jet fighter, you may want to put each sub-assembly—the wings, engine, cockpit, landing gear, and so on—in a separate layer, preserving each subassembly for individual attention, transformation, and animation.

All of the features mentioned in this chapter are discussed in greater detail in following chapters, as you employ them in tutorial exercises that are designed to develop second-hand familiarity.

Chapter 3

Getting Your First Job
in an Animation Studio

In this chapter, you will learn how to make a resume, and how to use it to get an internship in an animation production studio that will provide you with top-notch training and hardware for no money—maybe even for pay.

Okay, it's time to get you into an animation studio so you can start learning on the job.

"But I don't know enough about animation to get a job!", I hear you screaming through the screen of my laptop. "What do *I* know that some studio boss is going to pay me to do?"

Yep, that's one of the questions a potential employer might ask you: "What can you do for me?" For about four out of five people, it's a real nightmare to sit in front of a stranger and brag about what you can do to make that stranger money. But that's what the stranger is sizing you up for.

Consequently, strangers don't want to open their doors to someone they aren't sure will be useful from the get-go. They don't want to waste their time evaluating people with little experience, because people with little experience probably won't produce immediate cash flow. Hence, you—the newbie, the novice, the entry-level person—are walking around with a serious liability: lack of experience.

The Old Catch-22

Novelist Joseph Heller, in his 1961 book about World War II, *Catch-22*, referred to a fictional Air Force regulation whereby a pilot continuing to fly dangerous combat missions without asking for relief is regarded to be insane. Since insane airmen could be relieved of duty, this would have been an excellent way for a sane airman to get out of flying dangerous missions. But a second part of the regulation—the Catch-22—stated that if an airman *requested* the exemption from flying dangerous missions on the basis that he was insane, the request itself was proof that the airman was sane. Therefore, the airman could be ordered to continue to fly dangerous missions.

In our business, a Catch-22 refers to a situation that makes it difficult to find a job. For instance, you might come across the union Catch-22: "You can join the union if you have a union job, but you have to be a member of the union to get a union job." This book gives you a method to escape the Catch-22: "You can have the job if you have experience, but you need experience to get the job."

Sometimes Catch-22s are used to protect a few privileged individuals and their chosen cronies. It may get to that point one day in animation, but there are still plenty of jobs and not enough talented animators. If you come up against a Catch-22, most likely it's because of unique pressures that employers face in this business.

Animation studio bosses are like one-armed paperhangers. They have no time to go to the bathroom, much less time to interview a prospective employee who probably doesn't have enough experience to increase the studio's cash flow.

Even when you get an interview, you still have to convince the boss that you can do something worthwhile without a lot of education or handholding. Nobody in the studio will be able to spend too much time showing you how to do the things you gotta do! Get it? You can get an interview and then maybe a job if you have experience, but you need experience to get an interview. Catch-22.

So you have to find a way of convincing the boss you are worth the time to interview. Once you get the interview, you have a foot in the door. So let's start to think about things you already know. Things you feel confident about. Things you could talk confidently about to a stranger. Things you can *do* for somebody.

Maybe you think you know nothing about the animation business. This isn't true. You can make great coffee, answer phones, sweep floors, write letters, file, and make annoying calls to collect on delinquent invoices! That may not seem like much, but I don't know many people who would turn down a well-spoken phone caller who offered to provide such humble services. You know what? In 20 years, only two or three people have ever called *me* offering to do these humble tasks and each of them was granted an interview within a week (all three became interns and one of those three is now running his own animation studio in Tribeca).

And if you have some computer-related skill, like building a network, defragging hard drives, repairing computers, building a render farm, designing a Web site, or working on any of the ancillary software products that animators use—eyeon's Digital Fusion or Adobe Photoshop, Illustrator and After Effects, or Sonic Foundry's Sound Forge, or its MAC OS competitor, ProTools—you might get yourself an attractive offer.

Of course, there are the traditional skills that any employer desires, such as writing proposals and—God forbid you should stoop so low—salesmanship. (I don't know any studio boss that would turn you down if you offered your time to call new clients on the phone!) Or perhaps you can bring some of the traditional animation skills to the bargaining table, like sculpting, illustrating, modeling, plotting, storyboarding, coloring, or scenic designing.

Any one of these tasks answers the employer's question, "What can you do for me?" But before you get to answer this question, you have to hook up with someone who will ask it; someone who can offer you some kind of job. If you don't already have a job in the animation market, your task is to get one. Here's how you are going to do that.

Seven Simple Steps to a Successful Internship

You might look at the daunting task of getting hired by a professional animation studio as something so monumental, so awesome, that the idea itself is keeping you from getting the job done.

I'm way past the point in my career where I need an internship, but I face monumental tasks too. They appear just as awesome and scary to me as getting an internship may be to you. I like to take a big task and break it down into a list of "to-do's," or the task's simplest elements.

For instance, I've got this big production starting next month. It's for a company for whom I've never worked before, and the job itself is a little strange. So I took out a legal pad and pencil, and I started writing down each task that needed to be done. I triple-spaced, because often, I'd think of a task that needed to be done in between two other tasks I'd already listed. Eventually, I had about 35 tasks. That was everything I could anticipate I had to do. Then, to the right of each task, I put a deadline date—the day I had to finish that task. I was generous with the time allotments, just in case I got stuck on a task along the way.

After breaking down the huge task into little, unscary bits, the big job didn't feel so frightening. Eventually, I gave this list to my client. Being wiser than I, the client added a few more tasks between some of mine. (Good thing I allotted enough time, because my client didn't!)

So let's break down the huge task of getting an internship into a concise to-do list. It comes down to seven easy steps. After we review each one, I'll ask you to write the steps on your own pad of paper and establish your own schedule to get each task done. For now, let me show you the steps, and then we'll examine each step in greater detail. Here are the seven steps:

1. Create a resume.
2. Make a list of possible employers.
3. Call contacts periodically, and offer your services as an intern.
4. Set up and take job interviews.
5. When interning, work for real.
6. Watch for opportunities.
7. Ask for a letter of recommendation.

Hold on, dear. I know you've bought this very nice book about starting a career as an animator, and that's all very good. But your father and I have been talking, and . . . well, your father thinks perhaps you need to go to school to learn these things. He's even willing to pay for tuition, aren't you, Honey?

It's a loan, Honey. We're going to *loan* the kid the money for tuition.

Do You Need a College Degree?

Let me be give you some honest information that your teachers, friends, and parents—*especially* your parents—may not be able to provide. It's kind of a middle-class American expectation that a young person should get a college degree before going out to earn a living. This is a good thing. I did it. My kids did it. But you should know this: Animation is an *artistic trade*. It is not an academic pursuit.

Sure, you can take animation courses in college, and I'm sure some university is even offering a doctorate in the topic. That's fine if you want to teach animation. Getting a college degree is also good if you want a full educational background, so that if you fail at the trade of animation, you might have some credentials that will support a different career. But just to be an animator, you don't need a college degree, or even a high school diploma.

There are people who will argue with me vigorously on this point. What no one will dispute, however, is that if you want to be an animator, you most certainly need to know how to animate. So maybe you learn how to animate in college, or high school, or at a specialized institute for the arts. Or maybe you teach yourself with a computer and books.

Considering the current level of technology and what you need to know to get—and hold onto—your first job, it may take you a good six months to a year of full-time study. That's assuming you're mature and have some basic talent and skills in art, like sketching, painting, sculpture, or even photography.

Now, you could do a lot worse than to spend an additional three years taking courses in life drawing, anatomy, cell animation, plastic arts, oil & acrylics, and art history, and even some computer programming courses. This is the kind of rounded-out program a college offers, along with courses in accounting, English composition, and a foreign language. If you are like most American students between the ages of 17 and 22, you might also need to learn how to live on your own without Mommy and Daddy paying your bills, washing your clothes, making your meals, and teaching you what a closet and clothes drawer are used for. These are things you also learn in college. In other words, you learn maturity. This is a real necessary career skill, if not life skill.

So, you have to be honest with yourself. Are you mature, or do you need to learn these skills at a sleepaway sort of institution? Do you have a good foundation in the liberal arts, or do you need someone to hold your hand and teach you the difference between an Impressionist and an Expressionist? And most important of all, are you financially prepared for either college or a year or two of technical school, and prepared for the time it will take to pound the street for a job? Only you have the answers to these questions. But at least now you know that you need to answer them.

If you want to explore a career in animation, but you still need the structure and discipline of an institution of higher learning, keep in mind that a top-flight college or institute (such as Pratt Institute, Rhode Island School of Design, or Parsons) can cost as much as $120,000 in tuition alone for a four-year degree. You could pay a lot less for a regular college or community college, but then you'd be leaning more toward the maturity part of the package than the animation part. Learning animation in a college or university is going to cost you serious lucre.

On the other hand, if you are already a mature young adult, have some money saved from part-time or summer work, and have good discipline and focus, you might want to strip down your education to the bare animation requirements. In such a situation, a trade school specializing in animation might be your best choice. There, you can study with real animators who teach as a sideline (as opposed to tenured professors who animate as a sideline), and might even recommend you for a job or even hire you. Such schools offer a limited curriculum with precisely designed goals. You don't get a degree or even college credits, but you pay just as much per hour of class (sometimes more) to learn what you need to know. And the time you spend is a lot less than at a college. You're out on the street looking for work three years ahead of the rest of your cronies.

If this is more to your nature, I will recommend three such schools:

- **Gnomon (www.gnomon3d.com):** Located in Hollywood, California, Gnomon starts your education in the global center of digital content creation. In addition to animation, Gnomon offers a variety of short and long courses in several areas of entertainment arts, such as film and audio production. In addition to its faculty, Gnomon has an Advisory Board, which is composed of seasoned professionals who not only participate in the education of Gnomon students, but also serve as mentors and occasionally employers.

- **Full Sail (www.fullsail.com):** Full Sail offers six-month diploma courses in such topics as Animation, Digital Media, Film, Game Design and Development, Recording Arts, and Show Production and Touring. Animators can also take courses leading to an accredited Associate of Science degree in Computer Animation, which includes courses in Character Design, Compositing and Editing, Shading and Lighting, and Entertainment and Business Law. The most important course of all, in my opinion, is Business of Living/General Education, which teaches the skills one needs to get and keep a real job. The Associate degree program takes about 12 to 16 months to complete, based on the program selected. There are about 3,000 students in Full Sail at any given time, with most housed off-campus. The entrance and graduation schedules are staggered on a monthly basis to avoid releasing large groups of graduates in June and December, thus enhancing the probability of professional placement.

- **Future Media Concepts (www.fmctraining.com):** FMC is headquartered in New York City, with branches in Boston, Philadelphia, Washington D.C., Orlando, and Miami. FMC was the brainchild of an editor from CBS and a second-generation NYC commercial producer. FMC began as the only factory-authorized training center for Avid nonlinear editing systems on the East Coast. The TV networks, however, increased FMC's demand for qualified artists and technicians, so FMC expanded to include factory-authorized courses in 3dsMax, Lightwave, and SOFTIMAGE|XSI. Today, FMC offers courses in Nonlinear Editing, Sound Editing, Web Design, Web Programming, Streaming Video, DVD Authoring, Graphics, Compositing, 3D Animation, and Color Correction. A maximum of 6 students are permitted in each class, so instruction is highly individualized. Beginner, intermediate, and expert courses are taught on weekdays and weekends, but no degrees or college credits are offered.

FMC does not offer a set curriculum, but allows students to enroll in any one or more courses for which the instructor feels each student is qualified after a review of previous coursework or a showreel.

FMC is a factory-authorized training center for Adobe, Apple, Avid/Softimage, Boris, Discreet, Macromedia, NewTek, Pinnacle, Quark, Sonic, and Sony. Instructors are highly trained and qualified by the software manufacturers. Almost all of them are practicing professionals who produce media in addition to teaching at FMC.

Responding to the needs of individuals who cannot afford to take courses, FMC offers non-paid, three-month internships. Performing various office and logistical functions, FMC interns enjoy free access to all levels of training courses and unlimited practice time at the school's facilities. Contact FMC for more information on interning.

Okay, enough about schools. Let's get back to the Seven Simple Steps to a Successful Internship.

Step One: Create a Resume

Basically, there are two kinds of resumes: the traditional resume and the weird resume. A traditional resume is printed in black on one page of white paper (or offered as an email or Adobe PDF document), conforms to a traditional format established over decades, and presents your name, address, phone number, work history, educational background, and interesting facts about you. A weird resume is anything else that presents your name, address, phone number, work history, educational background, and interesting facts about you.

Here are the rules for the traditional resume:

- 12 point type (preferably Times Roman, but Helvetica and Arial are acceptable).
- Approximately one-inch margins on the top, bottom, and sides.
- Name, address, phone number (note if you have a service), and email, centered at top, boldface recommended.
- A short, one-sentence statement, left-justified, following the word Objective.
- A listing of recent jobs, latest job first, follows Objective. Each listing is two lines. The first line, right-left justified, states the company name, company address, and the dates of your tenure. The second line, left-justified, describes your duties on the job.
- A listing of educational institutions you have attended. Each listing is two lines. The first line, right-left justified, states the institution's name, the institution's address, and the dates of your attendance. The second line, left-justified, lists the courses you studied, your degree (if any), your grade-point average, and any honors you achieved.
- A listing of personal information, such as languages you speak, unusual hobbies or skills, and marital status (optional—but be aware that being married is better than being single, and being married with children is better than being married without children). This listing usually ends with the statement "References upon request."
- Special notes for media-related resumes: If you are seeking a position as a creator of media, it is customary to list some of your significant credits, if you *have* significant credits. This listing should appear below your listing of recent jobs. In addition to references being available on request, the final line may read, "References and showreel on request."

Here is what a traditional media creator's resume might look like:

ROSWELL T. CUMBERBUN
10 Turtledove Square
Bubbling Brook, NY 11005
914-555-5125 Mobile: 917-555-5577
email:

OBJECTIVE: An entry-level position in a media production company, in which I can learn to create 3D computer animation.

PROFESSIONAL EXPERIENCE:

Telephone Sales: Rizzi Catering, Seattle, WA, July 2004 – Present

Make 50-60 cold calls per day, from various data sources, to convince newly engaged women to use this catering house to host their weddings. Generated approximately $150,000 in bookings the first quarter.

Asst. Bookkeeper: Mason's Meat Supplies, Portland, OR, Sept. 1999 – June 2004

Night shift during college. Began as janitor, promoted to front office. Trained by book-keeper to record accounts payable, log income statements, and take cash to bank.

Hamburger Flipper: McDouglins, Las Vegas, NV, June 1998 – Sept. 2002

Night shift grill cook during high school. Reported to General Manager, who noted in exit evaluation, "The best hamburger flipper we ever had." Also assisted in bookkeeping.

SIGNIFICANT MEDIA CREDITS:

A Wedding at Rizzi	Interactive CD	Produced to enhance sales of a catering hall.
Heresthebeef.com	Web Site	Site for a metropolitan meat wholesaler.
You Go Girl	Video Documentary	Struggles of a paraplegic high school student.

EDUCATION:

University of Nevada   Las Vegas, NV   June 1998—Sept. 2002

BA: Media Studies major, Business minor, 3.5 GPA, Honors Society, Band.

PERSONAL:

Fluent in Spanish and Portuguese. Can repair computers. NV truck driver's license. Amateur Radio operator's technician license. Hobbies: Scuba, baseball, track, jazz trumpet.

References and showreel on request.

Some Notes on Editing Your Resume

Objective: Some experts do not suggest an objective. I think it helps readers who are quickly scanning resumes to understand that your objective is focused and realistic. If you think you can direct, write, animate, and paint murals, make a different resume for each, and include only one of these skills in each objective.

Professional Experience: Did you notice that I have created the career of someone who has never done media production? Probably a lot like you! But notice that I have extracted from each job two qualities that I think an animation studio boss will want to see—practical experience as a bookkeeper and sales work. Every business needs salespeople and bookkeepers! Notice also that I demonstrated initiative by noting that the candidate worked nights during the time he attended school. Notice also that I demonstrated a progression of job categories up the ladder of responsibility.

Obviously, your own career history will differ greatly from this fictitious example. However, you should examine your own career history and give the facts that indicate a similar progression of skill over time, a list of skills that would be useful (even if they are not media-related), and an underlying philosophy of wanting to work hard and please your boss.

Significant Media Credits: Keep in mind that this is an entry-level resume. Later, when you have a few years of experience, you will have credits that are significant enough to list. You may not have any now. If so, create some by offering free production services to friends, schools, charities, or your favorite band. This is what this fictitious job hunter has done, and there is no attempt to hide this inexperience by creating fictitious clients that differ from the job listings above. No one expects you to have produced an Emmy Award-winning show (*I* haven't even done that). But a potential employer might be impressed to know you went the extra mile to produce a showreel by offering your free services to your current employers. Three listings here would be the maximum. Don't create this category if you only have one example. Move that example into the job descriptions if you can.

Education: I would not include high school here, unless you have not completed college. If you changed colleges during the pursuit of a degree, or went from a junior college for an AA degree to a full college for a degree, list both institutions. If you went to any trade schools in addition to or instead of college, list the trade schools. but keep the list to a maximum of two, unless they are significant. For instance, don't list a two-week course in Softimage at FMC and then another one-month course at FMC. Join the two listings together under "Various courses taken in Softimage, Maya, etc."

Personal: This section is here for two reasons. First, you want to hint at some skills that you have not been able to apply to your job descriptions yet, but that might be useful to an employer—such as computer repair or truck driving. Second, it creates an opportunity for the employer to find something in common with you on a personal level. With that goal, list your personal interests that might be the same as those of an employer. Obviously, you would avoid putting down Sherman's Union Reenactors of the Civil War if you were pitching your resume in Atlanta. You might even go so far as to research what a specific employer does for a hobby, and then list the same hobby if you participate in it as well—in a specific resume for that employer!

NOTE

If you do make a specific resume for a potential employer, be sure to make two copies. Send one copy, and keep the other in a safe place to use when you go to visit that employer. See "Step Five" later in this chapter.

Step Two: Make a List of Employers You Could Call

Creating a list of potential employers is the most important thing you will do in the process of starting and developing your career. This step is often overlooked by new job seekers because of the work it takes, and because of . . . well, ignorance. Many new job seekers think employers will contact them after the resume is sent. Not so. You have to build a large database of potential employers, send resumes to each one, and then follow up to make sure the resumes were received, read, and evaluated. In the process of calling, your objective is to get job interviews. *I repeat: Your goal in building a list is to get job interviews.*

Before you start to build this list, you need a notepad to keep notes while speaking on the phone or doing research. Obviously, you will need a few sharpened pencils (not pens, which you cannot erase). Next, you need a loose-leaf binder full of blank *contact sheets*. I will show you how to make contact sheets in a minute. Finally, you need a date book, such as a Day-Timer, or a Personal Digital Assistant (PDA) to record the appointments you make and other very important information. Do not—I repeat—*do not* start making phone calls or send a single resume until you have obtained these items and set them up in a secure workplace that will remain undisturbed by the dog, your little sister, or your roommates.

You'll notice that this list of supplies is very inexpensive to obtain. You can even substitute the Day-Timer with any pocket-sized schedule book you can buy at Staples. However, you should know that for a few hundred dollars, you could buy a software tool that is, in my opinion, worth ten times the price. If you can afford it, buy it, but it's not necessary if you are just starting out with just a few dollars to your name. This tool goes under the generic title of *Contact Relation Management (CRM)* software.

Contact Relation Management Software

Computers make superb assistants in building and maintaining effective lists of contacts, which you can use to find a job and then sell to clients when you have your own production company. The two biggest brand names of CRM software are ACT! (www.act.com) and Gold Mine (www.frontrange.com/goldmine/).

CRM programs are sophisticated, easy-to-use databases that allow you to enter all the information on an employer (or client) and access it on a convenient, scheduled basis. For instance, you can store a studio's name, address, phone numbers, and any other information, such as their significant credits, Web site, and so on. Within the company, you can list all of the people for whom you might work. Below this information, you can list every contact you have made with each person, including phone calls, meetings, letters sent, and so on.

In addition to the stored information, the CRM includes a calendar in which you enter your planned actions, such as "Call Mr. Thomas" or "Meeting with Bill at New Sensory." When the target day comes around, the system will warn you in advance of the event to remind you to execute it.

There is even a library of template letters you can use (or you can create your own). While you have a particular contact on the screen, you just click a button or two and select the letter you want to mail. Instantly, the software creates the letter with all the specific information, like the person's name and address, already added in. Click the Print button and the letter is sent to your printer, while a notation that the letter was printed is added to your notes on the target person's data page.

CRM software is by far the best way to build an employer or client list and achieve any sales objective. And let's be frank: Getting a job is a job in itself. It's selling yourself. If you can afford CRM software right now, keep this information in the back of your mind and proceed to making the contact sheets I referred to earlier.

The Contact Sheet

You can easily create a master contact sheet using a standard sheet of copier paper, a pencil, and a ruler, or you can use any word processing program's Create Table function. Be sure to leave space in the left margin for the three punched holes that you will use to mount the pages, alphabetically according to company name, in a loose leaf binder.

Here's how a contact sheet can look:

Company Name: _____

Address: _____

City, State, ZIP: _____

Main Phone: _____

Specialty: _____   **Web site:** _____

Contact A: _____   **Phone:** _____

Title: _____   **Fax:** _____

Contact B: _____   **Phone:** _____

Title: _____   **Fax:** _____

Contact C: _____   **Phone:** _____

Title: _____   **Fax:** _____

Contact Notes: _____

_____

_____

_____

_____

These pages, when filled in with information, are a *paper database*, the most primitive kind. This is exactly what I used when I formed my media production company in 1982—long before there were computers to do this work. Later, I hired a programmer to make a software program that would extract the contact information I typed when I wrote my first letter, thus creating a database of names and addresses. A little more than a year after I spent $1,000 on that software, the first CRM program was offered for sale! I made much more than that $1,000, however, using the information from the database I commissioned. And I still have all my paper data pages, which are useful in doing historical research on contacts that I made years ago.

Notice how this paper database is based on the company name. You could choose a different method, but I find it easier to group individuals under companies, even when it is possible that these individuals leave the company and others enter. You'll see that this method is best, and that adding, changing, or deleting names is easy—if you use a pencil!

Each data page uses the top 1/3rd for generic company information and for listing just three persons' names. Each person is given a letter code for that page: A, B, or C. Don't put more than three individuals on a page. Below the generic company data and names list, you reserve 2/3rds of the page for contact notes. This area is composed of simple horizontal lines, like a notepad. A little later, I'll show you what you do with this part of your contact page, but for now, just concentrate on generating one page for each company you will attempt to serve.

Getting a job (or a client) is simply a matter of percentages. You will get an appointment to meet with, say, one percent of the people you contact (actually the percentage is higher). If that is believable, consider that if you contact 100 people, chances are you will get one appointment. Increase your contact list to 1,000 people and your chances of getting a job go up ten times.

Of course, you only need to get one job. But what happens when you get some experience, ask for a raise, and get refused? Are you out of luck, destined to be manipulated by a cruel boss with no compassion for your growing economic needs? No! You go back to that database and quickly find a better job. In fact, you never stop using the database. Even when you're fully employed (or totally booked with freelance or contract work), you should take a little part of each day to make contacts with the names in your database. This keeps you professionally active and always at the peak of your money-earning ability.

Step Three: Call Contacts Periodically, and Offer Your Services as an Intern

Okay, here's how you work the contact sheets and the date book. First day—get out a Yellow Pages or log onto the Internet, and start searching for the kinds of studios you want to work for. Begin with your immediate geographic area, and slowly work outward in ever-widening circles. If, like me, you live in a major metropolitan area, you will never need to go more than 50 miles. If, however, you have the bad luck to be a potential animator in the middle of the Kansas plains, you need to either start making long-distance contacts or move your home base.

For instance, if you're going to search the Internet, type in "animation studio" and your nearest city, such as "Harrisburg." If you're willing to relocate, don't type a city. Your results will produce studio references from every corner of the English-speaking world. For that matter, if you want to work in a foreign language, use the words for "animation studio" in Italian, French, or Chinese—whatever.

Whether you use the Yellow Pages, another directory from the library, or the Internet, you object is to get just 10 good potential listings. Even in Rats Nest, Idaho, there are at least 10 cable stations, corporations, religious institutions, schools, or small production companies that may offer you the prospect of an internship to learn your craft. If not, face it: You're living in the wrong place to start work as an animator. Later in life, when you're successful and have a long list of clients, you can move back to that babbling brook in Smuggler's Cove, Utah. But for now, consider that no one is going to hire an intern or entry-level worker who has to fly or take a train to come to the first interview.

Once you have 10 initial listings, call the employer's main number. Your objective is to identify the person who can offer you an internship (or, later, a job). In this quest, it helps if you can become friendly with the person who answers the phone.

I've prepared two telephone scripts for you here. I've developed these scripts carefully over more than 15 years of experimentation with both male and female callers, so I know they work. Start with these and then, if you like, experiment with your own individual routines.

The first is for small animation studios of 3-10 employees, where the receptionist is likely to know the target individual personally. The second script is for large companies, like Sony Pictures. I find that interns have better luck with small companies, but don't let that opinion sway you. Give each type a try.

Here's the Small Company Script:

> "Hi, what's your name? I'm ___(first name only)___. [Let's say she answers Judy.] Um, Judy, I wonder if you could please help me out. I want to kind of offer my services to your studio for free as an intern and then, you know, kind of learn 3D animation in my spare time there. Can you tell me the name of the person who might be able to use someone like me? And, oh yes, I'd better get the person's title too, because I'll need that for the resume letter."

I added an, "um" and "kind of" to the script to break up your speech pattern and keep you from sounding like you're reading a script. Even if you're a professional actor, you don't want to sound that way. It would make it harder for someone to take pity on you and help you out. This is a little like begging for money on the streets of New York City. You can't be wearing a new suit and polished shoes, and your voice can't sound like you've done this a hundred times before. Eventually, you'll get the hang of this. If you don't, you won't get any help!

If you're calling a large company (more than 10 employees), use the Big Company Script:

> "Hello. I'm ___(first and last name)_____, and I wonder if you can connect me to the person in charge of creative interns. But before you connect me, can you please give me the person's name and the person's title? I'll probably have to send a letter, and I want to get it right."

Notice that in each script, you asked the receptionist for both the name and the title of the person to whom you are being connected. Be sure to have your pencil and notepad ready to take this down. Don't rely on your shabby memory. By making the receptionist work a little, you also help avoid being sent to the wrong person and thus spending days, maybe weeks of contact work.

Once you get the name of a target person, you are ready for the next script, the Target Employer script. This is the same for small or big companies:

> "Hi Mr./Ms. _____. My name is _____(first and last name)___, and I'm calling to offer you my work for free in return for the opportunity of improving my resume. Do you have room in your studio for a hard-working apprentice?"

Most of the time, this script will elicit a favorable response, but in a moment or two, the person may begin to generate objections. You don't want this to happen. Before the person starts to think about objections, you have to press for your objective—the personal face-to-face meeting. So as soon as the initial surprise from your pitch is absorbed, you say something like this:

"I know this might come as a surprise to you, but in order to get a good job, I have to first make a good showreel. I figure if I do stuff like sweeping your floors, making coffee, or running errands, you can let me spend some time on one of your spare machines to learn the software on my own time and get my skills up to speed. How about letting me come by to visit so you can see how I present myself? I'm free next Tuesday, all day. Can we make an appointment?"

Often, the response will still be an objection, and this is natural. Most people do not want to open their doors to a stranger, no matter how charming and persuasive you are. It's part of the professional studio manager's demeanor. In such cases, when the person is polite, interested, and just wants to know more about you, they will ask for a resume. You have it. Send it. Before you hang up, be sure to confirm the spelling of the person's name (you should have it from the receptionist), title, and address. Often, mail will get lost in a large company, so ask if the person has a "mail code." Of course, write all this information down on your notepad.

Once you hang up, transfer the essential information to your contact database sheet. Then prepare a resume. You might send a mass produced resume, or one specifically crafted for that person. Be sure to include with the resume a *cover letter*.

The Cover Letter

In addition to your resume, the cover letter is another opportunity to show your personality and professional courtesy. You want to be courteous and acknowledge that the recipient's time is very valuable. Therefore, make the letter as short as possible, with the text set in the center of the page and lots of space above and below.

You can use personal stationery if you have it, with your name, address, and perhaps a logo at the top of the page. One word of serious warning: Do not under any circumstances send anything to a potential employer that implies you own or run a production company. I see a lot of business cards from entry-level professionals who want to enhance their image by presenting themselves as proprietors of production companies (President, CEO, and Director titles abound). This is a good idea if you're looking for a client and positioning yourself as an independent company, but it is a big mistake if you are looking for a job. No one wants to hire someone who looks like a competitor.

This is a good sample of a cover letter. Don't copy it—make something like it.

Your First Name, Second Name
Street Address
City, State, Zip

Mr./Ms. Firstname Lastname
333 Street Name
City, State Zip

Dear Firstname:

I would like to offer you my services for free as an intern in return for the opportunity to sit at one of your workstations and teach myself 3D animation. I am available from June 1, 2005 and can work from 8:00 a.m. to 1:00 p.m., Tuesday through Friday.

The enclosed resume briefly outlines my background, which, as you can see, needs more experience.

Please help me get the experience I need to be of greater service.

Sincerely,

[Your Signature]
[Your Name Printed]

What If Your Call Gets a Negative Response?

If your phone call is charming and pleasant, you should receive at least a polite response and possibly an interview. Often a call will produce a request to see your resume. Never *offer* to send the resume. The resume step, which entails at least a week to send and receive, only delays the inevitable necessity of getting that interview. But if the resume is requested, you can't say no. So you say:

> "Good, Mr./Ms. _____. I'll send that today. And may I call you
> to verify its arrival and follow up with you in a week or so?"

What cruel curmudgeon would say "No, you may not" to that request? I'll tell you, quite a few. The classic negative response is, "No need to call. We'll put it in our files and get back to you if we have a need."

Here's what you do with that response. Enter the person's name in your data sheet, and then schedule another call to that person six months from now and make whatever pitch you are pitching. Chances are, that person won't be there when you call back. If you've identified the correct person in the company, and that person's job is to interview interns and new people, their cold-hearted attitude to your internship inquiry is inappropriate.

My experience has shown that people like that don't continue to be employed for very long. In fact, 9 out of 10 of these six-month or one-year postponed calls result in finding someone entirely new in the position once occupied by the numbskull. If the bonehead is still there after six months, your first call will be completely forgotten anyway, and you get another chance to pitch yourself a different way. In six months, you'll probably have a better presentation and showreel anyway.

I wouldn't bother sending a resume to any person who's thick-headed enough not to respond nicely to an energetic novice like you. Most likely, your resume will get filed . . . in the circular file. Why bother wasting the postage? Even if they do file the resumes they get, and even if they do review them periodically (wouldn't that be a fantasy come true?), they probably only do it every six months, so your next call will probably come just in time.

Step Four: Set Up and Take Job Interviews

Once you have talked to someone who you believe to be a genuine contact, that's the time to fill in the lines in the bottom 2/3rds of your contact sheet. What is a *genuine contact*? It's either a person who has the power to hire you or a legitimate influence on the person who has the power to hire you. How do you know if the person you are talking to has the power or is an influencer? Simple. You ask.

Obviously, there is a polite way and a crude way to do this. The crude way is to ask in any way that implies that the person responding is of no interest to you if the response is negative. For instance, what if I were to ask you, "Are you rich enough to contribute to my charity?" You'd probably find that offensive, unless you were pretty rich. To say "No" would make you sad that you weren't rich.

However, what if I asked you, "Would I be offending you to ask if you could afford to contribute to my charity?" The answer could be yes or no without risking offense. It's sort of like asking, "Can you please do me a favor?" I could or I couldn't, and I might or I might not.

So when you ask if a person has the capability to hire you, you might ask, "Are you the person whose responsibility it is to hire interns?" I might say "Yes" or "No" without specifically addressing the issue of hiring you.

There are many other ways of determining the validity of a contact. The contact could be referred to you by someone who knows, if you are aggressive enough to ask if they know anyone who could offer you an internship. This is called *networking*.

I know a lad at the club, son, who hires interns for his company. They don't do media per se, but hey, you never know, and the interview could give you practice.

Okay, let's assume you have a genuine contact and you've put the name on one of your contact pages. You've made the first call to this person, but you got their voicemail. (I am convinced that voicemail and cockroaches will be the only things left behind by our civilization, so once in awhile, record something on a voicemail that tells the aliens what really went on here.) Leaving voicemail is like leaving a radio advertisement for yourself. Think it out ahead of time—make a script.

And after you leave the message, here's what you do. When you make your first call to person A, start a blank line with a large letter A, add the current date, like 8/21/05, and carefully write your notes. Use shorthand abbreviations, like LMCB for "left message to call back" and CBd for "Called me back." This saves space. If you continue past the first line, add another A to the next line and continue your notes. If you end up talking to person B, however, start a new line with a B, the date, and notes like "Spk about a website, call 1 mo."

If any of your notes require you to do something in the future, such as CB or APT (set an appointment), be *sure* you go to your date book and enter the task on the appropriate date. To be absolutely certain you don't forget the date, consult your date book every evening before going to sleep and every morning before starting work. You can even add an extra date before the key date to "Confirm apt."

Keep in mind that the notes area of your contact page is not for research notes or quick jottings about an employer or client, which would quickly fill the pages with useless garbage. Use your notepad for this task. For instance, if you are making several first calls to prospective studios out of the Yellow Pages, use your notebook to write the name of each company, the phone number, and notes on anything that happens during your first call. You will often get a phone receptionist who will quickly switch your call over to someone who will address your initial inquiry. If you are clever, you will quickly say, "Before you switch my call over, can you tell me the name of the person you are going to connect me to?"

The receptionist will say the name. Let's say it's a long name, like mine. Are you going to guess how to spell it, and then risk making a mistake when you mail your resume? Of course not. So you ask the receptionist, "How do you spell that, please?" And you spell the name carefully in your notebook. You might also ask for the local phone extension or even the person's email address.

These are all valuable pieces of information that you won't have time to carefully add to your database page. In fact, the person may turn out to be the wrong person! You certainly don't want to go through the trouble of adding this name to your data page without first ascertaining if the person is a bona fide contact. Those are just a few reasons to use a notebook when doing initial calls.

After you have made initial contact with the employer, or at least verified that he or she is the correct person to contact, *then* enter the person on your data page. In fact, you can do all the data page creation in the evening, using your notes, long after you make the calls.

All of this recordkeeping and date-making is part of a simple, aggressive, and very professional way of finding a job. Considering that it will not only lead to your first job, but create the foundation for finding more and better jobs as your career develops, this professional work is even more important than the job itself!

By carefully integrating your notebook notes, your contact pages (or CRM), and your daily date book, you can easily increase your contact network up to hundreds, even thousands of names, while keeping regular contact with each and every one of them!

By the way, *never* write anything bad about anyone in your contact notes. After trying for years to get a certain client on the phone, for example, you may be tempted to write an epithet that satisfies your urge for revenge. Not a good idea. Someday, someone may open your notes and read them. They might know the person you dissed. They might *be* the person you dissed. The worst I ever write in my notes is, "Fired yet?"

How Often Should You Call?

You should be adding several new genuine contacts to your database every day. As you add them, you will also be adding follow-up directives to your date book. Eventually, you will find that each day in your book has several notations to make a followup call. However, if you are really smart, you will note that if you write nothing in your date book after adding a contact to your database, chances are you will never call that contact again! Nothing in your database drives you to make calls—it's your date book that does this.

Therefore, no matter what, you have to add at least one regular followup call to every contact, the day you enter the contact, and after *every* followup call. This assures you of never losing track of any contact. But how often should you call?

Unless you are told by the contact or the contact's administrative assistant, never call more than once a month. Nothing ever happens within any company that a monthly call will be too late to serve.

What about emergencies? An emergency need for my darling could come up between two of those monthly calls.

Oh, there are emergencies that pop up, honey, but do you think that calling every week will help you be the one who is remembered in an emergency? Yes, you will be remembered. Remembered as the person *not* to call.

Calling more often than once a month shows you are hungry and needy. These aren't attractive attributes for anyone. You want to be of service, but you don't want to be a pest.

With that down, what about the least number of times to call a contact? I'd say once a year. A lot can happen in a year, and the contact might be replaced or moved up the corporate ladder from a position of being useful to you. Check in before that happens.

Now, you may realize that soon, your database and date book are going to be generating a lot of obligations for you. I expect that within three months, you will have found your first internship. When you do, keep making as many calls as you can, even though the internship will be eating up a lot of your time. Eventually, you will be using the database to find a permanent job, and perhaps after that, you will be using the very same database to find clients for your own production studio. *Never lose that database!*

As soon as you have a name, title, and phone extension, fill in the contact sheet. If you leave a message, put LMCB (left message to call back) on the Action line. If you speak to a person, write Spk and add the person's initials. Then write some notes to remind you what the conversation was about.

Next, immediately go to your daily appointment book and add a "to do" on the page that is most appropriate. An LMCB might require a call back in two weeks. A "call me back in the fall" would require you to put a "to do" into the book some months into the future. An appointment, of course, must not be forgotten—so use an appointment book. Always, always, *always* put in something about the appointment at some future date to remind you to call the person again. Nothing impresses an employer more than when you remember to call when they've forgotten. It shows real professionalism.

Attending a Job Interview

If you follow these directions so far and try to add 10 people to your database every day, in less than two weeks you could have as many as 100 names in your database. Statistically speaking, you should now be able to set at least one appointment with someone about being an intern. Now that you have someone who has agreed to meet with you, you must set the stage for a successful meeting.

We Greeks have a custom of never visiting anyone without bringing a gift. This doesn't apply to business, but it's never a good idea to walk through the door without something in your hand to give to the person who is courteous enough to see you. What do you hand over? Your resume!

Present Your Resume

It doesn't matter if you already sent the resume. Chances are, the person has lost it. In any case, have a fresh resume. (And it had better be the same resume as the one you sent, which is why I suggested making a copy of any custom written resume.)

Don't go in empty-handed. Prepare something to hand to the person when you walk in. This can be another copy of your resume—a good idea, since most people will lose it (or write something on it before the interview that they won't want you to see—like "see this guy when you can").

Prepare Your Reel/Portfolio

One of the best incentives to get your showreel or portfolio ready for presentation is to schedule a meeting with a potential employer or client. Nothing gets a presentation or job interview off to a good start than placing your work on the table.

Check the Facilities

Often, I've found that a person with whom I am meeting has no equipment or facilities to show my work! If you need a large table to unfold your portfolio, or a VCR and TV to show your reel, be sure you ask the person you are going to meet to have these facilities ready when you arrive. You can often contact the secretary or administrative assistant and politely ask him/her if the boss has these facilities on hand, or to book a conference room for your meeting. Try not to bother the boss with these details unless it comes up naturally in the conversation. Of course, if you can put everything you want to show on a laptop (that's what I do), you can dispense with this obligation.

Confirm the Appointment

Appointments can often be set weeks in advance. If, in your successful appointment-making call, you don't make the date a few days hence, be sure to call the person a few days before the appointment and confirm the date and time. You are not an important person on the boss's radar screen. It is common for people to completely forget their appointments with unimportant characters like potential interns. You don't want to get washed and dressed and make a long trip to a meeting only to find out that your contact flew off to Algeria the day before. Always confirm any appointments made more than a week in advance.

Be on Time

I've created most of the training videos for Brink's, the world's largest armored delivery company, and that company has an unofficial motto regarding the definition of "being on time" that you should adopt. Being on time at Brink's means being 15 minutes early. The worst thing you can do to start an interview is arrive late. But you can also arrive too soon. Just right on time is 15 minutes early. That way, if you run into a snag getting there, you have 15 minutes leeway before you're just "on time" by everyone else's standards, and 30 minutes leeway before you are *really* late by anyone's standards. (In the USA, that is; some countries consider a half-hour late as on time. Don't you wish you lived there?) And if you are going to be late, at least take a moment and call the person to tell them so, asking if it would be better to reschedule the appointment at their convenience.

Dress Appropriately

I've always been a nut for really expensive custom-made suits, fine watches, handmade shoes, and a car that makes a doctor drool. My belief is that we sell an intangible asset—our services, our attitude, etc. Therefore, bringing any tangible evidence of our quality to the meeting is important. People judge how good we are by how good we look. Animation bosses, however, are famous for looking grungy and appreciating grunge. I've heard one boss say he would most definitely *not* hire anyone who showed up in a suit or wearing a tie.

Well, then, how should you dress for your interview? My best advice, above all, is to be clean: freshly showered, deodorized, and hair and nails trimmed. Secondly, dress with quality. Even if you decide on jeans and sneakers, wear new sneakers and fresh jeans. (Is there such a thing as new jeans anymore?) You might be really smart and visit the facility in advance, not revealing who you are, just to see how people there dress. Then dress just a tad better than that, so you can show respect for the house. Most of the time, you dress better on your interview than on any day on the job, so don't copy exactly what you see being worn by the rank and file. They are already working there. You aren't.

Step Five: When Interning, Work for Real

If you follow the instructions I've given you here so far, you will get an internship. Now the task remains for you to take advantage of the opportunities an internship affords. If you don't, you will be looking for another internship in a few months. There are two things you want to achieve in your internship:

- Get enough experience (and a reel) to get a paying job.
- Get hired by the firm you are interning for (or get a good recommendation).

There are five basic keys to a successful internship, which I've listed below. However, the basic mission is to treat the internship like a real job. That is, you should work for real. (Or work for the reel!) Too many interns either misinterpret their responsibilities (to themselves, mostly) or assume that an internship is a half-job or a hobby or a playtime. It's work. If you treat it that way, you'll be respected as a worker and maybe, just maybe, you'll get hired.

1. **Work diligently.** Do the job you are given, and if you finish that job, immediately report to your supervisor and ask for more work. The more you do, the more you are going to learn. If there isn't someone to give you more work, find some on your own. Be careful, however. Don't go into the engineering room and start washing the wires with soapy water! But you know the sorts of jobs—clean the kitchen, organize the tape library, collect the empty coffee cups and donut bags, run for pizzas . . . be a helping fool.

2. **Be pleasant.** Most of the successful people I know in the business—in life, for that matter—have one overwhelming personal quality. They are people that other people want to have around. When I'm crewing an assignment, it's a natural thing to remember the best people I could call. Always at the top of the list are people I enjoy having around me. Be one of these people. It's not hard. You're an intern, so nobody expects you to be a great conversationalist or entertainer. Just be nice. Listen a lot. Be sympathetic. Don't gossip, brag, or even talk a lot. Look how the best-liked people in your workplace act, and emulate them.

3. **Take opportunities to learn.** Since most likely you aren't getting paid in cash to be an intern, you have to take your payment in learning opportunities. You should check with your boss on what these opportunities are going to be on the first day of the job, and periodically throughout your internship. For instance, you should be allowed to use the company's

unused computers as training workstations. Probably, no one will be available to teach you, but you should have access to all the software documentation. Use it to learn new programs and advance the knowledge you already have. If you get in a bind, courteously ask for help from one of the studio's experts. Listen in, if you can, to creative or technical sessions so you can learn the terminology and current state of progress in your shop. Sometimes a job will open up, temporarily or even permanently, that you can fill with your limited learning. Let it be known, in a polite way, that you are willing to stretch into the job and then leave it at that. Don't be a pest. Often the intern is first in line for an entry-level position. If you've already demonstrated your abilities in new tasks, it won't be hard for the management to see that you could "fit."

4. **Follow the rules.** Lots of interns move into a shop and assume the rules are the same as at home. At home it's okay to use the phone for personal calls, the computer to download music and games, the floor or couch to store your jacket and backpack. Chances are, the rules are really different at work. Ask what the rules are and follow them. What time are you expected to arrive for work? You may not be getting paid to be an intern, but if you're there, someone is probably relying on you for something. Don't disappoint them. If you can't make it or are going to be late, call in and let someone know.

5. **Adopt a mentor.** Or better yet, get adopted! A mentor is a person in the company who takes an interest in you and will help you learn and grow. The role of mentor is not usually a paid or defined role—it's just a personal thing that some people do out of the goodness of their hearts. Most healthy workplaces have one or more mentor types. Sometimes they step up and make themselves known to you, offering their assistance. Other times, you just have to discover one on your own. Always remember that having a mentor entails great responsibility. You have to return the kindness of your mentor by following their advice and never doing anything to embarrass them. The old saying "What goes around, comes around" applies strongly in a mentoring relationship. Don't forget to be good to others as well. One day, you might be a mentor yourself.

6. **Make (or improve) a showreel.** This is one of the most important tasks in an internship. Do not let the opportunity to add to or improve your show reel pass you by. If you work on legitimate productions, ask your supervisor if you can put your part of those productions on your reel. If the answer is yes, be sure you get a copy on some professional-gauge media.

(Not VHS or a DVD!) In your spare time, edit the new production into your reel and eliminate some of the speculative work that was on the reel before your internship. If you entered the internship without a reel, these professional productions you do in an internship will be excellent material for building your career and proving yourself to the next employer who interviews you.

7. **Ask for regular performance reviews.** You don't want too much time to pass without getting some appraisal of your work. If you are working for a good studio, your boss should take you aside once in awhile to advise you and appraise your performance. If this doesn't happen after three to four weeks, initiate the meeting yourself. When it's not too busy, simply ask your supervisor for a brief meeting in a private place. During the meeting, simply say, "I've been here three weeks or so, and I appreciate all you and the studio have done to help me learn the software and build a showreel. Now, I'd like to know how I'm doing?"

Your goal is to open the door of communication so the supervisor can give you honest advice and validate your work. Some employers have a habit of forgetting their interns or relegating them to second-class status. By asking for a meeting, you've said that the supervisor's opinions are important to you and implied that you too are important to your supervisor. Obviously, you expect some constructive criticism, because no intern's work is perfect. So when you get what you've asked for, follow these three rules:

- Show that you understand the criticism by repeating it back to your supervisor in your own words. For instance, if you have been criticized for talking too loudly while other workers are trying to concentrate, say something like, "What you're telling me is that my loud talking is keeping your workers from concentrating on their assignments, right? This costs you money." This establishes that you have assimilated the criticism and understand its implications.

- Apologize sincerely for the loss or damage you have caused, however little it may seem to you. You might say, "I'm sorry I let you down. You run a tight ship and I've been causing it to leak profits. I'm really sorry."

- Give your supervisor some assurance that you will not repeat the transgression. If you've been repeatedly late for work, for instance, you could say, "I'm going to buy a better alarm clock and subscribe to an Internet wake-up service."

This simple, three-step procedure has been used for centuries by ethical individuals, and is recognized by several religions as a means of self-improvement. It ensures that you and your supervisor have identified any issues that prevent you from being accepted as a member of the corporate community, and puts you on the road to eliminating any problems. If you follow your words with actions, you will change those things about you that may prevent your employment, and promote the best relationship you can have with the workplace. In fact, this method of conflict resolution is an excellent means of improving all of your life relationships and being a happier, more productive individual.

It's not a bad idea, if you've received serious criticism, to schedule another meeting of this sort a month later. Make it a point to review from memory the issues your supervisor enumerated before. Ask if these issues have been improved, and be prepared to politely show what sorts of concrete things you have done to address each one.

Keep up this pattern of meeting, identifying issues, and correction until your meetings are full of praise, and there are no issues your supervisor can identify as needing improvement.

Step Six: Watch for Opportunities

Consider this: As an intern, you have an inside track on everything that goes on around you in the shop. Someone else on the outside who's also looking for a job in your company won't have the view that you do. Who's got the advantage? You!

You can exploit this advantage by keeping an eye on the action around your company. Clients will be coming and going, your managers will be presenting proposals and bids, storyboards will be sketched, characters and objects will be designed, motions will be captured, scenes will be built, and frames will be rendered. All these jobs will be flying around you, within your vision and understanding. Try to learn how it all works, and more importantly, how it *doesn't* work from time to time.

What makes it not work? Does an assistant show up late frequently, or is there something missing in the lower echelon of the company's services? Is someone planning to leave the company and take a job elsewhere? Can you learn something about a recurring problem with the computers and offer assistance? Is the boss always complaining about something that you know how to solve? Opportunities like these are the doors through which an intern can adroitly step up to the level of valued employee. Look for these opportunities, and prepare yourself to serve your benefactors.

Once you see the possibility to serve, make a careful presentation of your offer. Keep in mind that there may be others who will be upset by your efforts. You might take an opportunity that someone else saw but failed to realize. Also, through no fault of yours, your offer may be refused. Perhaps the boss has other plans or faults of her own that disturb the flow toward perfection. If you make an effort and fail, don't show your disappointment. Shrug it off and move on. There will be other opportunities, and your initiative the first time will be remembered. Know this: More opportunities arise than people to take them. This is true in any animation studio, any job, anywhere in life. Most people are mediocre. If you strive to be better than average, better-than-average awards will be yours.

Step Seven: Ask for a Letter of Recommendation

Sometimes a good intern will just naturally be offered a job after a month or more of unpaid work. The job offered may be full-time, part-time, or freelance. Full-time work, also called a salaried position, entails a specific definition of work, called a job description, that should be given to you as part of your indoctrination. In return for doing the job described, you get a regular salary, from which the company will deduct certain taxes and fees as defined by federal, local, and city laws. In addition to salary, you may also receive benefits, such as health insurance, retirement benefits, death and dismemberment benefits, and perquisites or *perks* such as a company car, gym membership, etc. Often, salaried positions do not include overtime, since you are expected to complete your job description within the regular 36-40 hour workweek.

As the name would imply, part-time work offers fewer hours and rewards than full-time, but has some regularity to it. Usually, part-time work does not include healthcare or benefits, but it may include provisions for overtime. You are usually required to fill out tax deduction forms, and the company will deduct taxes from your income. If a company requires you to come in on a regular basis, but not enough to warrant a salaried position, it may offer you a part-time position. The implication, of course, is that you are free to find additional part-time work elsewhere to round out your career requirements.

Freelancing is like totally unregulated part-time work. There are no benefits and no tax deductions. Some people prefer freelancing over salaried or part-time work, because it affords them complete flexibility to come and go, work or not work, and vacation when they like. Freelancing usually pays the most per hour of any form of employment, because freelancers are expected to pay their own healthcare, benefits, and taxes. Usually young people like freelance work the best, because they see little use in healthcare or many of the other benefits that companies offer older employees with spouses and children.

You should also be aware that all U.S. states and territories require an employer to offer any worker, salaried, part-time, or freelance, some form of workers' compensation. This is a form of government-supplied insurance that covers you for accidents that may happen to you while on the job.

When I lecture on the topic of interning, one question always comes up: "How long should I intern before I ask for a job?" The answer is that you should *never* ask the company for a job. The very act of your interning is a regular, daily request for full-time work. Every day you show up and work for free, you are saying, "Isn't my work worth something? Won't you hire me?" To actually come out and ask for the same thing would be a redundant mistake.

On the other hand, if you have been interning for a long time (say, six months) and no one has asked you to fill out an employment form, something is wrong. Chances are, if you've been there that long, they need you. If they need you, they should hire you. But you've already given them something for nothing, so some places might just get complacent and figure, "Why mess up a good thing?"

If you believe you have learned everything you're going to learn as an intern, and you are ready to either get that job offer or move on, here is what you do: Ask your boss for a letter of recommendation.

A letter of recommendation is commonly written by the boss of a departing employee, addressed to anyone the employee wishes to consider as a potential employer. You will take this letter and include it with your resume when you apply for a new job. By asking your boss for a letter of recommendation, you are essentially saying, "I'm preparing to quit soon and I want your blessing."

This will often be enough to cause a boss to offer you a job. Just as often, the request is accepted by the boss, the letter is written, and it is expected that you will give notice of your departure in one or two weeks. BTW, you *never* leave a job on less than a week's notice—not even an internship!

If your internship employer has not hired you, which will most likely be the case, what should you have gained for your months of free work? First, you should have learned a great deal about working in a professional environment. Second, you should have learned at least one 3D animation product well enough to get a real, paying job. Third, you should have made at least three animations, which are suitable to constitute a showreel that demonstrates your capabilities. Finally, you should have some written documentation of your work and achievements thus far: the letter of recommendation.

Equipped with experience, practical software skills, a minimal showreel, and a letter of recommendation, you will have leaped over the Catch-22 and will be ready to look for a job as an animator. So how do you ask for that letter of recommendation?

If, as I suggested above, you have been having regular meetings with your supervisor about your progress in the company, this final meeting should not be difficult to arrange. The difference with this meeting is that you are going to imply a departure by asking for the letter of recommendation.

Now it will be the supervisor's turn to act. Three choices are possible. The supervisor can agree to write the letter, offer you some form of paid work to keep you employed, or refuse to write the letter.

It is extremely rare to be refused a letter of recommendation. At worst, you may get a very terse letter with no emotional content. But if you're refused, it means you've really fouled up somehow. In all my years, I have only refused a letter once, and that was when I caught an intern stealing.

Don't be disappointed if you are not offered employment. There are many factors that go into hiring a new employee, and most of them have nothing to do with you or the quality of your work. Most of the time, the company just doesn't have enough money to pay you. In such cases, if your work has been exemplary and the letter of recommendation is effusive, you may also ask for references. The employer will most likely offer them without prompting. References are simply a list of the employer's contacts in the business that he or she may believe you should call. Thank your employer generously for these. They are little treasures, because the employer is inviting you into his or her circle of friends. While you may not have been employed, you have been accepted into a network, and sometimes this can be much more valuable than a job.

Now, assuming you have completed your internship and are equipped with work experience, knowledge of at least one 3D animation software program, a showreel, and a letter of recommendation, you are ready to go out and look for a real job. As you take on these career-oriented tasks, let's return to the task of actually learning SOFTIMAGE|XSI. The next chapter gets back to the practicalities of animating.

Chapter 4

Scratching the Surface— The Storyboard, Previsualization, and Creating and Understanding Surfaces in Softimage

This chapter will start you on the course of producing your first animation. This will help you produce work to start your showreel. The work itself will be given to you as if I was your studio boss and you were one of my chief animators. Hopefully, the exercise will give you the impression of being in a real, professional situation. So let's begin fresh in the morning (whatever "morning" may be to you), as you sit in my office and take notes that I pass to you from my client.

We meet in the conference room, where I have a sketch board between us. I tell you that we have a new client that wants a simple "flying logo" animation. This is the most common type of short animation project, and it is entirely appropriate for you to have one on your showreel.

The Creative Envelope

Whenever you get a project from a supervisor or client, the project will come with specifications and directions that are more or less inflexible. We call this set of specifications and directions the *design envelope*. This envelope is a configuration outside of which you should not venture. For instance, I tell you that the specifications of this flying logo job are that the animation will be 30 seconds long and will end with a 10-second hold on the logo. The logo must feature the crest of the company and the name of the company below that. These instructions are specifications and directions that comprise the design envelope. You don't go and make the animation 31.5 seconds long, and you don't put the name of the company above the crest. That would be *exceeding the envelope.* That is a bad thing.

KEY POINT

A key requirement for any professional artist is to establish the design envelope as soon as a project begins, and make sure that you and the client/supervisor agree to it in writing, if possible. Try to include as many specifications or directions as possible to avoid misunderstandings and redos later.

Many young artists feel that a design envelope is a constrictive, oppressive thing. Sometimes it is, but there is one nice thing about having a design envelope: you are completely free to design anything within it! For instance, although the crest has to come to rest above the name of the company, there's nothing preventing you from warping, twisting, coloring, reflecting, bumping, spinning, or jittering the crest.

Often, strict limitations on the specifications of a work of art drive the artist to new and greater heights of achievement. After all, why do you think Shakespeare loved to write sonnets, and Musashi loved to pen haikus? They loved the restrictions!

So now that you have your own design envelope, it's time for you to sketch some ideas for me. The pressure is on here.

Figure 4.1 shows the logo design. This is the logo as it will appear in the final hold position. You can substitute your own design, of course, if you are building something on spec for a local client or if you want to make something for your showreel using the logo of a famous company.

Figure 4.1 *The basic logo design.*

For this book, I am using a hypothetical company crest and name. When you start to animate this logo, I would expect you to substitute whatever crest and company name you wish. It can be that of a local restaurant or dry cleaning store, for instance. You might even go visit the owner and tell him you'd like to make an animated logo for free. This could be the beginning of a real client relationship. Or, you could pick a well-known company (like IBM) and put this on your showreel as a *spec piece*. This means you did the work speculatively, without any prior relationship with the client. If you include this logo on your showreel, it is important that you inform the viewer that this is spec work, because you don't want to misrepresent that you actually have IBM as your client. (Yet!)

Now your job is to think of some ideas about how to animate the logo. If this job were on a tight deadline, I might ask you to sketch out these ideas on the pad between us. Would you be ready to be creative? I hope so. On the other hand, not wanting to put you under unnecessary pressure to perform, I might ask you to return to your workplace and ponder the challenge privately for a while. I could go either way.

Exercise 4.1: Making Thumbnail Sketches

Using the design envelope, choose a logo or crest and an accompanying name. Sketch the logo over the name as the final frame of animation, and then develop at least three ways of developing that frame by animating any of the elements.

KEY POINT

Perhaps the name of the company or the product that the company produces can give you an idea how to animate the elements. For instance, if it's a pizza restaurant, you might twirl the letters like flying pizza dough. Making animation that connects with the client's bottom-line interest (in this case, selling pizzas) helps make your concept stronger.

Figure 4.2 shows some ideas I sketched out to show you what your work might look like.

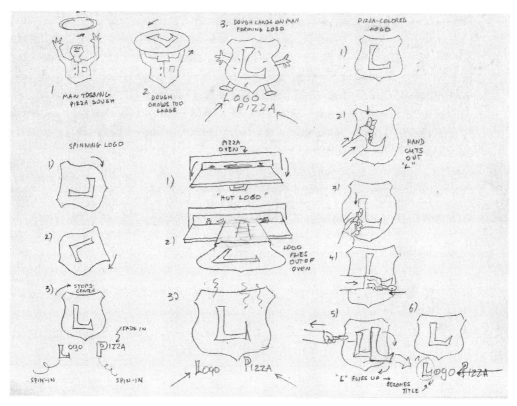

Figure 4.2 *Thumbnail sketches help you visualize your ideas.*

These sketches can be any size that is comfortable for you to draw. Traditionally, artists would draw them about 1 to 3 inches in size, and so they came to be known as *thumbnail sketches*.

The normal procedure of submitting creative work is to produce at least three, maybe dozens, of thumbnail sketches to your client or supervisor. Not a great deal of work goes into these sketches, so the artist feels no loss over having most of them rejected as the desires of the supervisor are realized.

At this step the work begins, and many artists choose to link this step with payment of some sort. Perhaps the first of three equal payments will be made before or just after the first presentation of thumbnails.

The Importance of Milestones

Incidentally, the production of thumbnails marks the first *milestone* of the creative process. A milestone is any significant point along a journey. In this case, it's your journey from a blank page to a finished animation that pleases your client or supervisor. One of the biggest problems in commercial art is the relationship between the effort of the artist and the satisfaction of the artist's client such that monetary reward is justified.

What an artist thinks is great may not be considered great by a client. In order that the artist doesn't venture too far along a path that will result in dissatisfaction, the traditional process of creation is interrupted frequently to allow the client to evaluate the work, make changes and suggestions, or outright reject the result and redirect the artist along a different path.

If the creative process were not interrupted in this way, the artist might expend great labor and arrive at a conclusion that would not please the client and thereby wouldn't justify payment. For this reason, you should always establish three or more points of interruption in your creative flow, so that your client or supervisor can judge your efforts before work continues. In animation, the typical milestones are as follows:

Thumbnails

Storyboard

Previsualization

Basic objects and scenes

Motion scripting

Rendered keyframes

Low-resolution rendered animation

Final rendered animation

Of course, on large projects, each stage may have many sub-milestones, during which various levels of supervisors (such as the client's assistants) may participate in guiding the artists' efforts.

The Storyboard

Let's say that the studio boss goes through your thumbnails and chooses one that particularly amuses her. Your next step may be to render this concept in a more complete form — the *storyboard*.

Since this is just an exercise, you will have to select the thumbnail you like best (or perhaps you can ask someone you trust to act as your supervisor and select one).

Now it's time to make a storyboard of your chosen thumbnail. At this point, I suggest you use your computer to design a blank storyboard page. This is simply a white page of paper from your printer, with 3-4 frames drawn along the left margin. You can make these easily using the table functions of Microsoft Word, or any other common word processing program.

Pay attention to the ratio of height to width of your frames, which is called the *aspect ratio*. The most common aspect ratio in video is that of standard definition (SD) or 4:3, where the width is 4 units and the height is 3 units. Feature film ratios are often wider, and the increasing popularity of high definition (HD) television uses an aspect ratio of 16:9. Therefore, you should design your blank storyboard appropriately to your chosen aspect ratio.

Exercise 4.2: Making a Storyboard Template in Microsoft Word

Using Microsoft Word, here is how I make my storyboard template:

1. Start with a new document in Print Layout View (View > Print Layout). Set the page zoom to 50% so you can see the entire page on your computer screen. Under the View menu, Ruler should be checked.

2. Under File > Page Setup, set the top margin to .5", the bottom margin to .5", the header height to .25", the footer height to .25", the left margin to 1.5" (to allow your pages to be three-hole punched), and your right margin to .25" (or just leave it at whatever setting you find it).

3. Use Table > Insert > Table to open the Insert Table window.

4. Under Number of Columns, type 1. Under Number of Rows, type 7. The Fixed Column Width radio button should be checked, and in the window to the right, replace the word Auto with the number 3 and the inches symbol ("). (The Set as Default for New Tables command should be left unchecked). Click OK.

5. The resulting table shows seven rectangles that are one line high and three inches wide. Click your cursor in the top rectangle to park the cursor there. Then go to Table > Table Properties, and in the pop-up window, select the Row tab.

6. Click in the box labeled Specify Row Height, and type in the amount, 2.25". Click two times on the Next Row button. This will change the height of the first rectangle to a 4:3 aspect ratio and park the cursor in the third rectangle.

7. Again, click the Specify Row Height box and set the height to 2.25". Click the Next Row button two times, and repeat the 2.25" height settings for the fifth rectangle. Click Next Row two more times, set the height for the last rectangle to 2.25", and then click the OK button to exit the Table Properties menu.

8. Now, with your cursor in the topmost small rectangle, go to the Lines and Borders control button in the toolbar at the top of your Word interface. Click on the No Border button. Repeat this command for each of the narrow rectangles. This will make the narrow rectangle invisible when you print the page. Unfortunately, it will also delete some of the lines necessary to make the large rectangles print. To correct this, click within each large rectangle and click the Outside Border command. This will put a printable border around each of the large rectangles.

9. Finally, click View > Header Footer. Type your name in the header, and the words Client, Title, and Page spaced across one line. In the footer, type Copyright, Your Name 2005 or whatever year this happens to be. This automatically copyright-protects anything you draw on this paper!

10. Save this page under an easy name to remember, like Storyboard_Template.doc, and store it where you can always find it.

Figure 4.3 shows the Lines and Borders tool open on the Microsoft Word toolbar. The No Border button is the second from the left on the bottom row. The Outside Border button is the first on the left in the top row.

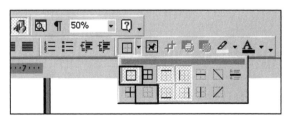

Figure 4.3 *The Lines and Borders tool open on the Microsoft Word toolbar.*

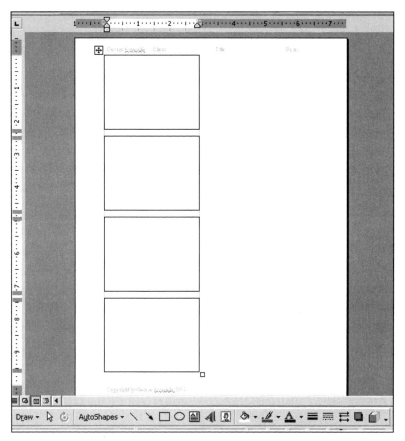

Figure 4.4 *A typical blank storyboard page in Microsoft Windows.*

Your page should now look like Figure 4.4. This is a typical blank storyboard page in Microsoft Windows. It's ready for mass printing and can be used as a template for all your storyboards. Notice the use of the header and footer to print text that will be useful on every storyboard.

You can print out as many of these blank storyboard template pages as you need. Now let's make a storyboard.

Sketching a Storyboard

The easiest way to make a storyboard is to use your template page, a pencil, and a good eraser (not the kind on the back of the pencil, but an inch-long eraser). Use as many blank panels as you need to draw each significant stage of the animation. Each of these drawings could also be called a *keyframe*. You needn't keep your drawing within the bounds of the black border. If you have elements that are zooming in from behind the camera, for instance, it is common to draw them halfway into the border, with an arrow indicating the direction they are moving. Curved arrows can also be used to denote an object that is spinning.

You might find that you've drawn three frames on a page perfectly, but botched up the fourth. Don't worry, and don't mess around with erasing and smudging your work. Simply take another template page, draw your fourth frame on it, scan both pages, cut the bad frame out, and paste the good frame into your original page. Or just use scissors and paste, and then scan it all in later for touch-ups. No one expects you to draw four perfect frames without a mistake. (Although there are many artists who do!) Cutting and pasting are common, as long as you wind up with a smooth-looking final product.

Another method of creating a storyboard is to create all elements in Adobe Illustrator or Photoshop, save the elements as individual picture files, and then import them into Microsoft Word or another word processing program. By carefully positioning these elements on the page, you can avoid a great deal of pencil sketching. Then add your text to the right of the frames using the word processor's text typing capability. This produces a very refined storyboard that is easy to read and professional-looking. Which method you use depends on your drawing skill, available time, and programming resources.

Figures 4.5 and 4.6 show two methods of making a storyboard. The left one was totally illustrated in pencil and touched up using Photoshop's cut and paste functions. The right one was created almost entirely using Photoshop elements imported into Microsoft Word, with a few pencil lines to denote the movement of elements.

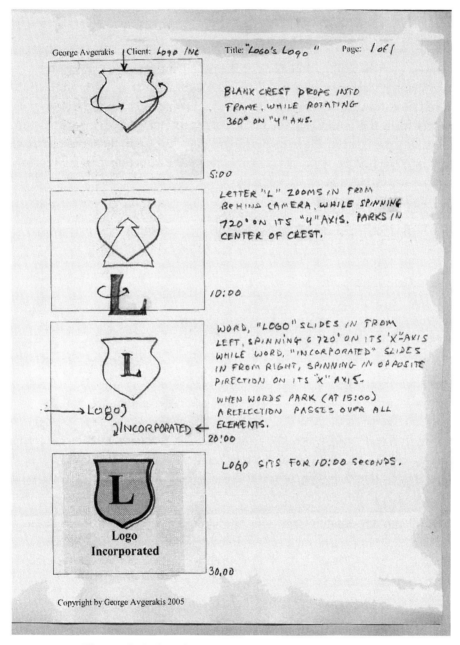

George Avgerakis | Client: *Logo Inc*   Title: "*Logo's Logo*"   Page: *1 of 1*

BLANK CREST DROPS INTO FRAME, WHILE ROTATING 360° ON "Y" AXIS.

5:00

LETTER "L" ZOOMS IN FROM BEHIND CAMERA, WHILE SPINNING 720° ON ITS "Y" AXIS. PARKS IN CENTER OF CREST.

10:00

WORD, "LOGO" SLIDES IN FROM LEFT, SPINNING @ 720° ON ITS "X"-AXIS WHILE WORD, "INCORPORATED" SLIDES IN FROM RIGHT, SPINNING IN OPPOSITE DIRECTION ON ITS "X" AXIS.

WHEN WORDS PARK (AT 15:00) A REFLECTION PASSES OVER ALL ELEMENTS.

20:00

LOGO SITS FOR 10:00 SECONDS.

Logo)
2)INCORPORATED

Logo
Incorporated

30,00

Copyright by George Avgerakis 2005

Figures 4.5 *First method of making a storyboard.*

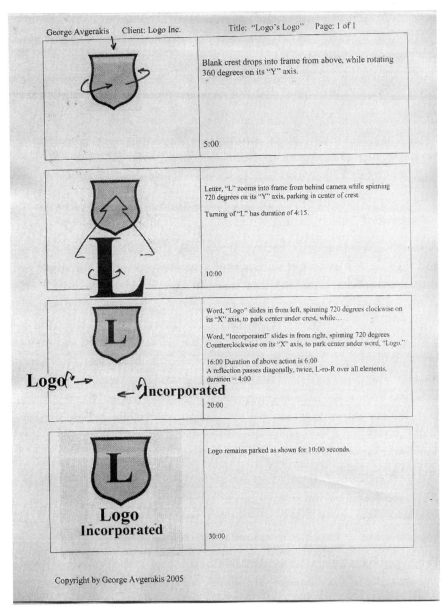

Figures 4.6 *Second method of making a storyboard.*

In order for you and anyone else who sees the storyboard to know how much time is signified by each frame, a time number is usually drawn to the right of the keyframe. This number should indicate the number of seconds and frames that have transpired since the beginning of the animation. So in this project, you will never have a number higher than 30:00, which means 30 seconds and zero frames.

In the area to the right of the frame, you might also indicate the number of seconds and frames, and other information regarding specific effects within a keyframe, such as the rotation of an object. In the example, I indicate that the letter L will rotate 720 degrees in 1:15, or one second and 15 frames.

The area to the right of the frame can also be used to address audio elements of the animation, such as music, sound effects, narration, and dialogue.

A storyboard is important because it acts as a kind of blueprint for the animator and the client. I try to put as much information as I can in my storyboards. If a storyboard is done prior to contracting a project, I include the board in the body of my contract, and refer to it in the text of the contract as a contractual element upon which all parties to the contract agree. In such cases, I may also include a line at the bottom of each page of the storyboard for the client and me to sign or initial, indicating that both of us have reviewed the board and agreed to produce the animation as described. This kind of paperwork may seem unimportant to you now, and even years later as you produce many animations. But it only takes one high-budget project to go awry—you disagree with a client about what was originally storyboarded, you go back to your boards for support of your position, and you find that you never had your boards signed by the client—to realize the importance of this step.

The loose-leaf book you start to create today can also be used as part of your portfolio when you go out looking for a job. Careful documentation and planning are important assets that employers look for in an animator.

When you have finished your storyboard, compare it with mine below and see if you are missing any elements. You should have each panel drawn as a keyframe. To the right of each frame, you should have cumulative time notations, element notations including time and text details, and any sound effects, music, or spoken words displayed.

If you are satisfied with your storyboard, punch three holes in the left margin and store it in a loose-leaf binder. In front of your storyboard, add a few pages of ordinary lined notebook paper. On this paper, list the elements you will need to make this animation. For instance, I know you are going to need a logo, so write "Logo graphic." You will also need the company name, so add "Company name." And if you need music, sound effects, or voice recordings, list them also. You have just used your storyboard as a resource to create a list of things you need to do to finish the animation. Someday, when you are working on very complex storyboards, this habit I have instilled in you of listing your requirements will serve you well in keeping your work organized and well documented.

Previsualization

Previsualization (or *previz*) is a process of creating your work quickly in a "scratch" form, in low resolution, at low cost, for client approval. There are many programs on the market that execute some form of previsualization. All of them offer access to a library of scene elements like trees, buildings, roads, and bushes; props like desks, beds, guns, and cars; set elements like walls, windows, and doors; and living figures like men, women, children, and dogs. For instance, FrameForge 3D Studio (www.frameforge3d.com) offers a library of over 300 objects, including hills, trees, fully poseable actors, cars, and snap-together walls.

In addition to elements that will appear in front of the camera, previz programs also offer one or more cameras. A previz camera should be able to precisely emulate a real film or video camera and its associated lenses. Some previz programs even have libraries of specific cameras and lenses, grouped by brand name.

Using these elements, the operator builds a scene, filling it with sets, props, and living figures. Then, using the script, the operator selects various angles from which to view the scene. These views can be saved and printed to form highly accurate previz storyboards.

Previz storyboards are more valuable to a director and film crew than hand-drawn storyboards, because they represent real-world results. Even a highly skilled storyboard artist, working from visual memory, cannot exactly duplicate the viewpoint of a 35mm Arriflex camera, equipped with a 12-120 Angenieux zoom lens set at 33.5mm and focused at a car passing the camera at 45 feet. A good previz program can do this perfectly.

On the other hand, no previz software can replace the drama, color, action, and intensity of a good storyboard. Therefore, a higher-budget production will avail itself of both media. Usually the hand-drawn storyboard is shown to investors and others who need to see the dramatic portrayal of the script, while the previz is used for the more technical aspects of planning the shoot.

Figure 4.7 shows how the precise placement of props, actors, and cameras can all be done in a bird's-eye two-dimensional view using the FrameForge 3D Studio previz software.

A more expensive previz program, Antics from Antics Software in England, (www.antics3d.com) employs intelligent actors that walk, open doors, and even climb into bed when you place targets on the floor that the actors follow.

Figure 4.8 shows the Antics interface, which features multiple views and an extensive menu of easy-to-understand icon controls that allow the user to make floors, walls, windows, and doors, and then populate the virtual set with actors, props, and actions.

Using Antics, the operator designs the master scene and then gives each actor a path to follow. Instantly, the actor walks the path, opening and closing doors that are in the way, climbing stairs, getting into and out of bed, whatever! Once all the

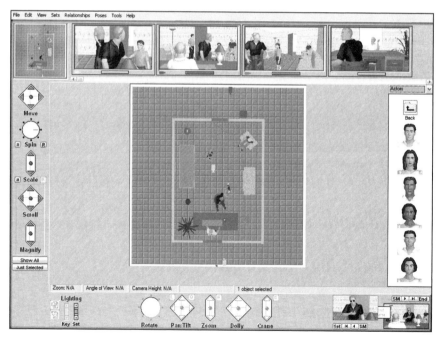

Figure 4.7 *The FrameForge 3D Studio previz software.*

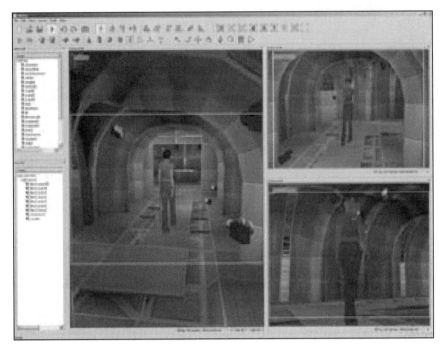

Figure 4.8 *A more expensive previz program, Antics from Antics Software.*

action is plotted, the operator can choose any number of camera angles, storing each camera position on the program's timeline.

As shown in Figure 4.9, camera choreography and sceneplay can be created using the Action Director in Antics. Using point-and-click operation, the initial actions of the characters, props, and cameras can be created and recorded, eliminating the need for laborious keyframing or complex scripting.

The Antics timeline works just like a nonlinear editing program's timeline. The length of a camera's view can be slid in time or trimmed to length. When the previz artist is done with an Antics timeline, the entire show can be recorded to videotape or emailed to the creative staff. Using a simple OS playback window or VCR, the staff can see a low-resolution version of the movie, complete with music and dialogue, that they haven't even shot yet!

Whether a previz is used for animation or live-action film, it is an invaluable resource for preplanning every aspect of a production at low cost, before the higher-cost elements of animation or location production come into play.

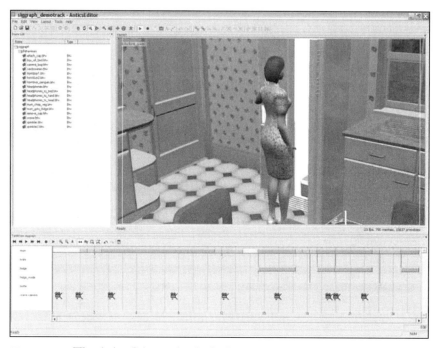

Figure 4.9 *The Action Director in Antics helps you create camera choreography and sceneplay.*

Obviously, the expense of the software, and the time taken to execute a previz, may not be appropriate for a quick 30-second cable TV animation, but for longer productions, previz can't be beat.

Building a Simple Logo Animation in Softimage

We are now going to realize your imaginative storyboard in Softimage. However, before we begin, we need to attend to some simple Softimage housekeeping.

SOFTIMAGE|XSI is highly customizable. Before beginning any tutorials, it is important to make sure that certain options are set up so that your results will look like those in my tutorials. These are the same settings that you will need for most of the tutorials that ship with the software package.

Standardizing the Options

1. First, make sure you are using the XSI keyboard settings. Check this by selecting File > Keyboard Mapping and checking the drop-down menu in the upper-left corner (see Figure 4.10). When you are more experienced, you will be able to create your own keyboard layout if you wish. For now, make sure it says XSI Key Map.

2. Next, make sure that none of the special selection modes are switched on. Click the gray *Select* tab in the Master Control Panel (that's the long panel that runs down the right side for your screen), and make sure there are no checkmarks next to the options at the bottom of the drop-down menu.

3. Finally, make sure that the *Enable Transform Manipulators* option is active. These are the "handles" that allow you to directly manipulate the icons for Translate (position), Rotate, and Scale. Some people prefer to switch these off, and you are welcome to do so if that makes you more comfortable, but I will be using them in this tutorial. So, click on the gray Transform tab in the MCP (Master Control Panel), and make sure that Enable Transform Manipulators is checked.

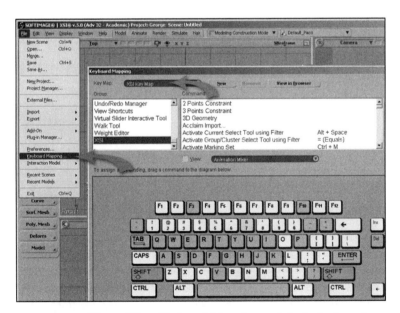

Figure 4.10 *Choose File > Keyboard Mapping and check the drop-down menu.*

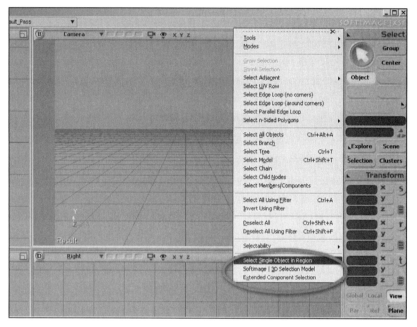

Figure 4.11 *The Master Control Panel.*

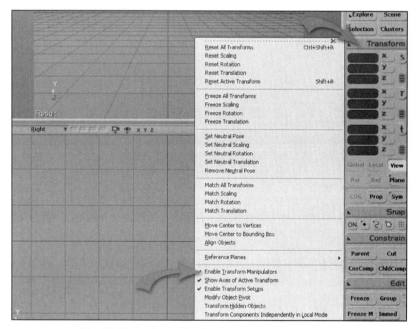

Figure 4.12 *Enable Transform Manipulators.*

Setting Up Projects

Before you begin any new project in SOFTIMAGE|XSI, you ought to create a dedicated project folder that will contain all of the images, models, textures, scene files, and so on. It is not so important what you call the project, but it is important that you can click the Save button frequently as you work and be certain of the location of your files.

The first time you start the software, you will find yourself in the Create New Project area, and you probably won't have any idea what to do. So you skip it[el] Afterwards, when you figure out that you need projects to organize your work, you have no idea how to get back there.

1. Not to worry. From your open XSI interface, go to the menu bar and select File > New Project. You will see a window that looks like the one in Figure 4.13.

2. Type in the name of your project on the top line, and take note of its location on line 2. If you have installed XSI anywhere other than the default location, you should edit the path on line 2. You may specify any location for your project files, but this book will assume that you have placed them in the default location (C:\Softimage\XSI_version\Data).

3. When you click OK, you will see the name of your project and your scene listed in the title bar at the top of your window.

4. Give your scene a name right now by selecting File > Save and typing something meaningful, like CH4_Crest. The title bar will now read something like Project: My First Project, Scene: CH4_Crest.

TONY'S TIP

When you use File > Save, XSI overwrites your scene files with the current version. While you are learning, or if you ever have any doubt about the steps that you have performed since the last save, use File > Save As instead and give your scene a sequential number (or whatever your favorite naming convention is). This will allow you to reload your previous scene if the results are not to your liking. It is important to save new versions frequently while you are learning so that you do not have to go back to square one (unless, of course, you like the practice).

You are now ready to proceed with your Softimage tutorial.

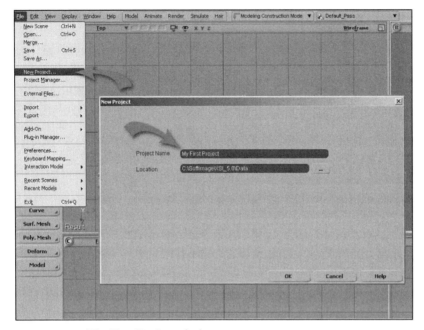

Figure 4.13 *The New Project window.*

Importing a Template Drawing

For this exercise, we are going to need a fairly clean drawing of the crest that you created previously in the thumbnail and storyboard drawing exercises. If you don't have a clean enough drawing of the crest, you'll have to make one now. It can be any size, as long as it fits in your scanner. Try to save your image at about 400 by 400 pixels, and at a low resolution—about 100 dpi is fine. This will load well into your SOFTIMAGE|XSI viewport.

1. Use your computer's scanner to scan in your drawing of the crest that you drew. Save it as CrestOnly in a separate subdirectory called Pizza Logo.

2. In the SOFTIMAGE|XSI interface, make sure you have just opened a new scene (File > New Scene). We will now set up a few things to make your modeling tasks easier. First, check that you are in the Modeling module. There are four modules: Modeling, Animation, Rendering, and

Simulation. You can easily switch between these modules by pressing the number keys 1–4 on your keyboard (not the number pad keys). Try this out. You may also change the modules by clicking on the name of the current module and selecting from a drop-down menu. Next, make sure your construction mode is set to Modeling. This is located at the bottom of the Modeling toolbar on the left side of your screen.

TONY'S TIP

This may seem a little complicated at this point, but these construction modes will help get you out of all kinds of trouble when you get into more complicated tasks.

3. Now, focus your attention on the front viewport. In the upper-right corner, the display type should read Wireframe.

   If not, click on the display type window to open the drop-down menu, and select Wireframe. The menu will disappear and you will see Wireframe in the display type window. Click on it again.

4. At the bottom of the drop-down menu that appears, you will see Rotoscope. Click on this selection. A utility window will open. This window allows you to import a wide range of digital picture file types.

5. Under Image, there will be a gray title window. To the right of this window is the New button. Click it to and select New From File. This opens an XSI Browser window. Find the graphic you stored as CrestOnly, click on it, and the file will load into the small preview window of the utility (see Figure 4.14). If you are happy with the image as captured, close the utility window.

   If you are not happy, you can edit the picture outside Softimage and import it again, or you can edit it within Softimage. You can edit within Softimage by clicking the Edit button. Here you will find several tabs that allow you to crop the image, adjust its hue, saturation, exposure, and gamma (contrast), and transform its size and dimensions (or texture, but that goes beyond the tutorial). Now that you're happy, close the utility and return to the Softimage interface.

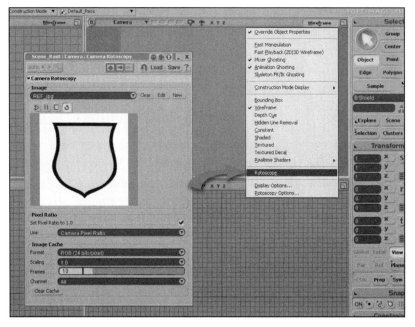

Figure 4.14 *The CrestOnly graphic.*

Modeling a Curved Line

6. Back in the Softimage interface, you will see your image imposed on the Front viewport. Now you will model a curved line, using the image as a tracing template. Place your cursor over the Front viewport and maximize it by pressing F12.

7. Before you begin to draw, you should zoom (Z) in on the front window to adjust the resolution of Softimage workspace. When you hold down any key in Softimage, you will see what each of your mouse buttons does at the very bottom of the screen.

   If you do not, you may need to set your windows taskbar to autohide. Zoom in and out over the Front window until you have a smaller grid pattern displayed over your image template. This will allow you to create a larger 3D object. When you are happy with the relative scale of image to grid, click the magnifying glass at the top of the screen. This will lock your image to your camera and allow you to move around in the viewport without losing registration. Last but not least, middle-click on the first of the four indents (MemoCams) at the top of your Front (Rotoscope) viewport.

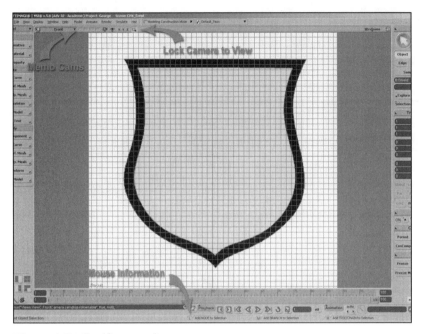

Figure 4.15 *Locking your image to your camera.*

This memorizes the camera position just in case you accidentally lose your place. Left-clicking the MemoCam snaps to that position, and right-clicking erases the data. Save your scene.

8. Select Curve > Draw Linear, and click at the top center of the crest. Click again at the corner, and continue setting points every couple of grid units as you trace the outline of the logo until you get to the point at the bottom. You only have to draw half of the crest!

Mirroring and Merging

9. With the curve selected, press Ctrl+D to duplicate the curve. Softimage features blank windows beside most controls that enable you to actually type numerical values into the control. These windows are called *fields*. You'll notice such fields beside the X, Y, and Z controls in the Transform menu. Now, type −1 in the *X* field of Transform > Scale on the MCP. The duplicate curve will flip along the x-axis, giving you a perfect mirror of the original curve. (See Figure 4.16.) Select both halves of your crest.

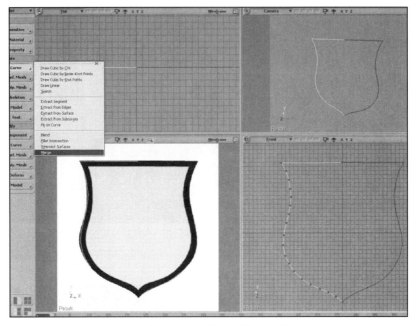

Figure 4.16 *Select both halves of your Crest. Simply drag your cursor over some piece of both curves, or hold down Shift to add to your selection.*

Simply drag your cursor over some piece of both curves, or hold down Shift to add to your selection.

TONY'S TIP

If you ever have trouble selecting objects, you may need to press the spacebar to toggle back to Object Selection mode. Notice that there are also buttons at the top of the MCP for changing selection modes.

10. Press 8 on your keyboard to open a floating explorer window.

TONY'S TIP

Aside from keys 1–4, which change modules, the number keys in Softimage, both when typed alone and in conjunction with the Alt key, open floating windows. Click on one of the View selection tabs (like Front), and you will see the number shortcuts listed next to the View description in the menu. This is handy if you don't want to "dock" a view in one of the viewports. You can double-click on the header of a floating window to roll it up. Neat, huh?

11. You will see the two curves listed there. Click the Point selection button in the MCP or press T on your keyboard. Your curves will turn yellow and the points will become visible. Draw a marquee with your mouse around the point(s) at the center top of your crest. Multi (2) will appear in the Selection field of the MCP and the points will turn red.

12. Now, choose Create > Curve > Merge from the modeling tool panel. The word Pick will appear on your mouse cursor. Select the same red points again, and a new curve will appear that contains the entire outline of your logo. You will see this reflected in the Explorer window as well. Select the two originals in the explorer window and press the H (Hide) key. This will remove them from the screen, but you can access them later if necessary. You may also uncheck the Rotoscopy option in the Front view menu; we will work in Wireframe and Shaded modes from now on.

TONY'S TIP

If you have switched between two display types in any viewport (for example: Wireframe and Shaded) you can middle-click with your mouse over the current display name to toggle back and forth between them. This is a real timesaver. You can middle-click over any menu button to repeat an action. For example, if I choose Get > Primitive > Poly Mesh > Cube, that is four steps. The next time I middle–click on Get > Primitive, I will generate another cube automatically.

Creating and Extruding Polygons

13. With your new curve selected, choose Create > Poly Mesh > Curves to Mesh. A Property Page (PPG) will pop up that allows you to create a polygon face from your curve with options for extrude, bevel, tessellation, and so on. If these terms aren't familiar to you yet, don't worry. You need only click the Extrude tab and set the Length option to a value of 1 or 2 (depending on the size of your crest), and leave all of the other options set to their default values. This gives us a solid 3D crest that has a thickness (z-depth) of 1 or 2 Softimage units (grid spaces).

14. At this point, you should have something that looks like Figure 4.17. Press the Enter key and type a name for your new Polymesh object. Save your scene!

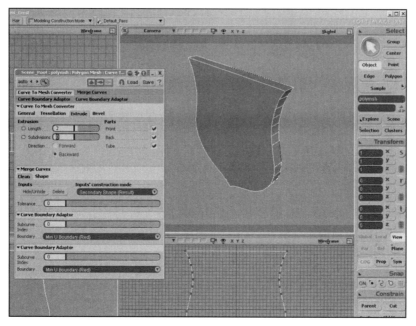

Figure 4.17 *Creating a solid 3D crest that has a thickness.*

TONY'S TIP

A few notes about your interface: You are already aware that you may toggle a view between its normal size and full screen by pressing F12. If you need to frame a selected object in any viewport, place your mouse over that view and press F (Frame). To frame all objects in a view, press A. To do either of the above in all views simultaneously, hold down the Shift key while pressing F or A. You may resize your windows by dragging on the separator bars or by grabbing the intersection and dragging it.

15. Now you are going to going to make the logo a little fancier by creating an inset for your crest. Frame the crest in the camera view by clicking it and pressing F. You may maximize the camera view any time you wish, or just keep working in the four-view layout. It is a good idea to get used to switching views to optimize your workflow. Some tasks will be much easier in one view than in another. However, always check the result in the Camera view, because that is what you will eventually render. If the grid is

bothering you, press the G key to toggle the grid off (and back on when you need it). Hold down the S key and examine the L, M, and R (left, middle, and right mouse button) descriptions at the bottom of your screen. You will notice that with this single key, you can orbit, dolly, and track your camera. If you hold the mouse over a non-camera view, you will see the options change to Track and Zoom. Always use Dolly instead of Zoom in the Camera view, or else you will change the perspective (lens angle) of your camera.

16. Now for the fun part. Hold down the U key and click on the front face of your crest. It should turn pink, and the Polygon button should light up in the MCP. This is called *raycasting* (not to be confused with *raytracing*, which we will discuss later). Point your mouse at a polygon surface and click. The selection process stops when the first surface is hit, preventing any polygons on the back of your object from being selected. Orbit around and see for yourself! The back of the crest is probably dark because of the default lighting. Not to worry, you can do a simple trick to model in the camera view.

17. Open the display menu in the Camera view (the one that says Wireframe or Shaded). At the bottom you will see Display Options. Click this. Eek, another huge menu. . . . Don't worry. Scroll down to the bottom and look for a check box that says Enable Head Light (see Figure 4.18).

18. Now you can orbit anywhere and see what you are doing. If you ever get really messed up in the Camera view, you can press R to reset it (don't forget the MemoCam buttons either). Okay, enough playing around. Back at the front of your crest, with the front face (polygon) selected, press Ctrl+D. You have duplicated the front face. Switch to Scale Manipulation by clicking on the S under Transforms in the MCP, or by pressing X. Make sure that Global is selected.

TONY'S TIP

Sticky keys: If you only press a hotkey such as X (scale), C (rotation), or V (translation), the effect is temporary. (It is only scaling for as long as you hold the button down.) If you press firmly (or tap) the hotkey, you enter sticky mode and the scaling remains on until you press another key. For instance, I can tap X to enter scale mode, press and hold the V key to reposition the selection, and when I release the V key, I will return to scaling. Nifty, no?

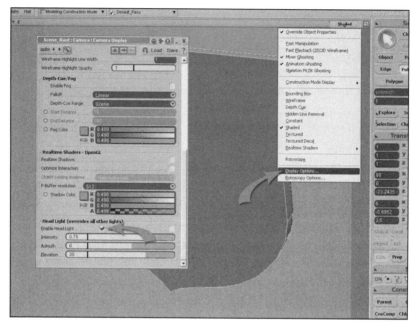

Figure 4.18 *Find the Enable Head Light check box.*

19. Move your mouse around until the cursor indicates that you are affecting the X and Y-axis together, and scale down the copy of the front face. Use the V key to reposition it if necessary. Use one scale handle at a time to reapportion it (see Figure 4.19).

20. Next, press Ctrl+D again to duplicate once more, and translate (V key) in Local mode using the Y (green) handle. Push it in slightly to create an indented surface.

TONY'S TIP

When you use local mode with polygons, the y-axis is always perpendicular to the face. So, translation in Local y allows you to work in the camera view with complete confidence that you are always moving the face perpendicular to its original position.

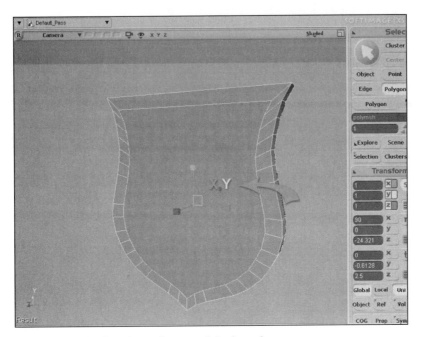

Figure 4.19 *Scaling down the copy of the front face.*

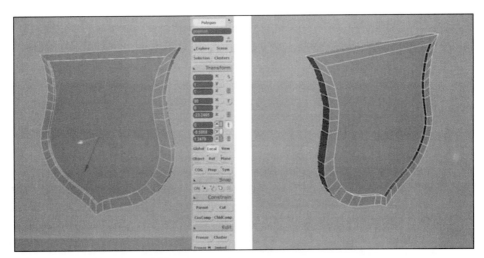

Figure 4.20 *It's looking good!*

21. Admire your creation. This is a good time to save your scene.

Adding 3D Text

So far, you have been adding elements to your design by drawing them from scratch. But when it comes to adding 3D text, Softimage has tools that make the job very easy. Now you will create the raised letter that goes inside your crest. This is easy in XSI because a text function is built into the interface.

1. Make sure that you are still in Model mode.
2. Select Create > Text > Solid Mesh. You will see a Text PPG pop up that is very similar to the one you used when creating the face of your crest. At the bottom of the pop-up are the default words 3D Text.
3. Simply overwrite the letters with whatever text you wish (in this case, L), and click Apply.
4. You may then use the Fit Size adjustment to resize the letters, or you may scale them later in the 3D interface.
5. If the letters are not thick enough, select the Extrude tab and adjust the length until you are satisfied.

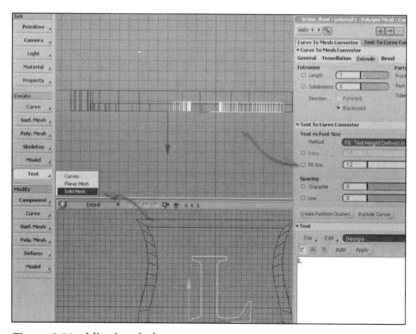

Figure 4.21 *Adjusting the letters.*

5.1 If you accidentally close any PPG or need to get back to one after you have closed it for further adjustments . . .

5.2 Select the object that is affected and click the Select button on the Master Control Panel.

5.3 You will see a list of all of the operators that have been applied. Click the little gear icon next to the one you want to reopen in the associated PPG.

NOTE

This will not work if you have pushed the Freeze buttons at the bottom of the MPC. Freezing erases the operator stack, making your scene lighter but preventing you from editing those properties further via the PPG. See Figure 4.22.

---

6. Use the Transformation handles to position and scale the text until you are pleased with the look.

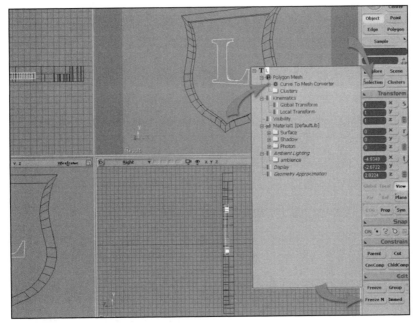

Figure 4.22 *Using the Freeze buttons.*

TONY'S TIP

Get used to using multiple orthographic views (front, side, top, and so on) when manipulating your objects in 3D space. These views have no perspective (vanishing point), so that you can see the true relationship between your scene objects. Do *not* use the Camera view by itself, at least until you know a lot more tools. This is akin to positioning an object by reaching through the lens of your camera, and it can have unpredictable results.

7. When you are happy with what you see, parent the letter to the shield, completing the modeling stage of your crest. You may parent in one of two ways. You can open an explorer window (8), as you did earlier, and drag the child on top of the parent. This will cause the child to disappear and a plus sign to appear next to the parent object (a la windows). Or, use the Parent button in the MCP.

8. For this method, select the parent object (the shield), turn on the Parent button, and click on the child (letter).

9. Turn off the Parent button.

10. Save your scene.

11. Take a break.

Adding a Basic Material and Texture

So far, you've been learning how to produce an object with a small degree of complexity. You now have enough experience to start making your own objects. However, all of these objects would have a dull gray luster to them, with no color or texture. A world made of such objects would be a kind of artist's hell. Obviously, you need to impart some properties to the surfaces of your objects. In the final part of this exercise, you will learn how to add color and texture. Crack those knuckles, me maties! It's time to get back to work.

There are many ways to add color and texture to your objects in SOFTIMAGE|XSI. For this first look, you will use the tools that are built into the interface.

1. Begin by switching from the Model module to the Render module. Press the number 3 on your keyboard, or click on the word Model at the top of the model toolbar and choose Render from the drop-down menu.

2. If you haven't done so already, let's name the objects. Select the shield object by clicking on it, and check the info window in the MCP to make

sure that you have only one object selected. If you have only the shield selected, you will see Polymesh displayed. If you accidentally selected something else as well, you will see MULTI (2).

3. When you have just the one object selected, press the Enter key and type Shield in the dialog box.

4. Next, select the letter object, press Enter, and name it Letter (or something appropriate if you are making something different).

5. Click the shield and select Get > Material > Phong. A PPG will open that allows you to define the diffuse (main surface) color, ambient (shadow surface) color, and specular (highlight) color of your object.

6. Drag the RGB sliders around until you find a color you like. (I picked a nice red.)

7. Now copy the color from the diffuse to the ambient (or vice versa) by dragging one color swatch over another. It's okay to make the ambient and diffuse color the same, because these both represent the surface color. You might adjust the ambient if you wanted to deepen or lighten the shadow on a specific object. See Figure 4.23.

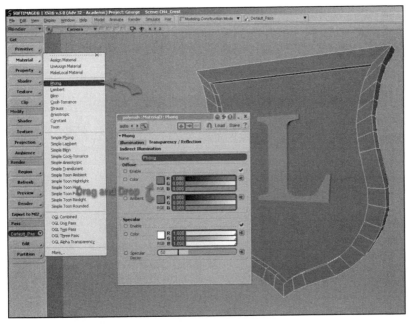

Figure 4.23 *Adding color to your image.*

8. The Specular Decay slider affects how shiny the surface looks. You would set it high for a pool ball and low for a rubber ball, for example.

9. Next, press the U key to enable raycasting (as you did earlier when creating the sunken face), and click on the inset polygon. This puts you in Polygon mode and makes the selected face pink. If you have trouble seeing this, you may want to toggle back to Wireframe display temporarily.

10. Repeat the previous steps for applying a Phong material, and dial up a different color for the selected face. (I picked a shiny yellow.)

11. While the Material PPG is open, name the second material something clever like Yellow.

TONY'S TIP

When you selected the face and then applied the new material to it, you created a *polygon cluster*, a unique selection that can be recalled at a later time by selecting it from the cluster list. You may manually create clusters of points, edges, or polygons by making your selection in the appropriate selection mode and pressing the Edit > Cluster button at the bottom of the MCP. If you wish to view or select the clusters that you have created, select the object in question (in object mode) and click the Cluster button in the middle of the MCP. You may also use an Explorer window.

You now know one way to apply different materials to different areas of an object (see Figure 4.24).

12. To view these different materials, open an Explorer window and adjust the focus to Materials and Shaders.

13. Or if you prefer, click the Selection button in the MCP. You will see the red material attached to the main object and the yellow material attached to the cluster.

14. Select the Text object and repeat the steps to put an interesting color on that object. (I picked blue.)

15. In order to better judge the look of your creation, you should look at it in rendered form. In most software packages, this would involve a separate step and would interrupt your workflow. In XSI, however, you can preview a portion of any view at any time in any module to see what the final product will look like when you are done. Simply press the Q key and drag a marquee around the area you want to render.

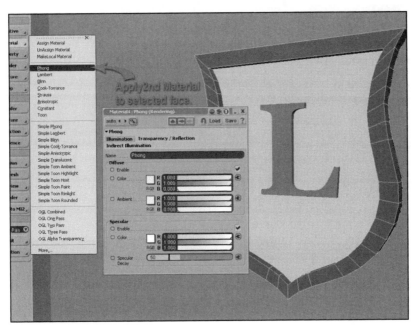

Figure 4.24 *Applying different materials to different areas of an object.*

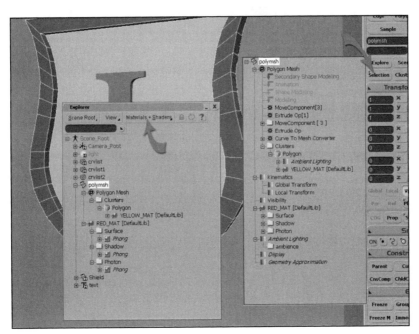

Figure 4.25 *The red material is attached to the main object and the yellow material is attached to the cluster.*

16. If the image looks a bit ratty, this is due to low anti-aliasing settings and may be adjusted by clicking in the box at the side of your *render region*.

17. Save your scene.

18. If you've ever fiddled with a real policeman's shield, you might remember that the front surface has a kind of molded, pebbly texture. This texture is a common technique of metal fabricators to add value to an object. Let's put a little value into your object by adding a bit of texture on the inset face. With the shield object selected, click the selection button and open the polygon cluster.

19. Click on the blue ball for the yellow material, and the PPG for the yellow material will open.

20. Click on the little plug icon next to the diffuse property, and select More from the menu that drops down (see Figure 4.27). This should take you to the Preset Texture area. (If not, navigate to it using this path: C:\Softimage\XSI_4.2\Data\DSPresets\Shaders\Texture.)

Figure 4.26 *The Quality Slider.*

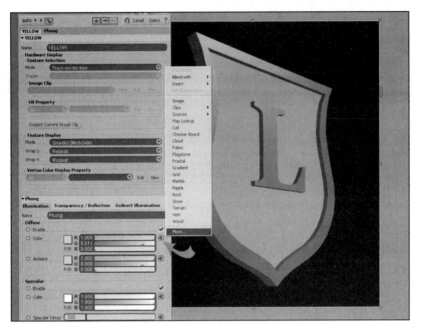

Figure 4.27 *The Preset Texture area.*

From the list of presets, select Grid. This is usually used for creating grids (duh), but you are going to use it for the more glorious purpose of adding a texture to your crest. You could actually use any black and white drawing produced in a program like Adobe Photoshop. However, I can't walk you through a tour of Photoshop, so we're going to cheat and use one of the tools in XSI.

As you'll soon see, most animation programs can take the tonal values of a black and white drawing and convert them to physical dimensions. For instance, if you drew a bunch of bumps and then converted the drawing into 3D space, a program like XSI would actually make the bumps form on any object's surface. This process, oddly enough, is called *bump mapping*.

You're going to modify the grid pattern to create a regular series of soft, rounded squares that you can use to create a regular bump map pattern on the inset surface.

21. From the Grid PPG Texture tab, click New and select Planar XY. This will cause the grid to be projected straight toward the selected face (the XY plane is the front view). If you have a render region open, you should see the default grid pattern on the face, as shown in Figure 4.28.

22. Now you will make some adjustments to make it appear as a soft bump.

23. While you are still on the Texture tab, enable the Bump check and set the factor to -1.

24. On the Grid tab, change the line color to something close to the yellow material (or whatever your face color is).

25. Make the fill color white or a light version of the line color.

26. Change Diffusion to .5, and the U and V widths to .025.

27. Finally, on the Advanced tab, change the three Repeats sliders to 5. If all is well, your crest should now look something like Figure 4.29.

28. Save your scene.

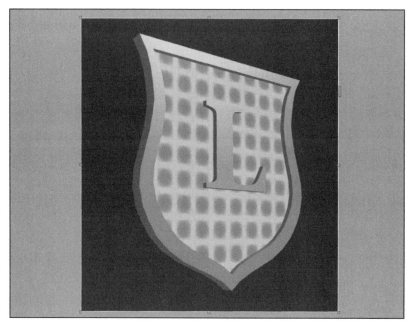

Figure 4.28 *The default grid pattern on the face.*

Figure 4.29 *The final crest, with patterned background.*

Congratulations. You have now completed a rather complex object with intricate detail, color, and texture. You've learned how to add 3D lettering and how to combine objects into clusters. You've also learned how to save your work.

If you feel up to it, start to branch out from what you've learned and experiment. Try importing a different storyboard element, like a traffic sign or a computer monitor. These are objects with about the same level of complexity as the crest. If you foul up, remember that you can always press Ctrl+Z to go back. And if you really foul up, get frustrated, and feel like giving up, you have exhausted the limitations of this exercise and it's time for you to move on to Chapter 5!

In Chapter 5, we're going to switch gears and once more explore the business side of being an animator. I can imagine that you are building a library of objects. Soon, you will learn how to make them move about, as if they have lives of their own. So I figure it's time to teach you how to make a killer showreel—because soon, you're going to need it!

Chapter 5

Making a Killer Showreel

I n this chapter, you will learn how to organize your completed projects into a visual presentation that gets you work.

We, as practitioners in the media business in general and the animation business specifically, must understand that our product—talent and energy—is somewhat *intangible*. Unlike a butcher or used car salesman, our product cannot be touched, smelled, or tasted, and with the exception of work we have already done for others, it cannot be seen or heard either.

Talent and energy are so elusive and difficult to demonstrate to a customer. People hire us because they *trust* us when we say we are what we are. What other professions have this handicap? Well, most highly paid professions—lawyers, doctors, stock brokers—also suffer the effect of selling intangible assets. We can't take a lawyer's trial record out for a test spin around the block. We can't taste a surgeon's bedside manner to see if we'd like to dine on it. And we can't smell a stock broker's claims of financial growth to see if it was netted on this morning's tide or left sitting on the dock to rot for three days.

Since we have so much in common with lawyers, doctors, and stock brokers, doesn't it make sense for us to observe how they engender trust in their potential customers, and perhaps emulate them? How do these professionals dress? What cars do they drive? With what accoutrements do they adorn themselves? And, most importantly, how do they present their professional capabilities, such that you are prone to trust them with your freedom, life, and savings?

Essentially, every successful professional who sells an intangible asset must offer some tangible evidence of his success. These professionals dress impressively in the accustomed style of their social class.

Selling Intangible Assets

Lawyers wear conservative, often hand-tailored dark suits. Doctors also wear conservative suits, but often embellish them with a stethoscope around the neck and a white lab coat (notice the embroidered name, and the name of a prestigious medical institution below that). Stockbrokers wear somewhat louder, more ornately tailored suits, often with distinctive ties and suspenders. If you invite them to your home, each of these professionals will arrive in a Mercedes, Cadillac, or BMW of the latest vintage. Lawyers and doctors will sport at least three pieces of gold jewelry, one of which bears the signet of a prestigious institute of higher learning, the other the brand name of a Swiss timepiece manufacturer. The stockbroker may sport more gold, usually in the form of some frivolous jewelry, like a bracelet, perhaps adorned with diamonds of significant size.

Why do I bother mentioning this to you, in a book about how to become a successful animator?

The reason is that you, too, sell an intangible asset, and you, too, must learn how to adorn yourself, like the lawyer, doctor, and stockbroker, with the symbols of success in your craft.

Now, don't go off and buy a custom-made suit, Rolex watch, and Z4 Roadster (although I will not criticize you for the Z4) with the expectation of getting a job at Disney. That is not my point. My point is that you must examine what your customers expect you to bring to the table, in terms of tangible evidence of your success, before you will be allowed to dine.

Animators do not wear suits or much gold jewelry, or drive expensive cars to their demo appointments. Later, in Chapter 9, I discuss just how a successful animator should dress, accessorize, and arrive at a presentation. But for now, let's concentrate on the one tangible thing that you, as a media creator, can bring to the table—and that is your showreel.

The Reel Is Real

A showreel is a brief compilation of your most stunning work, edited in such a way as to compel the viewer to demand more—more reel, more you. A showreel is best presented by you in person, but it can also be delivered or mailed to a client, or even presented on a Web site (yours or some agency's).

You will not get a job as an animator without a showreel. Therefore, as soon as you are able to animate, you should set out to create your first showreel. So how do you begin? Well, you begin by watching.

Unlike a lawyer, doctor, or stockbroker, who would certainly benefit from having a showreel (but who, in my experience, are usually too frugal to invest in one), you are a media professional. You must watch TV programs, movies, commercials, music videos, and video games every day, regardless of what your Mom or room-mate tell you. But you don't do all this watching for pleasure—it is work!

You must learn, by watching and even taking notes, what makes a great presentation; what motivates a viewer to get up and act; what makes the viewer sit on the edge of his seat and spill popcorn all over his hot date's lap.

In addition to watching the end product of other animators—films, programs, and games—you must get your hands on other animators' showreels. This is simple to do. Just go on the Internet and Google keywords like "animator showreel," or visit the Web sites of established animation houses like Blue Sky (www.blueskystudios.com) and ComputerCafe Group (www.computercafe.com) to see their showreels. Once you've got an idea of what a good reel looks like, two things will happen.

First, you will feel depressed and think you can never make a great showreel like the ones you've just seen. Second, you will begin to understand what you have to do to make a showreel like the ones you've just seen, and hopefully you'll be enthusiastic to get started. Great reels are not made in a week or two. They are evolved over many years of trial and error, as your career begins, gets better, and matures. Every time you make a new animation, on spec or for a client, you will judge it for inclusion in your reel.

"Is the project good enough for the reel?", you will ask yourself. And if the answer is "No," you'd better know the reason why. Too many "No's" in a row is a definite warning that your career is not heading in the right direction.

So, you've now seen some good reels. You just have to learn how to make *your* showreel do all these things. Now, I'm going to show you how.

Ditto's Lesson

I am going to tell you a little story that led me to the secret of making a killer showreel. It doesn't begin in an animation studio or a client's posh conference room. It begins at the back door of my house, one early morning as I set out to walk my young Dalmatian puppy, Ditto.

I never had a dog as a kid, and the one I finally bought for my kids was the first dog I ever cared for. Obviously, one of the main things you do to care for a dog is take it for a daily walk. I looked forward to my first dog walk, dressing up in sweats and anticipating getting some exercise.

So I started walking at a nice, brisk pace, and I was thinking about a lecture I was going to do later that week about how to edit a killer showreel. I was just getting my breath, walking fast and thinking about the lecture, when suddenly, Ditto stopped in his tracks to pay attention to a lamp post. As he bounded off again, I thought we were going to get some good exercise. *Wham*, Ditto stopped at a fire hydrant. Off we went again, and again he interrupted my otherwise highly motivated morning walk!

What is this? I thought, never having walked a dog before. *Can't we just have a good walk without stopping at every vertical object?*

So the next day I joined my friend Aldo, who had a German Shepherd named Sable, and we walked our dogs together. I decided to lead both dogs to a very large parking lot, free from any vertical intrusions, to see what would happen. We started our walk by going directly across this large space, me thinking I was finally going to get an uninterrupted workout. Guess what? Ditto refused to take the direct path through the center of the lot. Instead, he started walking around the perimeter of the lot, pausing at the corners. Sable, a female, gleefully went across the middle of the lot.

As we met at the far end of the lot, Aldo told me all about male dogs, and it caused me to have an epiphany about how showreels should be made. Aldo told me that male dogs are *territorial*. This means they like to mark a geographic area with their scent, so that other dogs will not intrude on their area. Instinctively, Ditto was marking the entire parking lot, surrounding the female, Sable! He was claiming Sable—and any other females in the parking lot—as his property.

Now why did this cause me to have an epiphany about how showreels should be made? The answer is *gestalt*. A gestalt is a configuration of physical, biological, or psychological phenomena so integrated as to constitute a functional unit with properties not derivable from its parts in summation. In other words, a gestalt is something that is more than the sum of its parts. If you're going to make a showreel, wouldn't it be nice if it could be a gestalt, not just a simple collection of animation clips?

In psychology class back in college, I was taught that a gestalt pattern could be made up of two or more dots on a paper. (Dots—could the Dalmatian be a coincidence?) If you had only one dot, there could be no gestalt effect because the human eye does not perceive a configuration.

Consider Figure 5.1, for example. On the left, a single dot can represent just a dot, or a single example of your work—say, a clay animation with a fat, red-faced character. On the right (the gestalt), the dot (or the single animation clip) does not provoke the brain to imagine anything more. It is just a dot or a single animation clip.

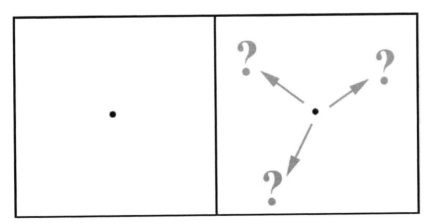

Figure 5.1 *Two dots representing a gestalt.*

Two dots are kind of weak for a gestalt. Your mind might configure a line, but it would depend on the similarity of the dots and whether they were arranged horizontally, vertically, or diagonally.

Now consider Figure 5.2. On the left, two identical dots, displayed horizontally, can be just two dots or two similar examples of your work—say, two clay animations, one with a fat, red-faced character and one with a skinny old lady. On the right (the gestalt), the two dots (or two animation clips) might provoke the brain to make a connection, thus forming the gestalt of a line between the dots. The probability (and strength) of the gestalt is based on the similarity of the dots (or clips) and the relationship between them as displayed.

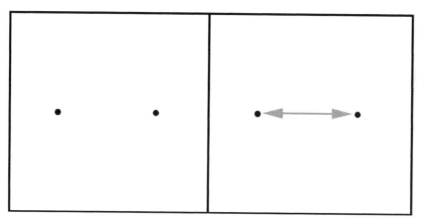

Figure 5.2 *The probability (and strength) of the gestalt is based on the similarity of the dots (or clips) and the relationship between them as displayed.*

For instance, if the two dots were not identical and were not displayed horizontally, the gestalt relationship between them would be weak. Our minds would not readily see a line. Similarly, if the two animation clips were not similar—for instance, if one was a short clay animation of a fat, red-faced character and the other was a long spaceship sequence—the viewer would not tend to perceive these two clips as being related in any important way (important meaning that they represent the scope of your career to date).

Figure 5.3 shows two dissimilar dots, displayed diagonally. Right (the gestalt): Notice how, when the two dots are of different sizes and are not aligned horizontally or vertically (the way our minds want to see simple order), the relationship between them and the gestalt effect of a line weakens.

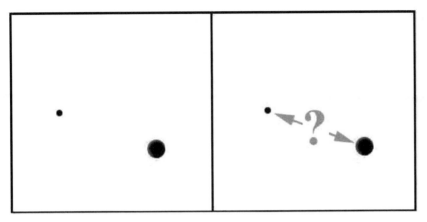

Figure 5.3 *Two dissimilar dots, displayed diagonally.*

Now see what happens when we arrange three identical dots an equal distance from each other. By gestalt, our minds easily imagine an equilateral triangle. Three or more dots, spread out in space—*that's* a gestalt. No matter how you spread the dots, the mind sees some kind of triangle. Even though there are just three dots, the gestalt configuration is perceived as a sum that is greater than its parts.

Now take a look at Figure 5.4. On the left three identical dots, an equal distance from a central point, can be just three dots or three similar examples of your work—say, three clay animations, one with a fat, red-faced character, one with a

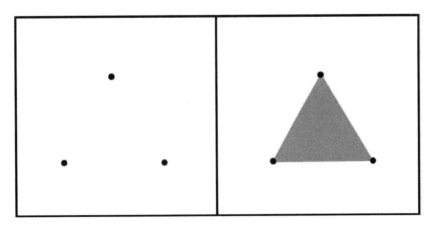

Figure 5.4 *These three dots might provoke the brain to make a connection, thus forming the gestalt of a geometrical shape between the dots.*

skinny old lady, and one with a blonde in a bathing suit. On the right (the gestalt) the three dots (or three animation clips) might provoke the brain to make a connection, thus forming the gestalt of a geometrical shape between the dots.

Even if we take the dots, change their sizes, and move them around randomly, the power of the gestalt phenomenon causes our minds to imagine a triangle—a *relationship* between the dots. This relationship persists, even if we line up the dissimilar dots, eliminating the space between them, because our minds now imagine a line.

Now look at Figure 5.5. On the left are dissimilar sized dots arranged in an irregular shape that still evokes a triangle, although the evocation is not as strong as in Figure 5.4. On the right, dissimilar dots arranged in a line evoke a line, which would be stronger if the dots were the same size.

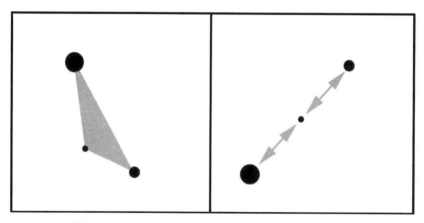

Figure 5.5 *The triangle relationship persists, even if we line up the dissimilar dots, eliminating the space between them, because our minds now imagine a line.*

So what about Figure 5.6? It's just for fun—to show that dots can be fun, and loyal too!

Figure 5.6 *The author, shown with his dog, Ditto. Here, Ditto demonstrates that a minimum of three feet is necessary to imitate a puppy and sit on the master's lap.*

The Power of Gestalt

The power of gestalt can be applied very effectively to the composition of your showreel. If the viewer of your reel sees a strong relationship between your clips, this gestalt impression will evoke wholeness, a sense of quality, and a powerful statement from you to the viewer that is greater than the mere sum of the clips.

For instance, note that the preceding examples I used were all clay animations that varied from each other only in the type of character presented. The symbols for these clips were identical dots, symbolizing the similarity between the clips. I also placed the clips equal distances from each other. These distances symbolized the length of time of each clip in the showreel.

Although this reel could be considered a weak reel, since it only has one specific type of animation and only three clips, it is stronger than the sum of its parts. The viewer would undeniably understand that the animator was somewhat of an expert in creating characters in clay! This understanding is supported by the gestalt phenomenon, working within the viewer's mind.

By virtue of gestalt, this reel would be a strong example of clay character animation. The animator could expect to be evaluated according to the criteria of a clay character animator, and if the viewer were an employer of clay character animators, the animator could reasonably expect to be granted a job interview.

Now, let's assume that this hypothetical clay animator got a job, not as a clay animator, but as a 3D spaceship designer. She spent a few months on a film project, and at the end of the project, she was given a Betacam tape of her best spaceship design, flying through the Crab Nebula. What would happen if our animator edited this clip into her showreel? Would the reel become stronger or weaker?

Figure 5.7 illustrates three similar character clay animation clips in a showreel after a fourth clip, depicting a 3D spaceship flying through the Crab Nebula, has been added. On the right, the gestalt of this new showreel depicts the strong relationship between the three similar clips being diluted by the addition of the fourth, dissimilar clip.

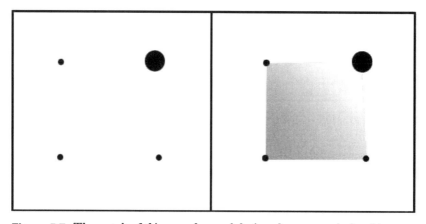

Figure 5.7 *The gestalt of this new showreel depicts the strong relationship between the three similar clips being diluted by the addition of the fourth, dissimilar clip.*

As you can see, although the animator assumed that the reel would become stronger because it has four instead of three clips, it has become weaker because the gestalt effect has been diminished.

As Figure 5.8 shows, the original showreel is weak because it has only three clips, but strong because it has a powerful gestalt. On the right, the new showreel is stronger than the reel symbolized on the left because it has four clips, but weaker because its gestalt has been weakened. Which clip would you send to a potential employer?

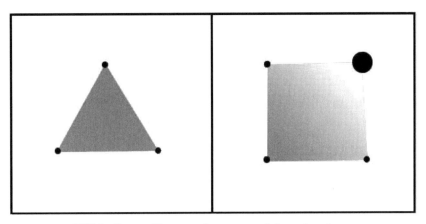

Figure 5.8 *Which clip would you send to a potential employer?*

I am not saying that if you were in the same position as this animator, or if you had three similar clips and a new clip that was dissimilar, you could not add this clip to your reel. I am simply showing you how the addition of the clip will tend to weaken the previous reel. If the weakening were offset by some incredible quality of the new clip, you might decide to edit the new clip into the reel without regard to the loss of gestalt power. But then again, you might decide to disregard gestalt entirely, throw away the three similar clips, and send out a reel with just the one clip of incredible quality.

Let's say you aren't *that* stubborn, but you still want to include that fourth clip of incredible quality. Now, your concern is not *inclusion* by *order*. We will take up how you order your clips a little later. For the moment, let's consider the criteria by which you would evaluate the similarity or dissimilarity of clips.

How many descriptive criteria can you think of to describe any animation clip? Let's see:

2D vs. 3D

Cartoon vs. Realistic

Dramatic vs. Comical

Space vs. Earth

Character vs. Scenic

. . . and on and on.

When evaluating the raw material of a showreel, your task is to carefully describe each clip in terms *that your viewers will recognize with the least effort*. A clip is only a few seconds long, and the viewer will be distracted by whatever distractions prevail in the viewer's environment, so he probably won't notice that your three clips all include a rusty wingnut. The clips you display must have a unifying similarity that is immediately apparent. (That's why, in my example, I made all the clips one striking form of animation.) Until you have an understanding of this principle and can demonstrate it with actual clips, you do not have the strongest reel you can have. In fact, many animators go through the trouble of making speculative animations, just so they can create three or more of a particular type and thereby establish a stronger gestalt. (Although they may not be consciously following the suggestions or terminology that I've described here.)

Now, before we go on to the concept of ordering your clips, let's consider what happens when you get a lot more than three clips. Let's say you've worked as an intern for a few months, during which time you've used your evenings to cobble together a bunch of showreel clips. Maybe after that, you got a few freelance jobs. So now, you have your three clay animation clips and 10 others.

After careful examination of your clips, you group them into the following list:

Clay Animation

1. Fat, red-faced character
2. Skinny old lady
3. Blonde in a bathing suit

3D Animation

1. Crab Nebula spaceship
2. Octopus character
3. Flying pizza logo
4. Dancing pumpkins

Adobe After Effects Sequences

1. Channel 9 News
2. Animated bullet points
3. Sepia-toned historical photos
4. Dance theater introduction
5. Panda zoo exhibit
6. Pharmaceutical diagram

How would you organize these clips? You could, of course, jumble them all up and spit them out in some random order. Would that create the impression of a myriad variety of clips, such that the viewer would be astounded by the sheer magnitude of your work? I think not. More likely, the viewer would get the impression that there was a collection of clips here fitting three general categories, but without any intelligent order.

Figure 5.9 shows a diagrammatic expression of the 13 clips in a hypothetical showreel, grouped according to their category of animation. Notice the visual pattern of the gestalt and how your eyes see three distinct shapes that have little relationship to each other. A reel composed of these clip groups, arranged in any order, will present a weak impression on the viewer. The visual pattern is imbalanced. The viewer will be distracted by one category that is too small, and one that is too large. This grouping cannot produce a showreel that will work to maximum effect.

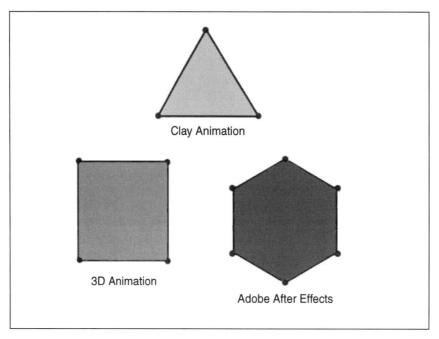

Figure 5.9 *A diagrammatic expression of the 13 clips in a hypothetical showreel, grouped according to their category of animation.*

Gestalt and Editing

Now let's apply the gestalt principle to editing and organizing these clips, and see how the pattern can be changed to create a highly balanced visual pattern. When carried to the edit suite, this pattern will produce a reel that flows without causing the viewer to dwell on any one category.

Certainly, at some point in your career, you might have enough clips that a mind-boggling myriad could be created. But my guess is that your top-notch clips would stand out significantly, causing the viewer's mind to hang onto those while he pushed the rest back into some viewer-invented subcategory.

You see, if *you* don't organize your clips, the viewer will! If he follows the natural mental order of things, chances are he will employ some gestalt principle, slicing and dicing your "random" design into his own mental diagram. And you might not like how the viewer does your job for you.

So, with all respect, may I bring you back to the task of organizing your clips? Good.

What have we got? How can we organize the preceding list to exploit the maximum gestalt effect? If we decide to assemble a first-draft diagram, we could easily start with a nice triangle for the Clay Animation sequence, as noted before. The four works of 3D would form a square space, and then the six After Effects clips . . . hmmm.

A series of six clips so heavily outweighs the smaller groups that it would cause imbalance in the reel. What if we cut up this series into two series of three clips each? Instead of calling each of these series "Adobe After Effects," let's see if we can refine them into two subcategories.

If we grouped the Channel 9 News, the animated bullet points, and the dance theater introduction together, it could be called a series of "television clips." The remaining clips—the sepia-toned historical photos, the panda zoo exhibit, and the pharmaceutical diagram—could be considered "graphic designs."

Law and Order

Now that the two After Effects series are divided, you can separate them from each other. This suggests the order in which they will be shown and begins the process of actually editing the reel. You can put the "television clips" series first, then the clay animation, followed by the "graphic designs," and wrap up with the 3D animation—or any other order that neatly separates the two After Effects clip series.

Now, notice that you now have three series of three clips and one of four clips. You could go with this arrangement, but you must realize that a little bit of extra influence will be placed on the 3D clips because there is one more clip in that series. This is okay, but you might want to consider cutting the weakest example and creating four series of three clips. This provides the most balance. Now your diagram can be ordered in any one of 24 different ways. One of them would look like Figure 5.10. In this example, the two After Effects series have been placed on either side of the clay animation series to create the impression that they are two different categories of animation. Experimentation will tell you what the best order is for your purposes.

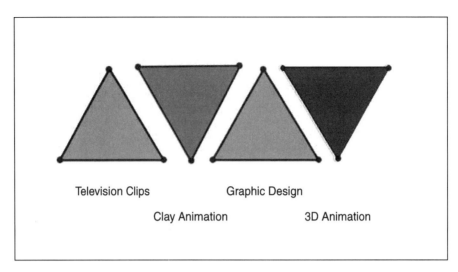

Figure 5.10 *The best gestalt balance for all the clips is four series of three clips each.*

In general editing as well as showreel editing, there are certain laws or customs that apply to the craft of making great edits. You already know one of the most important and subtle customs: the gestalt principle. Now here is another—the Rule of Three.

In gestalt, you need at least three points of reference to define a space. However, this works a bit differently when you work in a linear mode like video editing. In addition to the gestalt space perceived by the viewer, there is also the linear rhythm of the cuts, which are more apparent.

In rhythm, there are three kinds of events: happenstance, coincidence, and intent. (If you are a James Bond fan, you might remember these words used by Auric Goldfinger when summarizing his "coincidental" encounters with 007!) It goes like this:

If you sat down at Carnegie Hall to listen to a concert and the timpanist hit his kettle drum once, and that was it, you might think, *Was that a mistake? Is it the start of the symphony? What's up?*

Instead, the timpanist hits the drum two times and then leaves you in silence. Now your mind has more to work with. *Was one beat louder than the other? How long did he pause between beats?* You might think, *Well, that wasn't a mistake, cuz he did it twice. But what's up? Was it a coincidence?*

Finally, if this curious drummer hit the drum three times, you would certainly know the drumming was intentional. In addition to that, your mind, analyzing more information than two beats could provide, now measures the two intervals between the beats, comparing them to each other, as well as the intensity of the three beats.

For a moment, let's assume these three beats were of equal intensity (loud) and equally spaced:

Boom. Boom. Boom.

In a way, these beats could represent your first three clips—the "television clips."

Now, let's assume the drummer hits three more beats. These are soft, but spaced the same as the first three beats. Let's say these represent the "clay animation" clips. Next, the drummer returns to the same beat and interval as the first three. You're probably getting my point now, since these three beats represent the second set of After Effects clips! Finally, Ringo gives us three more beats, really loud on a bigger bass drum, played very close together.

What does the mind experience when this rhythm is heard? Here it is, expressed as a line of type:

- - - _ _ _ - - - + + +

Perhaps you remember your high school English teacher instructing you about the rhyme and rhythm of a poem. She might have expressed the drumbeat like this:

a a a b b b a a a CCC

Mathematicians might express the same thing like this.

1 1 1 2 2 2 1 1 1 3 3 3

Okay, if you're not a musician, a poet, or a mathematician, you'll just have to take my word for it, but each of these expressions represents a rhythm pattern, a cycle if you will, with a specific signature. This signature is created by the mind's natural tendency to anticipate what comes next.

The Rule of Three

This is a very strong tendency of the mind, evolved over thousands of years, because our ancestors survived by anticipating and predicting what at first appeared to be random events. The crack of a twig in the forest, a cold morning at the end of summer, a change in the river's current, all these could be parts of rhythms that, if ignored, might mean death. You can be very sure that your great[10]-grandfather didn't wait for the fourth twig-snap to grab a spear and gird his loins.

When you use rhythms, you're using one of the most deeply rooted instincts of the human race. Your showreel can make people dance, make them cry, or make them hand over a contract and hire you on the spot.

Getting back to our 1, 2, 1, 3 rhythm, if we had not added the final trio of three quick, hard, low beats—the last group—the mind would have expected another three loud beats, like the very first three. The mind would have expected 1, 2, 1, and then 2.

The arrival of the final quick, low beats at the end tells the mind that something has changed. Imagine if Grandpa Caveman heard a twig snap, then a breath, then a twig snap, then . . . "Hi, honey, it's me."

The new series at the end of the 1, 2, 1 signals the mind that either the 1, 2, 1 series is over or that, most probably, another series is about to begin, probably a repeat of the one just heard. In other words, instead of anticipating 1, 2, 1, 2, the mind is anticipating 1, 2, 1, 3, 1, 2, 1, 3.

Taking this realization back to our video editing (assuming we are editing just the 12 clips), the last three, which are unique 3D animation clips, would be a fitting way to end the reel.

While you had 24 different choices of how to order the four series on the reel (4x3x2x1), there is virtually an unlimited number of ways to edit the 12 clips. What you must realize, however, is that the most powerful versions will be those that observe the Rule of Three.

This rule applies to the three first cuts: 1 1 1

This rule applies also to the first three groups of cuts: 1 1 1 2 2 2 1 1 1

And if you take the entire cycle of 12 cuts and decide to make a much larger reel, your best version would exploit how the minds of your viewers will also be looking for the established rhythm to build upon itself in further permutations of the Rule of Three, or, if you are particularly skillful, in clever ways that you *violate* the Rule of Three.

A really great illustration of setting up a Rule of Three expectation may be found in the drum solo during Dave Brubeck's classic jazz number, "Take Five." A quick, short drum roll is followed by a heavy bass drum hit. This is repeated enough times that the mind expects that heavy beat every time, at precisely the same interval. Then drummer Joe Morello starts to stretch out the interval until the listener's mind is literally begging to hear the bass hit.

When you learn to play with the viewer's mind by feeding it and then depriving it of expectations, you turn your showreel (or any form of media) into art. It is the art—as Frank N. Furter in the *Rocky Horror Picture Show* puts it—of, "antici-

--pation."

How Long a Reel?

Since the invention of electronic media, the attention span of media watchers has decreased with every generation. When I was a kid, showreels were half an hour long and often included entire programs from beginning to end! When I worked as an assistant television commercial producer in a major advertising agency in the early '80s, reels were getting down to 10 minutes, and we usually yelled, "Cut. Next!" to the projectionist. (Yeah, get it? There was actually a projectionist running the reels!)

I have a feeling all this attention deficit disorder stuff is related to electronic media in some way. And I have a sneaking suspicion that animation is at the core, because out of all the reels, animation reels are the shortest. You want to know how long your reel should be? Try less than five minutes, dude.

People who screen reels are in your generation. You know how, like, CNN and FOX are so borrring with their news analysis that runs, what, 10 minutes? Well, Sherlock, nobody your age wants to look at your animation reel if the surf's up or someone in the next room is shouting for a rematch of *Half Life 3*.

You want to show brief clips of your best stuff and sign off ("Hasta la vista, baby") before the viewer knows what hit him. Assuming you threw in at least 12 distinctly different clips, your reel could be 30 seconds and no one would complain, really. They might even think you're playing hard-to-get, which of course makes you even more desirable. They might even call you up and say, "Hey, Judith, let's have some more of that good stuff!", and invite you in for a rad interview.

On the other hand, a long reel risks the ultimate diss: getting the Eject button pressed in mid-scene. That's Game Over. Don't expect them to return your calls or emails. I recently reviewed a reel from one of the guys who worked on *Star Wars* and *Men In Black*. It was a reel with Jar Jar Binks and the bad side of Lara Flynn Boyle. Clocked in at a minute forty-five. I whispered, "Wow," and pressed the replay.

Bust Your Best Cap

If you have honed your skills in one specific area of animation, such as modeling, be sure to highlight that skill in your reel. In fact, you might strive to exclude everything else, thereby showing extreme discipline. Of course, make sure that what you show is what you want to do. If you're great at modeling but have grown to hate it, don't send out reels with your lighting work or you'll only get more of the same.

I once made a reel composed completely of jobs where I'd saved the client's posterior, most often when the client had no budget. Guess what kinds of jobs I got from that reel? Lots and lots of headaches. The only person who wants to hire a hero is someone who's always getting into a jam. Know this: You will most likely get hired to do what is on your reel.

The Power of DVDs

Back in the days of VHS showreels (and we're still using these, so don't panic), the smart artist would line the inside of the plastic box (never use the slide-cardboard type) with a printed paper listing the clips on the reel. Using this paper, the viewer could see what she had in store for herself, fast-forward to various clips, and so on. The paper would also feature brief notes about each clip, perhaps listing the jobs the artist did on each clip.

Today, we have the marvelous interactive capabilities of the DVD to assist in the process of making a showreel conform to a viewer's expectations, whatever they might be. The short showreel described above could be designed to play automatically, as soon as the DVD was inserted in the player. At the conclusion, a menu screen might appear, offering longer examples of the clips, a biography and resume of the animator, whatever.

With DVD showreels, there is a compelling argument to at least annotate all your clips with a menu that clearly and simply lists what you did on each. And let's not forget—put your name, address, email, home phone, cell phone, IM address, and message service on the opening and closing screen, the disk or tape itself, the box in which the disk or tape gets delivered . . . heck, tattoo this stuff on the FedEx man's forehead if you can. One thing is for sure: If the viewer can't reach you, you are not going to get the job.

I think DVDs are the way to go with animation reels. They can be anything that anybody wants. The only trouble is that this can also be anything that anybody *doesn't* want. Let's say, for instance, a potential client is suitably awed by your quick intro piece and is ready to pick up the phone and hire you. Then the menu comes up and the client sees one of your lengthy clips, watches it, and hates it. What did your DVD do here? It killed the deal!

Now I've confused you. I said something was probably great *and* probably bad. Well, welcome to the real world, sonny boy. DVDs are a new technology. Guess what? Sometimes they don't work! VHS reels, on the other hand, have been around since dirt was invented and they work 99.99% of the time. So let's say that I am merely presenting you with the facts. You decide.

What to Expect

Here's some more sad news. Often, you will send out your reel and hear absolutely nothing in response. After 10 business days, you are certainly within your rights to call the recipient, and I suggest you do so. Simply say you are calling "to confirm receipt of the reel."

This doesn't imply that you expect the recipient to put everything aside and look at the reel, just that the person actually acknowledges receiving it. You see, just this little humble request is often enough to nudge someone in the right direction without getting them angry at you. Nothing is quite as effective as modesty and showing respect. It's twice as insulting as being insulting, and no one can get angry at you for it!

When the person acknowledges getting the reel, say something innocuous, such as, "I hope you like it when you see it." They will often respond with some kind of promise to look at it. You can respond with something like, "I know it's difficult to walk the line between being a pain in the neck and being of service to you, so I hope I haven't crossed the line."

This will usually get you a response as to what specifically the line is. If the person says, "Oh no. Don't worry. You can call me every month if you want," then you have a license to call every month if you want. If the person says, "Look, I haven't got time to take calls, frankly. If we want to see you, we'll call you," that happens as often as the nice response, so be ready for it. It usually has nothing to do with how good or bad your reel is—unless the person actually says they saw the reel and gives you the brush-off.

In that case, go back to the drawing board if this client is of value to you. Of course, the client may just be a bonehead. If you suspect this is so, mail out more reels and see if the bonehead's response is duplicated. If not, you've confirmed another bonehead. (Congratulations. I have about 500 of them in my database.) If so, maybe your reel really needs reworking.

Also keep in mind that you are trying to get a job that is fun to do, and everyone else has already figured this out and sent in their reels to the same companies you are calling. If you decided to be a sanitation worker, your sample of a well-thrown sack of goo would probably get a callback in 24 hours. That's because not many people want to be sanitation workers. In fact, I don't think you need a showsack to get the job. So the point is to be a little patient and a lot persistent.

Selling Yourself

Earlier, I mentioned making phone calls to your prospective employer or client. Does the idea of making a phone call to get work bother you? It bothers a lot of people I know. In fact, I have found that animators in general are the category of media worker that is the most reticent to make calls. I don't know why this is. Perhaps it fits that they like to put their nose into a computer screen all day because they don't want to do anything else. I don't know. But if you don't like selling yourself, whether it's by phone, sending reels, or writing letters, you are not going to achieve your highest level of professional rewards.

In general, creative workers fall into one of two categories: those who like selling themselves and those who don't. Usually, the ones who don't will end up working for the ones who do. If you like to sell—that is, pick up a phone and pitch your creativity to a stranger—there is an excellent chance you can make a pretty good living. Starting freelance animator wages in the New York metropolitan area are about $2,000 per week. That might sound like a lot, but keep in mind, this is free-lance work. You might go for weeks without work, so don't expect to multiply 2,000 by 52 weeks and think you're going to be raking in north of a hundred grand a year. To do that, you have to be the guy who hires animators.

If you don't like to sell, you might consider hiring a salesperson or engaging a rep-resentative. Of course, to do this, you need a pretty good reel—so file away this advice until you're ready. At the novice stage, you probably can't afford the salary of a salesperson (unless you marry one!), and no representative is going to take on a rank amateur. But you will be surprised at how little time it takes before one of these two options becomes possible. Maybe less than a year of good full-time work.

If you're the kind of creative person who doesn't like to sell, and if you're still rather new to the craft, you'll have to go to work for someone. To get that work, you're going to have to (my apologies) sell yourself. You have to take your reel and pitch it to a producer, animation supervisor, or animation studio owner. To get to make that pitch, you have to research the available workplaces, get the names of the people you need to meet, make some calls, and send some mail. *Oh lordy*, you think. *I can't sell myself!* Oh yes you can. I'll show you how. And it will be easy.

Consider this: When you work for somebody, chances are that the amount you get paid will be less than one half of what your employer will charge his clients for your work. It's a simple formula. To be profitable, most companies have to double your costs. If you get $400 per day, the client will pay more than $800 per hour to your boss. Your boss uses his share, $400, maybe more, to pay for the costs of run-ning his studio and making his sales calls, and still has a little bit left over to buy a Ferrari and a nice crib in the Hamptons. That's the real deal.

And if you have a representative, it isn't exactly Easy Street either. You will pay this representative anywhere from 10% to 15% of your gross billings. That includes the work your rep gets you, the work you get for yourself, and the work you get because your dad referred you to someone who once bounced you on her knee. Add to that what the representative will charge you for her allowance for lunches and other forms of entertainment, and inducements to get clients to meet with her on your behalf. If you're really good, you can hire a full-time representative, pay her a salary and benefits, and thereby eliminate the percentage deal on everything you make. But then, you're running your own animation studio, aren't you?

Categories of Animation Work

There are seven general categories of media that employ animation. You needn't feel obligated to make Hollywood features or television commercials. Those are just two categories. They happen to be the most lucrative, and hence are the hardest to get into. Consider finding a niche that's lower on the food chain, and then, as you gain experience, work your way up. The seven categories are:

Hollywood Feature Films

TV Commercials

Televised Entertainment

Games

Home Videos

Business Communications

E-media

Hollywood Feature Films

"Hollywood" animated feature films are rarely produced in Hollywood, a neighborhood in Los Angeles, California. There is a growing animation community up the coast in Santa Barbara, and everyone knows about George Lucas's new facility going up in San Francisco. Nevertheless, it really helps if you go where the work is, and feature films are being animated in Southern California and the Northeast of the U.S. A lot of work is also being done overseas in Russia, Romania, India, Australia, and New Zealand. I wouldn't suggest you emigrate—but if you happen to be from one of these countries, you might not have to negotiate with Homeland Security and come to the U.S.

The global market of the Internet makes locating your animation business anywhere in the world a practicality. If you're really good, the world will beat a digital pathway to your door.

Cracking your way into a position making 3D animation for feature films is kind of like getting a job as a feature film director. You have to be maniacally persistent, concentrate exclusively on the feature film market, and be kind of lucky. If you have a really good showreel, particularly with regard to character animation, lighting, or compositing, you might get a break if you find a new director or producer who is looking for new talent. Such a person will be looking to ride your coattails to stardom as much as you're looking to ride hers. Look for a low-budget production, and strive to make their sad little budget a reality. It's like in the music video business, where you find a band about to make it and then become their video person. Your client makes it big—and so do you.

Short of that great feat, simply send your reel to existing feature film shops and hope their needs match up with your capabilities. And don't believe Jim Morrison. You *can* petition the Lord with prayer.

TV Commercials

TV commercials are another hard market to crack, but not as hard as features. As the commercials get higher in budget, though, the market gets tougher. If you live in a second- or third-tier market (that is, a city that is not New York, Chicago, or Los Angeles), you can pitch your reel to advertising agencies and commercial producers. If your reel is a starter, you should still be able to get some work doing cable commercials, but if you have a stick of dynamite with a sizzling fuse, head for a top-tier market, hire a *rep* (representative), and go for broke.

The top markets are dominated by the big advertising agencies that have an established method of seeing new talent. You basically call producers, or better yet, their assistants, send your reel, and pester them a bit until they see it. It's a hit-or-miss proposition. Having a rep with existing client contacts helps enormously. Reps come in all flavors, from the ones who have their own businesses to the ones you hire yourself on full-time basis with salary and benefits. On second thought, maybe it's a good idea to get your start in a small town, build a good reel, and work your way to one of the three coasts.

Televised Entertainment

Televised entertainment includes TV shows that use 3D animation and composited effects as part of their weekly fare. Again, this is primarily a Los Angeles market, but there is no reason you can't create your own show in Smalltown, USA, pitch it to a network, and get a sale. Mike Judge did that with *Beavis and Butthead*, although he used primitive, 2D *cell animation* instead of sophisticated 3D computer techniques.

The cost of producing a half-hour or one-hour pilot using 3D animation is rather small compared to making a filmed presentation. Your biggest expense will be the voices. Mike Judge did several of his own!

Again, cable television is a great place to get started, especially the public access channels. You can test your production techniques, audience response, and enjoyment for the process with very little risk.

Games

Game devices, from arcades to set-top boxes (and computers in-between), continually increase in their capabilities to emulate photorealistic 3D action. The market for 3D animation in the gaming community is always growing and highly competitive. Skills that will place you at the head of the line include character and creature development, achieving photorealistic playback with minimum memory allocation, understanding moving camera dynamics, and of course, good teamwork.

You may consider designing your own game and using it to penetrate the market. Certain equipment requirements, such as a motion capture system, may be beyond your reach. But your creative concept, supported by less sophisticated choreography, may be adequate to earn you a significant production contract, or at least a great job.

Home Videos

Home videos are another outlet for creative 3D animation. If you decide to make your own televised entertainment, you can extend the selling opportunities of your work by making copies for the home market and testing their legs by sending your work to home video distributors.

You can also go to your local video rental house, look over the *special interest videos* section, and collect the names of key producers. These enterprising businesspeople are always looking for a way to spice up their productions, and if you can price a package of logos, graphics, special effects, and other fireworks for their productions, you will have found a friend and a long-lasting client.

Business Communications

Business communications is the largest category of application for 3D animation, especially videos and DVDs that are made to explain the arcane intricacies of medicine and high technology. Here, your market is composed of producers, marketing directors, human resource managers, venture capital entrepreneurs, and training directors, all of whom have a constant need to have their communications embellished by animation and graphics.

Many of these clients have very liberal criteria regarding the quality and complexity of the animations they purchase. If you are a beginner and your reel is not yet replete with the most original, cutting-edge work, you may still be able to make sales in this category if your client has not had the opportunity to look at more sophisticated work, or does not understand the difference between the reels of a beginner and those of a seasoned pro. This limited window of opportunity should not be exploited by laziness. If you are lucky to get a client after only a few months practice in 3D, don't rest on your laurels and take your good fortune for granted. Keep pushing your envelope of skills.

E-Media

E-media presentations that appear on the Internet are another large and growing market that temporarily offer advantages to the beginner. Because most e-media is streamed to the viewer at a low bandwidth compared to broadcast television, the complexity of the animation it can play is severely limited. Beginners, whose work is limited by their level of knowledge, can exploit a medium whose resolution is limited by its bandwidth, if the beginner is at least aware of how these two limitations overlap.

Low bandwidth means fewer colors and shading, fewer frames, simpler morphing, and less detail than full-bandwidth imagery. If you plan to get your start in this category, concentrate your initial skill set on achieving good results within the limitations of the medium, and expand your skill set as the medium's bandwidth increases. You just may get in on the ground floor of something big.

So now you're sitting by the phone, waiting for the call. You can do two things. First, move on to Chapter 6 and get back to learning SOFTIMAGE|XSI. Next, read Chapter 7, where I'll teach you what to do when you get the call, and how to handle the job interview. Hey, we're really moving now!

Chapter 6

Just In Time: Adding the Aspects of a Timeline, Keyframes, and Motion to Your Animation Project

So far, everything we have created in tutorials and interface exploration of SOFTIMAGE|XSI has been related to creating still pictures. But we are not photographers or fine art painters! We are animators! Animators create work in four dimensions: height, width, depth, and *time*.

Walking the Timeline

In order to address the passage of time in an animation, the interface of an animation program needs to have some kind of control mechanism. This is done with the *timeline*, a horizontal track, the length of which represents time. (You were introduced to it in Chapter 2.) It is graduated into minimal units of time called *frames*.

The word *frame* comes from cinema, where a strip of film is divided into frames. Each frame holds a still photograph. When the film is run through a projector, each frame is projected onto the cinema screen for a specific length of time, usually 1/24th of a second. Then the projector blocks the ray of light through the frame, the film is mechanically advanced to the next frame, and the projector's light is unblocked to project the next frame on the screen. The rapid exposure of frames, at a rate of 24 per second, has been established as a practical method of producing moving pictures based on the physiology of the human eyes and brain.

As cinema and its daughter video developed, many different frame sizes, aspect ratios (the ratio of height to width), and frame rates have been used. For instance, most of Europe uses 25 frames per second for video (their system is called PAL). High definition video uses both 60 and 30 frames per second. SOFTIMAGE|XSI allows you to choose the frame rate and aspect ratio of your animations, but for this book, we will stay with the most common rate in the U.S., 30 frames per second. (If you want to be really technical, it's actually 29.97 frames per second. That's the standard for NTSC, the North American television format. Explaining the complexity of this fraction is not within the scope of this book.)

Time, Frames, and Timecode

For the duration of this book, we will refer to the NTSC standard of 30 frames per second. You will see these frames indicated on your timeline at the bottom of the XSI control screen. At the far left, the timeline starts at frame zero and continues up to whatever limit you set in the duration of your animation.

In Softimage, the timeline can refer to frames or actual time increments. Time increments are according to a digital code known as the SMPTE timecode. (SMPTE stands for Society of Motion Picture and Television Engineers, an industry organization.) This code is expressed as a series of four pairs of numbers separated by three colons. Reading from left to right, the first pair of numbers represent hours, ranging from 00 to 23. The second pair represent minutes, ranging from 00 to 59. The third pair represent seconds, ranging from 00 to 59. And the final pair represent frames, which in NTSC range from 00 to 29.

You should become familiar with referring to animations in both total frames and in timecode, because your entire work path will often contain references to both. For instance, you may be assigned to create a 30-second logo, like the one referred to in Chapter 4. The ending timecode for that logo, as it will appear on the video-tape recorder that will record your final rendered sequence, would look like this:

00:00:30:00

However, the frame count will be 900 (30 frames × 30 seconds).

Let's bend your mind a moment to get you thinking about converting from time-code to frames and back again. To convert timecode into frames, you must first convert the hours into minutes (minutes × 60), and then add the result to whatever number is in the minutes pair. Convert this result into seconds (minutes ×60), and add this to whatever number is in the seconds pair. Convert this result into frames (seconds × 30) . . .

Pay attention here, kiddo!

. . . and add the result to whatever number is in the frames pair. Whew! That is the total number of frames represented by the timecode.

For example, a timecode of 01:33:21:18 will produce 60 seconds from the 01 of the hours pair, added to the 33 in the minutes pair, to yield 93 minutes. This will produce 5,580 seconds (93 minutes × 60), which, when added to the 21 seconds in the seconds pair, yields 5,601 seconds. This will produce 168,030 frames (5,601 seconds × 30), which, when added to the 18 frames in the frames pair, yields a total frame count of 168,048.

Exercise 6.1: Calculating Timecode and Frames

Convert the following SMPTE timecode references to frames:

00:00:28:00 _____   This is the actual length of many TV commercials.

01:50:00:00 _____   This is the most common length of feature films.

00:22:00:00 _____   This is the most common length of a 30-minute TV show without commercials.

00:45:00:00 _____   This is the most common length of a one-hour TV show.

(The answers are at the end of the chapter.)

Often it is necessary for you to convert frames into time. Obviously, the method for converting frame counts is the reverse of converting timecode. First, divide the total frame count by 30 to get the total number of seconds. If any number remains . . .

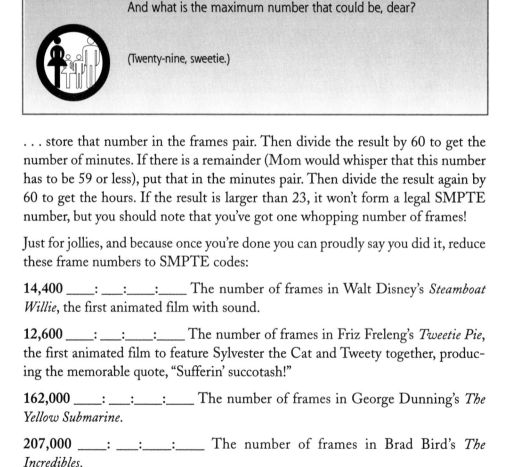

And what is the maximum number that could be, dear?

(Twenty-nine, sweetie.)

. . . store that number in the frames pair. Then divide the result by 60 to get the number of minutes. If there is a remainder (Mom would whisper that this number has to be 59 or less), put that in the minutes pair. Then divide the result again by 60 to get the hours. If the result is larger than 23, it won't form a legal SMPTE number, but you should note that you've got one whopping number of frames!

Just for jollies, and because once you're done you can proudly say you did it, reduce these frame numbers to SMPTE codes:

14,400 ____: ___:____:____ The number of frames in Walt Disney's *Steamboat Willie*, the first animated film with sound.

12,600 ____: ___:____:____ The number of frames in Friz Freleng's *Tweetie Pie*, the first animated film to feature Sylvester the Cat and Tweety together, producing the memorable quote, "Sufferin' succotash!"

162,000 ____: ___:____:____ The number of frames in George Dunning's *The Yellow Submarine*.

207,000 ____: ___:____:____ The number of frames in Brad Bird's *The Incredibles*.

126,452 ____: ___:____:____ A random number I pulled out of thin air, just to make you work a bit.

(The answers are at the end of the chapter.)

Keyframes Are the Key

Okay, enough hard work. Let's get back to animating things.

You already know that the main control area for animation in Softimage is the timeline, and that the timeline can be graduated in frames or increments of time. For most animation control, you will use the frame gradations. This is because frames are the smallest unit of time with which you may animate practically.

In order to make something happen over a period of time, you must tell Softimage how much time the program has to make the animation happen! For instance, if you want a ball to drop from the edge of a table down to the floor, you have to tell Softimage how many frames it will take, from the point where the ball leaves the table until it makes first contact with the floor.

Let's say that the art director who drew your storyboard wrote a timing suggestion on this panel that says "1 second." You know that there are 30 frames in 1 second. So wherever the ball starts—let's say it starts at frame zero—you're going to assign 30 frames to get the ball to the floor.

The animation is accomplished by putting the ball at the edge of the table and assigning the assemblage of objects and effects in that position (ball on table, over floor, and any other props, scenery, lights, and so on) to Frame 0. Then, you move the ball (probably only on the Y axis) down to the floor.

TONY'S TIP

If you were really clever, you would squash the ball a bit vertically for just a frame or two to make it look rubbery!

At the point the ball touches the floor, you assign the assemblage of objects to Frame 30. Instantly, Softimage measures the Y axis distance that you assigned to the ball between Frames 0 and 30, and calculates the ball's position for each of the in-between frames (1 through 29). This process is called *in-betweening* or just *tweening*. It used to take a lot of time for hand-drawing animators to draw these frames, but for you and Softimage, it only takes seconds.

This is basically how you make animations in Softimage and almost any other animation program. Each time you assign an object or effect to a specific frame on the timeline, this frame is called a *keyframe*. The frame contains key information necessary to create the illusion of motion and the passage of time.

Animation and the fourth dimension of cinematic art is based, very simply, on assigning specific events to occur at specific times (keyframes) along a graduated track, called the timeline.

If you understand this, you are ready to start animating, dude! Let's get it on!

Exercise 6.2: Animating the Logo

In this exercise, we will take a look at what is involved in animating the logo you designed in Chapter 4.

Before attempting any animation, it is a really good idea to have a plan. Whether it is your own idea or a predefined project for a client, it is essential that you have some idea of the timing involved before you start saving motion information. Let's go back and take a look at the original storyboard, shown in Figure 6.1.

You will notice that there are time notations at the bottom of each note section. These tell you exactly (or approximately, depending on your project) how long it should take for each section of the animation to be accomplished. There are additional notes on individual elements and effects that you can use to refine the motion later. When animating, it is always best to put in the broad strokes first, gradually adding more detail only when needed, thereby avoiding unnecessary keyframes (motion data) that may interrupt the smooth flow of your objects as they travel from place to place.

Since you will always be using a time measurement of 30 frames per second, the shield will spin into the frame over the first 5 seconds (or 150 frames) of animation. The L has landed after 10 seconds (or 300 frames), and the remaining elements are in place by 20 seconds (600 frames). That leaves a 10-second hold at the end, which results in a total length of 30 seconds or 900 frames.

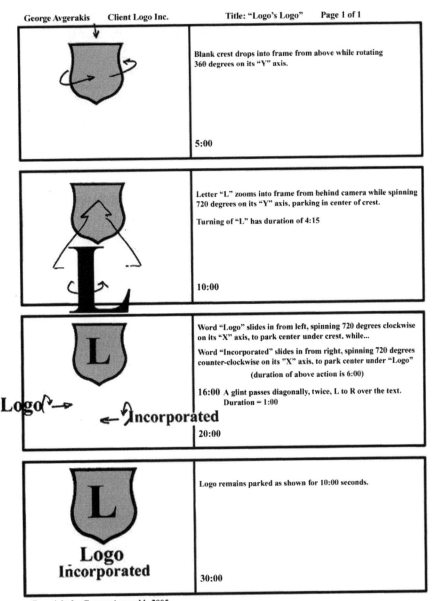

Figure 6.1 *The original storyboard.*

If you do not already have it open, load your scene from Chapter 4. The scene contains a shield element and the capital letter L, which make up your crest. At this point you will create the last remaining elements for your animation, the corporation's name. In this case, it's "Logo Incorporated."

1. In the Model module, select Create > Text > Solid Mesh. Follow the steps laid out in Chapter 4 when you created the capital L, and create the word "Logo."

2. Repeat the process for the word "Incorporated." I used the Georgia font, a fit size of 10, and an extrusion length of 2. You should feel free to experiment and choose whatever makes you happy.

3. Put a unique material on each of these items, as you did earlier. Select them one at a time and choose Get > Material > Phong. Accept the default settings.

You will edit these properties later, but for now you must ensure that you have replaced the scene material with one of your own.

4. Select both of the new text objects and click the Selection button in the Master Control Panel. Choose Move Center to Vertices. This will allow you to pivot these objects around their geometric centers later on.

Before you start setting keyframes, you need to make a few final adjustments.

5. First, select the L object and click the Cut button in the MCP. This unparents the L from the shield. Since it flies in separately from the shield, you don't want it to be influenced by the other object's coordinates.

6. Next, select the shield and click the Freeze button at the bottom of the MCP. This erases the operator stack (construction history) for the shield and "bakes" any texture coordinates onto the object. That way, you don't run the risk of moving your bumps around during the animation process.

7. Finally, set the last frame to 900 (or 30 seconds) so that you have the whole timeline available at a glance. Click in the text box to the right of the timeline and enter 900.

8. Press Enter to accept the value.

Now use the various viewports and translate (hotkey V) the various elements around until they look like the final frame in the storyboard (see Figure 6.2). It is often beneficial with logo components to pose everything as you know it should be when the animation is finished, and animate the objects off-camera. Also, if it helps you to keep track of your objects, open an Explorer window (8), and rename (F2) each of the objects to be animated. I highly recommend naming all of the components in your scene for the sake of clarity down the road. Make sure that your camera is in the correct position before starting. In Figure 6.2, my camera is at an angle to assist me in judging special relationships. Before I begin recording keyframes, I will reset the camera by pressing the R key and then dolly back into position. Do not zoom in the Camera view, or you will change the lens angle (perspective). If you are seeing too much perspective on the text, click on the camera icon in the Camera view and choose the settings (see Figure 6.3).

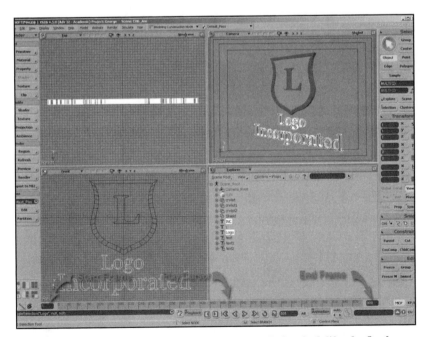

Figure 6.2 *Translating the elements around until they look like the final frame in the storyboard.*

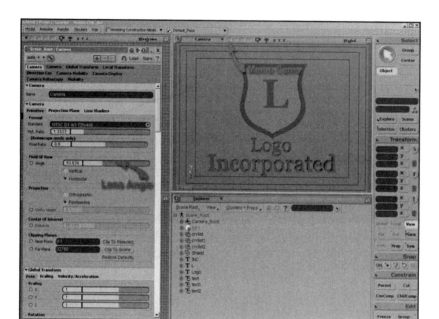

Figure 6.3 *Click on the camera icon in the Camera view to change the perspective.*

1. Adjust the angle here and take note of it. A smaller number will flatten out the text, but you may have unexpected results when you fly the objects by the camera later.

2. When you are done, middle-click on one of the MemoCam indents at the top of the Camera view. You may also click on the eyeball icon at the top of the Camera view, choose visibility options at the bottom, and click on the Visual Cues tab to access the Safe/Action/Title indicators.

3. Using Save As, save your scene under a different name (like Chapter 6 or Ani_Crest). This way, you can return to the earlier version if needed.

Entering Basic Keyframes to Control Animation

Now that you can see the scope of the whole project, you will begin by animating the shield object over the first 5 seconds (150 frames). It may help to hide (H) certain objects that you are not currently working with. I am going to select the L and hide it while I animate the shield.

4. Select the shield!

5. Drag the play cursor to frame 150 on the timeline.

6. Click the letter T (translate position) in the MCP, or firmly press V on the keyboard. You should see the x, y, and z letters light up next to the T icon, indicating that all three axis are available for keying.

    If x, y, and z are not all selected, click the little ladder icon under the T to activate them.

    You are now ready to keyframe the end position of the shield.

7. Click on the key icon just below the timeline, or press the K key. The key icon should turn pink, indicating that an active key exists for this property at this frame.

TONY'S TIP

A gray key icon indicates no keys for the selected property. Green indicates keys for this property, but not on this frame. Yellow indicates that a value has been changed, but not yet keyed on the current frame. It seems complicated, but you will quickly come to rely on this feedback.

8. Now change the play cursor to frame 1.

9. Zoom out in the front view if necessary.

10. Grab the green arrow icon (y axis) in the front view, and drag the shield straight up and out of sight of the camera. The key icon should now be green.

11. Click it to record the change of position. (It should change to pink.)

12. Scrub the play cursor back and forth between frames 1 and 150. You should see the shield move between the two positions that you've specified. If not, back up and try again (see Fig. 6.4).

TONY'S TIP

It is important to change the frame value before you change the property value. Otherwise, you will not create animation; you will just change the property value at the same point in time.

Once you have mastered changing position, it is time to add some rotation. Make sure you are back on frame 150 and the shield is still selected.

13. Click on the R (rotation) button in the MCP, or firmly press C on the keyboard. As before, you should see the x, y, and z buttons light up with their respective colors.

    If not, click the little ladder under the R button. Also, check to see that Add mode is selected in the cluster of buttons at the bottom of the Transformation Panel.

14. Click the key icon to set a key on this frame.

15. Drag the cursor back to frame 1.

Your storyboard tells you that the shield should rotate 360 degrees as it drops into place.

16. Since you set your original key at a value of 0, on frame 150 you will type -360 in the y text field in the rotation cluster.

17. Click the key icon. Now, if you scrub again, you should see the shield rotate as it drops into place.

18. Save your scene. See Figure 6.4.

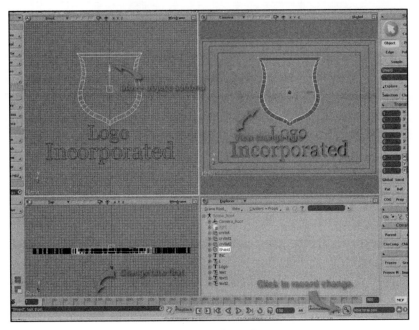

Figure 6.4 *The shield rotates as it drops into place.*

Staggering Events in Time

Now that you have the shield landing successfully on frame 150, you will follow it with the L. Since the L does pretty much the same thing as the shield, except along the z-axis instead of the y, you will learn how to finesse the motion rather than just how to set the keys. Let's rough in the motion first.

1. Move the cursor to frame 300 (10 seconds).

2. Un-hide the L by selecting it in the Explorer and pressing the H key.

3. Save a key for position and a key for rotation without moving off frame 300.

4. Next, change to frame 150 on the timeline.

5. This time, adjust the top view instead of the front view, so that you have room to maneuver. While watching the camera, drag the L forward along the z-axis until it scales past the camera and out of sight. Make sure that the T is selected and save a position key.

6. Click the R to change to rotation mode.

7. From the storyboard, you know that you need a 720-degree rotation as the L flies in, so type -720 in the y-axis next to the R (rotation) button.

8. Save a key.

9. Scrub the play cursor to check that everything is progressing as you expected.

The storyboard says that the rotation should end at SMPTE time 4:15 into this 5-second segment. Because your animation is playing at 30 fps, this means that although the position animation will continue to frame 300, the rotation should end on frame 285.

10. Make sure that the L is selected and the Rotation panel is active.

11. Press the number 0 on your keyboard.

Using the Animation Editor

This opens up the Animation (f-curve) Editor. This is a graphical representation of a property's change over time (see Fig 6.5). The horizontal axis is Frames (time), and the vertical axis is the property that you have animated. You can use this window to adjust the timing, acceleration, interpolation, and many other properties of your animation curves. The more horizontal the curve, the slower the motion is changing; the steeper the curve, the faster the change. A curve that is completely horizontal is not changing and therefore is not contributing to the animation. The default interpolation of an animation curve in XSI is called *spline interpolation*. Just like the curve in Figure 6.5, it starts changing slowly, reaches maximum velocity in the middle, and gradually slows to a stop.

You can select any keyframe and move it to a different time or value. You can also grab the handles at each keyframe and change the speed at which change is occurring at that moment.

1. In this case, you will select the frame for rotation in y that you set at frame 300.

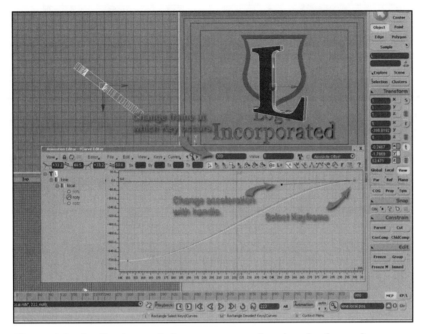

Figure 6.5 *A spline interpolation curve starts changing slowly, reaches maximum velocity in the middle, and gradually slows to a stop.*

2. Next, type a new frame number in the field at the top of the page (in this case 285), and press Enter. This fixes the timing in your animation so that it correctly matches the storyboard.

3. Just for fun, try pulling the handles at the keyframes to see how you can affect the speed of the rotation.

4. For more information on the animation editor, click the question mark (?) on the property page to access the manual.

TONY'S TIP

The question mark is available in all of the property pages and allows the user to quickly access the appropriate page in the XSI manuals. This is extremely helpful when you are exploring areas of the software that you want to read about on the fly. It assumes, of course, that you have a valid installation of the software, which includes the interactive help feature.

5. When you are done with the f-curves, close the animation editor and save your scene.

Compound Animations

The last part of the animation involves flying in the company name components from opposite sides of the screen while rotating them in opposite directions around their local x-axis. Follow the same techniques that you have used thus far.

1. According to the storyboard, set the final frame at 16 seconds (480 frames) with both words in their final resting place.
2. Then, work them back (off-screen) at frame 300.

The final instructions involve an animated highlight between frames 480 and 600 that we will address in a different module.

3. When you are satisfied with your animation, save your scene and take a break.

Incorporating Materials and Textures

The time has come to address the final notes in the storyboard. According to the third panel, the surface of the words "Logo" and "Incorporated" are reflective, and there is a moving highlight that crosses over the words twice between 10 and 20 seconds. There are several ways to accomplish this via lighting or post-production compositing. (Indeed, XSI offers a compositing module for that very reason.) However, since this is still early in your Softimage career, let's look at a way to achieve the whole effect using only materials and textures.

1. If it is not already open, open your animated crest scene now.
2. Press the number 3 on your keyboard to enter the render module.

You are going to add a little reflection to the L object to give it a bit of depth and make it more interesting as it flies in. Because we have already defined its material in an earlier tutorial, you will simply edit the material shader.

TONY'S TIP

You will see the term *shader* a lot in XSI, and at times it may seem a bit confusing. A shader is simply a description of how something should appear when rendered. In reality, a shader is really a simple text file containing instructions regarding a specific element's appearance. There are material shaders, surface shaders, camera shaders, and so forth. Shaders may be scripted, applied from presets, or created using the Render Tree in XSI.

1. Select the L and click Modify > Shader. The material PPG will open, showing the current material settings.

2. Click on the Transparency/Reflection tab.

3. Since you want to reflect all colors, hold down Ctrl and drag any of the RGBA sliders in the reflection portion of this PPG, as shown in Figure 6.6. This will lock the values together as you adjust the amount of reflection. Keep the number fairly small (I picked .2).

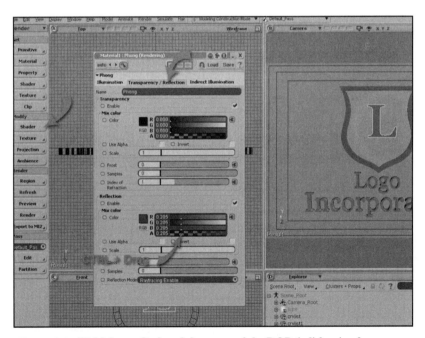

Figure 6.6 *Hold down Ctrl and drag any of the RGBA sliders in the reflection portion of this PPG.*

This is true raytraced reflection, meaning that Softimage will calculate every ray of light striking the object until it decays. The results of ray tracing are very accurate and realistic, but time-consuming. If there were a color range or an actual scene around the object, the bounced light would produce a version of that color range or scene on the surface of the object, similar to seeing the lights of a store in the shine of a new car. But since there is only a black void around the object, it will reflect the black void that surrounds your scene, causing the surface to become darker as it becomes more reflective.

You could also turn the sliders to full and use the Scale slider to adjust the overall amount. This is particularly handy when you have specified a unique color range that you wish to be reflective.

Using the Render Tree

You have just seen an easy way to make quick adjustments to simple shaders. In the next section, you are going to use the Render Tree to assemble a custom shader that will incorporate a custom reflection and an animated highlight for your text. You will then store it so that you can apply it a second time without re-creating it from scratch.

1. Start by selecting one of the text objects ("Logo" or "Incorporated" or whatever yours says).
2. You should have applied a basic gray Phong material earlier. If not, do it now.
3. Close all material PPGs and press number 7 on your keyboard. This opens the Render Tree, XSI's custom shader assembly area. It may look a bit strange at first unless you are familiar with other node-based programs, but the functionality should become quickly apparent. See Figure 6.7.

This is the way it works . . . The node that is farthest to the right (currently Material 2) represents connections to the surface of your object. If you ever see this node named scene_material, it indicates that you are about to edit the shared scene material. This is not good, because everything else that uses that scene material will be changed if you apply any modifications to it here. Instead, you should apply a scene material of your own.

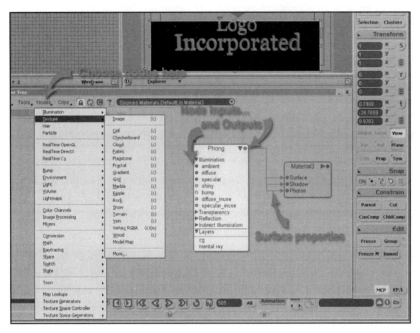

Figure 6.7 *The Render Tree.*

The next node to the left (which is plugged into the surface and shadow inputs of the rightmost node) is the material description (Phong, Lambert, Toon, and so on). This is the shader node that you just adjusted for the L. This node has inputs for all of the familiar material properties, such as Ambient, Diffuse, Transparency, and so on. All of the different types of nodes (shaders) can be accessed from the Node menu at the top of this page.

4. If you double-click on any node, it will open the associated PPG. You can click the gray arrow in the upper-right corner of any node to cycle through its three display modes (collapsed, expanded, and currently used inputs).

5. Just for practice, let's replace the current Phong with a new Phong node. Click on the Node menu, move to the Illumination submenu, and choose Phong.

6. A new Phong node appears in your window. Hold your mouse over the red dot on the right side of this new node, click, and drag an arrow from that dot over the top of the orange Material 2 node. When you release the mouse, a menu pops up that allows you to pick an input (hold down Shift to pick more than one at a time).

That's all there is to it. If you try to plug the wrong color dot into an input, either it will be rejected or a converter node will be placed in line with your connection. There are tons of nodes for textures, mixers, environments, math functions, and on and on. It will probably take you quite a while to become familiar with all of the neat things that the Render Tree can do. For now, just try to get a feel for working in this interface as you build your custom text surface.

TONY'S TIP

The different colors at the inputs and outputs on the nodes indicate the type of information expected. The most common are

Red—Color (RGB)

Green—Scalar (0 to 1, 0 to 100%)

Yellow—Vector (XYZ direction)

With the L object, you turned up the raytraced reflection setting in its Phong node. In the case of the "Logo" and the "Incorporated" object, you want them to look like highly reflective metal, so you will have to force them to reflect an environment of your choosing instead of the black void that surrounds your scene.

1. Go to the Node menu and select Environment > Environment. You will see an environment node with the default noIcon_pic plugged into the texture input. This is a multicolored grid that helps you to verify the correct orientation and alignment of image projections and texture supports before applying your own images. See Figure 6.8.

2. Drag the red dot on the environment node across to the orange material node, and select the Environment input.

3. If you do not already have one, draw a render region (Q) around the two word objects in the Camera view. Hmmm. . . . No change yet . . .

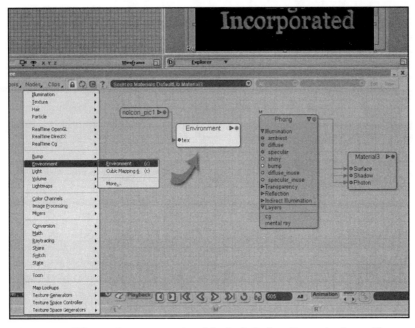

Figure 6.8 *The environment node with the default noIcon_pic plugged into the texture input.*

4. This is because you never turned on the Reflect property in the Phong node.

5. Double-click on the Phong node and select the Transparency/Reflection tab. See Figure 6.9.

6. Ctrl and drag all of the RGB reflection sliders to around .5 (50%). Now you should see a colorful pattern appear on the surface of your letters.

7. At the bottom of the reflection PPG, you will see a dialog box that is currently set to Raytracing Enable. Drop the selection menu and choose Environment Only. This stops the reflections from real scene objects from being calculated on the surface of your text.

8. Next, double-click on the Environment node.

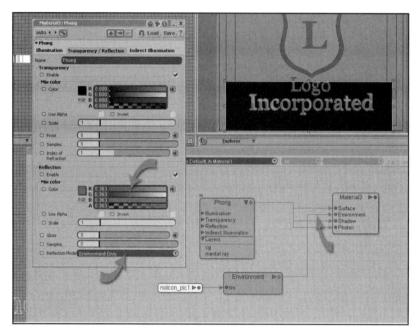

Figure 6.9 *The Transparency/Reflection tab of the Phong node.*

Here, you can see the relationship of the noIcon texture in the display window to the portion of the image reflected on the text object's surface. This feature is very handy when you are trying to apply a texture whose position is critical to the design, such as the label on a beer can. In such a case, you could use this information to precisely reposition your map with predictable results. Since precise positioning of a map is not required in this tutorial, instead you'll replace the default texture with one of your own.

9. Click on the New button next to the noIcon name in the Environment PPG.

10. In the upper-right corner of the browser that appears, click the Paths and choose XSI Samples from the menu. See Figure 6.10.

TIP

XSI Samples is installed with the default software installation. If you do not have access to it, you will need an environment image to use for this example. (Grayscale is best for these settings.)

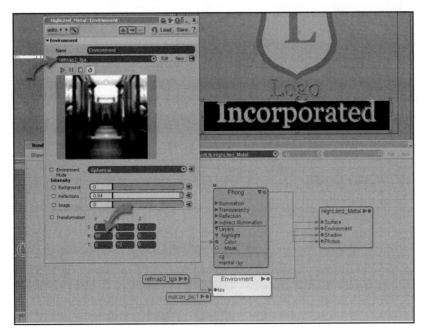

Figure 6.10 *Adjusting the Scale Rotation and Translation values.*

11. Navigate to the pictures directory and select the refmap2_tga file.

Because you are using the default Spherical projection method for your environment image, you can adjust the portion of this new image that is reflected on the surface by adjusting the Scale Rotation and Translation values on the Environment PPG (see Fig. 6.10). I chose to set Scale X to 2, Rotation X to 90, and Translation Y to 10. This gives me a nice metallic base for my highlight.

12. Choose your own settings now, or use mine if you're feeling wimpy.

13. Save your scene.

Now for that last note. . . . A left-to-right diagonal highlight runs over the text (twice) between frames 450 and 600. As I said earlier, there are many ways to achieve this effect, but since we have been discussing animation and the Render Tree, why not use those tools to achieve your glint?

14. Select "Incorporated" (or whatever you have placed the environment on) if the Render Tree is already open.

If not, press number 7 on your keyboard to open the Render Tree.

15. Close all other PPGs and click the recycle icon at the top of the Render Tree window. This will refresh the window and get rid of any nodes that are not currently connected to anything.

16. Go to the Node menu and select Texture > Gradient. In order to see more clearly as you adjust the settings, you will plug the gradient node directly into the surface input of Material 2.

17. Double-click the gradient node so that its PPG opens, showing a multi-colored vertical gradient.

18. Click the Texture tab and create a New > Planar XY Projection to support the gradient. Click the RGBA Gradient tab and select the preset for Black/White.

19. Change the Vertical setting to Horizontal.

Your display should now look like Figure 6.11.

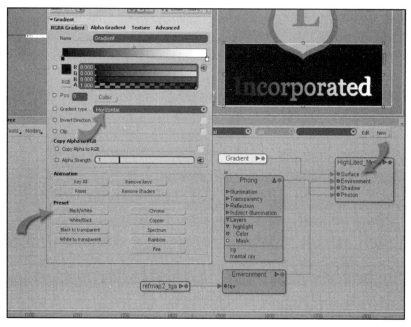

Figure 6.11 *The display so far . . .*

In order to create a glint, you need to sandwich the white slider between two black ones.

20. Click and drag the white slider to the center of the gradient display area.

21. Click again at the right side of the gradient swatch where the white slider was previously located. A new slider is created.

22. Make sure it is selected, and change its color to black.

23. Now you can adjust the position of the three sliders on the bottom and the two break point adjustments on top to create a soft or hard white bar of any width within your word.

24. Close the gradient PPG for a moment, and change the top-left viewport to a front view. You should see a green box (New > Planar XY support) around the selected text.

25. Select the texture support by itself, and then scale (x and y) and rotate (z) to tilt the gradient on the surface of the text.

26. Reposition as necessary. See Figure 6.12.

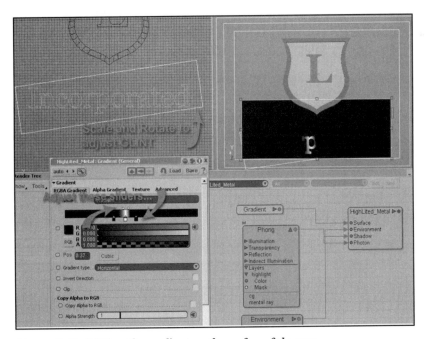

Figure 6.12 *Tilting the gradient on the surface of the text.*

Now for the magic! You may have noticed that there are small green dots in every PPG that you have opened. These dots allow each individual property to be keyframed. You see, not only can you use keyframes to animate objects, but you can also use them to animate any parameter of a node. The indication that a parameter may be animated is the green dot. In this case, you are going to animate the position of the three sliders to create a moving highlight.

27. Open the Gradient PPG again.

28. Click on one of the black sliders (a red box tells you that it is selected). Make sure that you are on frame 450.

29. In the Pos (position) box, type 0 (zero) and press Enter.

30. Click the green dot next to Pos. You will notice a tiny pink f-curve icon, denoting that a keyframe has been set (on frame 450).

31. Move the play cursor to frame 510, type 1 in the Pos box, and press Enter.

32. Click the dot next to Pos to set another key on frame 510.

33. Repeat these steps for the white slider, except that the first key is set on frame 455 (pos=0) and the second key is set at 515 (pos =1).

34. And once more, for the second black slider, set keys at 460 and 520.

35. Scrub the cursor, and you will notice that the highlight changes shape and moves at an uneven speed.

36. Right-click over the big key at the top of the PPG and select Animation Editor. Our old friend opens up, showing the three curves easing in and out of their keys. This is what is causing the odd motion.

37. Select all three curves (or all six keys) in the Animation Editor, and choose Curves > Linear Interpolation (see Figure 6.13).

This fixes the motion issue. Now you will create the second pass in the animation editor by copying and pasting keys.

38. Move the play cursor to frame 520, select each curve one at a time, and choose Keys > Insert Key at Current Frame.

39. Now move one frame ahead and repeat the procedure.

40. Zoom in if necessary. Choose all of the keys on frame 521 and type 0 (zero) in the value. Now you can select the first two keys on the first curve and choose Edit > Copy (Ctrl+C), move the play cursor to frame 530, and choose Edit > Paste (Ctrl+V).

41. Select the second curve. Paste the same keys at frame 535. The third gets the keys pasted at frame 540.

Your editor should now look like Figure 6.13.

42. Save your scene.

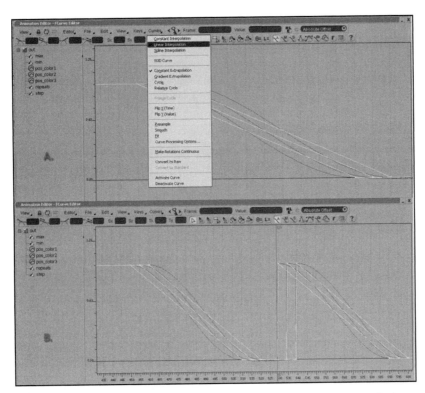

Figure 6.13 *Select all three curves and choose Curves > Linear Interpolation.*

Okay, it's time to put the metal back on your text and properly apply your fancy new highlight.

1. If necessary, reload your scene, select the text object, open your Render Tree (7), and draw a render region.

2. Click the little arrow in the corner of your Phong node to expand the options.

3. Right-click on the word "Layers" and choose Add Layer.

4. Click and drag the red output dot on the gradient node, and plug it into the color input of your new layer.

5. Now drag the Phong output back into the Surface input of your material node.

6. Double-click the Phong node to open its PPG.

7. Type "HighLite" in the name field for the new layer. You will notice that the input color sliders are missing. This is because you plugged the gradient in its place. This layer is on top of the base material layer, so you want to adjust the blending mode.

8. Turn the weight slider to 1. (This makes this layer 100 percent visible over the Phong.)

9. Now change the mode from Over to Plus.

This uses *additive blending*, which will affect a gradient such that where it's black, the color will actually be transparent, and where it's white, it will increase the intensity (luminance) of the underlying layers (the metal in this case). However, you'll notice that there's no change in the render region! How come? Well, when you add a new layer to a node, you must specify what inputs it affects. In this case, you want the new layer to boost the surface color.

10. So, right-click over the name of your new layer (on the Phong node) and pick Diffuse from the list. Now your highlight is contributing to the diffuse property of the text.

    If you don't see anything, make sure you are on a frame where the highlight is actually active (around 480 is good). You can increase the intensity of the effect if you type a slightly larger number in the Weight field.

    If you are still having trouble, check Figure 6.14 for reference.

11. Save your scene.

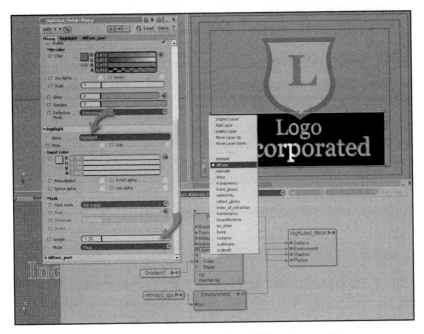

Figure 6.14 *Use this for a reference if you're still having trouble.*

Now, as much fun as that was, you're probably not in the mood to go through all of that work again for the second piece of text. That is where *presets* come in. You have created a custom shader that you want to use again, so you will save it. Your Render Trees may be saved in whole or in part. Since this shader involves an environment node that is applied at the surface level of the tree, you will need to save all of the nodes.

1. With your Render Tree window open, double-click on the Material 2 node. In the PPG Name field, give it a clever name like Highlighted Metal.

2. Click the Save button in the upper-right corner, and navigate to your project folder. Save the preset with the same name to make it easier to find later.

3. Select the other text object (in my case, Logo) and press 7, or refresh the Render Tree if it is already open. You should see a simple combination of a surface (material) node and a Phong node.

4. Double-click the orange material node and click the Load button in the upper-right corner.

5. Navigate to your project folder and select the preset that you saved a minute ago.

You should see the same node tree that you just saved appear in your Render Tree window. There are a couple of things that you will have to do to guarantee that this preset will function identically. First, you will need a texture support for your gradient on this object.

6. Double-click the gradient node.

7. Click the Texture tab and create a new planar XY projection.

8. Scale and rotate the support in the front view, as you did with the first object.

Now you must copy the animation. Don't worry, it's really simple this time. Whenever you need to copy between two identical properties, you can open both PPGs and drag the information across. Observe!

9. If it's not already open, double-click the current gradient node to bring up the PPG. This should be the gradient that needs animation.

10. Type a different name in the Name field (I'll use LogoGradient).

11. Now lock it by clicking the little keyhole symbol in the upper-right corner.

12. Push this PPG slightly out of the way.

13. Now select the other text object (in my case, Incorporated).

14. Refresh the Render Tree and double click this gradient node to open its PPG (check for a different name).

15. Lock it and move it so that you can see the RGBA Gradient tab in both PPGs. Notice that the original has keyframes but the copy does not (indicated by the little curve icon instead of a plain green dot).

16. Simply click on the same slider, let's say black 1, in both windows (don't worry if they shift slightly). Drag the Pos dot from the keyframed PPG on top of the Pos dot in the other (LogoGradient for me).

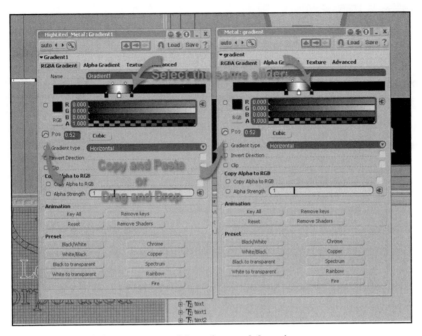

Figure 6.15 *It's just a matter of dragging and dropping.*

17. Repeat the step for each slider, and you're done. See Figure 6.15.

    If you don't believe that it's that simple, right-click on the big key icon at the top of the PPG and select Animation Editor. You will see the exact pattern that you edited on the original.

18. Save your scene.

Although I don't cover rendering until a bit later in the book, I'm sure you're dying to see your masterpiece right away. Here's a quick and dirty method!

1. Push number 3 on your keyboard to make sure you are in the render module.

2. Choose Render > Render > Options. You will keep most of the defaults.

3. On the first tab (Output), make sure that you have frames 1 through 600 selected (900 if you want to see the last 10 seconds of hold).

4. On the Format tab, click the Maintain Picture Ratio divot and enter 400 in the X Resolution.
5. On the Create Movie tab, enable the check box for Create Movie.
6. Enable the check box for Delete Source Images . . .
7. Click the three dots on the button following abs to specify a name and location for your movie (desktop, perhaps).
8. Click the Render button.

Answers to Exercise 6.1:

00:00:28:00 = 840 frames

01:50:00:00 = 198,000 frames

00:22:00:00 = 39,600 frames

00:45:00:00 = 81,000 frames

14,400 frames = 00:08:00:00

12,600 frames = 00:07:00:00

207,600 frames = 01:30:00:00

126,452 frames = 01:10:15:02

Chapter 7

Bowling for Dollars

In this chapter, you will learn how to apply some simple habits to the art of selling yourself and the works of art you wish to produce.

If you have never attended one of my lectures at the National Association of Broadcasters (NAB) convention, or any of the other shows and college engagements I do throughout the year, you might be surprised to learn that the lectures that comprise this chapter are among the most popular at each of these events. At NAB, thousands of people choose between classes on Final Cut Pro, Avid, Photoshop, and other production tools. Why would artists, people who make their living building an expertise in motion picture editing, compositing, and photo composition, want to know about how to sell? Listen to one editor, speaking to me after attending a series of lectures:

"I took eight courses this time. Eight. I learned so many things about my craft. But your course on how to get new clients, which I took last year, turned my business around and made this year possible."

Trying to be humble, I thanked the attendee and remarked that the course wasn't so unique, and that I had just cobbled together a bunch of ideas that I'd scooped up reading and trying things out over the years.

"But there's nobody teaching this stuff in our business category," he replied. "Maybe in real estate or life insurance, but not in media production. Certainly not in colleges or universities with big media departments."

Well, okay. I'll take a compliment. But what is it that this editor, and the others who popularize my classes, learn? Is there a theme, a key message? Yes. The message is this:

You will never reach your full potential as an artist if you don't learn how to sell yourself.

Artists have a difficult time buying into this statement. The most difficult part is the phrase (an imperative command, if you will) "sell yourself."

"I'm not a prostitute!", some have said, "I'm an artist!"

And then the debate begins. The artists' side of the debate is based on an assumption that an artist should not have to sell himself or his work, that the work should—in some magical way—sell itself. Furthermore, the argument goes, art and artists belong to some special class of substance and society that is almost religiously respected, and will be defiled by any contact with commerciality, commerce, or filthy lucre.

My side of the debate is based on a belief that art represents labor, labor represents value, and value represents money. There is no way to separate art from commerce. You can even go over to the Socialists and examine their historic struggles to come to terms with the definition of art and artists, as they tried to classify whether making art was labor or leisure. (Trotsky, in my opinion, had the best opinion of artists. At least he thought they should be allowed to live and practice their art.) Art is a commodity. It has values and can be judged and classified by these values. Consequently, artists are workers (they may not be laborers, but that is a subject I'll touch on later), and the product of their work is sellable.

The point of this debate, whether you stand with the artists or with me, is that you, as an artist, can and should learn to sell your work. And because your work is you, it is totally appropriate to teach you, the artist, how to sell yourself. It has nothing to do with prostitution, unless you regard a prostitute as an artist, and then you find yourself agreeing with me even more.

Of course, to go any further in discussing the selling of an artist, we must come to some mutual understanding of what an artist is. Is this possible? I think so.

What Is Art?

I can remember discussing this topic for hours and hours in film school, college teaching, and long drunken conversations with artists and "artistes." Then, alone, I gave it even more hours of thought. And finally, I came up with a definition that I think satisfies most of the people with whom I share it. The definition is in two parts. The first part defines an artist, and the second part attempts to apply the values of a commodity to art. Once we can agree that an artist produces a commodity, and can define what constitutes that commodity, we can also learn how to apply value to the commodity. (What is good art and bad art?) Consequently, we can apply value to the artist who created it. (What is a good artist and a bad artist?)

> **Part 1:** An artist is a person who replicates his emotions and personal truths, such that others feel these emotions and truths as if they were their own.

> **Part 2:** The quality of a work of art and the artist who created it may be determined by the number of people the art affects, as described in Part 1, the degree of similarity between the artist's experience and that of the recipient, and the depth of emotion engendered in the recipient.

For example, a story that affects two people profoundly in exactly the same way the artist intended is worth less than a story that affects 2,000 people profoundly in exactly the same way the artist intended.

I always get most of my arguments over Part 2, which many feel is not a necessary corollary to the definition of an artist. But without Part 2, a good spouse could be considered an artist, even though he shares a great depth of love with only one person. I do not consider a good spouse to be an artist, although such a person might love artistically. On the other hand, one might consider a true revolutionary to be a great artist, because she replicates her emotion and personal truth among a population to such an extent that the population takes up a common struggle, often at the cost of life and limb.

Incidentally, a religious leader might be considered an artist too, and here we get the glimpse of what really underlies the greatest art—a belief that the work is inspired by a power greater than the artist. But that is for another book.

Notice, however, that there are three components to Part 2: number, similarity, and depth. Different artists must succeed to varying degrees in all three components, but rarely does an artist succeed greatly in all three.

As you can see, there is no mention of talent in the above definition. Talent has very little to do with art. Edison said that invention is 1% inspiration and 99% perspiration; art is 1% talent and 99% hard work. In my opinion, "talent" is a fiction, perpetrated by those who would exploit the artist as a means of elevating artists and thereby generating fictional value. Artists are common people. Everyone is an artist, but few walk the path to fulfillment of the title.

Let's examine the stages that one must undergo to become an artist. There are many steps to this path, and even more temptations to depart from it at every step.

First, in order to replicate emotions and truth, an artist must dig deeply into oneself. In addition, the digging must be truthful and relentless. Otherwise, the depth one digs may not be the true center of one's being, but a fictional realm, produced in an effort to avoid finding one's true self. How can we know which self is the true self? When you get down deep in the true self, it usually hurts. It hurts so much you don't want to share it with anyone. But this is not art. This is merely self-discovery.

To approach art, you must take this hurt and learn to express it without shame or fear. But doing this successfully would still not be art. This would be honest confession. This might succeed in getting a clergyman to absolve you.

To get closer to art, you must make your confession understood by others. But doing this successfully would still not be art. This is craft. This would be a good letter or a documentary. This might succeed in getting another person to understand you.

You must make someone feel your emotion or truth on a deep level, the deeper the better. But although this is artistic, it is still not art. This might be a good newspaper article. This might succeed in getting another person to vote you into public office or loan you money.

To achieve art, you must make another person feel your emotion or truth as if it were his or her own. Let's say a straight guy writes a story about the heartbreak of losing his girlfriend. If what he creates is art, a gay guy could read it and weep, feeling the emotion of losing his boyfriend. This is art. But this is not _great_ art.

When anyone reads this story—whether that person is gay, straight, old, young, male, female, clever, stupid, selfish, generous, pious, sinful, the old man who lives with his balls of twine behind the boiler, the woman who has never had a love, the man who has been deeply in love with one woman for 50 years—when all these people and more read the story and weep like babies for having lost their love—that story is great art.

In addition to all of the above, I would agree that art is a special form of work, but it is not, after all sane considerations, labor. Labor is work that one would do only for money. Work is effort expended toward a goal that the worker wishes to achieve for some degree of self-satisfaction.

Because art draws so much out of artists, exposing them to an often-unsympathetic public, it deserves special consideration. This consideration is made because the act of art might, under extreme circumstances, become self-destructive and carry the artist across the threshold of sanity. It is necessary to be always vigilant, as artists and as appreciators of art, for evidence of artistic work that becomes obsessive or of obsessive people who might appear to be artists. Those who accept the gift of art must bear the responsibility of caring for those on both sides of the border between healthy work and destructive obsession.

Would you now choose to disagree with my definition? If so, send me a better one. Until then, for your benefit, let me continue with mine.

So, Are You a Great Artist?

Probably not. Do you aspire to be an artist? Yes, I hope. If so, you must take one of two paths. And now we are done with the metaphysical part of this chapter and ready to start work on making you a good career.

After many years of living the life of both an artist and a businessman, and counseling, hiring, and befriending many artists who were struggling to start their careers, I have narrowed down the two basic paths that artists follow when going from their training into a career. These are dedicated isolation and integrated compromise.

Path A: Dedicated Isolation

On this path, the artist preserves the creation of art as separate and isolated from the labor of earning a living. The risk of this path is that the artist never has sufficient time and quietude to concentrate on the task of art. Another risk is that the artist, choosing art over labor, fails to provide adequately for himself and suffers mentally and/or physically, often to the result of having a shortened artistic lifespan.

The rewards of this path are that the art is usually preserved from most influences of commerce, and that the artist, while never being able to live off his art, nevertheless enjoys an enriching, satisfying, well-balanced life.

Actors commonly take this path, preferring to work as waiters or waitresses to earn money for food, rent, health care, and incidentals, while refusing to get paid for acting unless the role satisfies some predefined level of artistic purity. On this path, the artist will be highly discriminating about what forms of art he will practice and what payment he will accept.

Path B: Integrated Compromise

On this path, the artist starts out exactly like the artist on Path A, except there is no distinction between work for hire as an artist and labor for hire in any other endeavor. The risks of this path are that the artist loses focus on the purpose of art, and instead begins to produce work that is calculated to bring the highest price. Eventually, the artist may find that her art has become shallow and commercialized, and that in order to keep food on the table, she has become more of a businessperson than an artist.

The reward of this path is that the individual is, ideally, always working as an artist at some level, shallow or profound. Such work improves the craft, at least, and keeps the artist's skills acute. If and when a purely artistic opportunity arises, the artist is practiced and ready to make the most of the opportunity. On this path, the difference between succumbing to risk and reaping rewards is largely dependent on the maturity of the artist. If the artist is self-aware and can resist the temptation to get lazy, this path may prove very fulfilling.

Artists who express themselves in a wide range of media, such as 3D animators, find this path the easiest to follow, because project specifications tend to be both commercially and artistically rewarding.

As you might surmise, my hope is that you will choose Path A. I didn't exactly write this chapter to help you get a job as a busboy. (Although you certainly could do so!) My hope is that you will employ this chapter to diligently explore your powers of personal persuasion. This chapter is going to teach you how to persuade people to listen to your ideas, and then to give you opportunities to convert your ideas into reality by paying you lots of money. In other words, I am trying to get you to the point on Path A where you are making art on your own terms and getting paid—even though you'd probably be doing the same work for free. Does that sound interesting? If so, let's take the next step.

Hard Work vs. Hard Labor

Let me now put forth a statement with which you may not agree. First, I want you to react. And second, I want to think.

"Artists don't like to work."

Some artists tend to rely on the myth of talent as a shortcut on the path to artistic realization. Others are just plain lazy and never respect the gift of their sensitivity or expressive hearts. Finally, there are the "artistes," a fancy word I use to define people who are not artists, but imitate artists in order to reap the benefits of the profession, usually in terms of amorous attention or ego gratification. All of these individuals reduce the stature and respect that are due to real artists and give a bad reputation to those of us who are dedicated, hard working, and benefactors to our communities. We, the real artists, must struggle to outdo the bad press of the lazy artists and crafty artistes. We must wake up early each morning, work hard at our chosen fields, be generous and compassionate, and above all, be true to ourselves and our missions.

If anybody tells you that artists don't like to work, proudly show them your work. Open your meticulous date book and show the hours you have logged learning your software, the LMCBs and tick-marks of your sales calls, the "to-do" lists full of brochures and showreel mailings, and the appointments you made for client presentations. "Work?", you can shout, indignantly. "I work! I work my butt off at my art, buster!"

What's that I hear you asking? What's an LMCB and a tick-mark? Ah, these are the footprints of a diligent 21st Century artist as she makes her way down the path of independent artistic freedom. Come with me now and learn how to put on boots that are made for walkin'.

What I am now going to describe to you will probably sound like labor. It *is* work. But with a bit of self-delusion (and heaven knows, that isn't hard to manufacture in an artist's studio), you might fool yourself into enjoying this work. Nahh, I'm jiving you. This is work. You do it because the alternative is much worse: always being poor or having someone else make a living from your sweat. If you follow my advice, this work will soon become just a regular, mildly annoying habit—like going to the gym for a daily workout before enjoying your day. Let's start out with 10 pounds on the bar and do a few simple bench presses to see if your pecs are up to the task.

What Is a Client?

Clients, quite simply, are people or companies that pay you money to practice your art. And before you think I'm blowing smoke up your kilt, let's be honest: Great art is a powerful force. Throughout history, it has moved populations to revolution, driven individuals to pinnacles of heroism, opened millions of people's hearts to alien points of view, and on one or two occasions, won the love of a beautiful princess for an ugly pauper. Is it any wonder that people look to artists when they want to persuade others to do their bidding?

"Selling cancer-causing cigarettes to innocent children? Hmmm. We better get ourselves one good artist for that." But designing a camel character who plays pool with a cigarette butt hanging from his generous lips—is that art? Nahh. It's just a little *taste* of art—but that's just enough for most persuaders, so strong is our medicine!

You, dear artist, get to choose which of these hungry little creatures of commerce you are going to help and which you will reject. You can pick and choose your clients. Tell the ciggy suit to pound sand. Pick up the phone and do a sales pitch to the American Cancer Society.

Either way, before you can earn a buck, you have to hook up with a client. I don't mean that literally. In fact, it's a bad idea to get on really personal terms with clients, much less to engage in physical relations. But it's hard not to use dating analogies when referring to the process of client pursuit. And the analogy is fun, so let's use it.

Like a member of the opposite gender (oh, jeez—maybe I'm not being diverse enough here, but I'm straight, so cut me some slack, okay?), a client is someone with whom you wish to relate on serious terms. A client is someone who represents a company's decision to hire you to create animation. You are what is called a "vendor."

If we employ a dating analogy, the vendor is sort of the active player, somewhat aggressively pursuing the client (although we all know there are clients who have their own insatiable needs, and therefore pursue vendors).

Either way, the vendor's goal is to "get out there," "hit the bar scene," whatever, to make first contract. The object is to develop some basic level of trust. If you establish trust, and there is a mutual need between you and the client, you might hook up in some low-risk engagement. It might be a little project, like doing a storyboard, or sketching some thumbnails. This is like going out with someone for the first time. Your come-on wasn't too strong, you had some fun, you tested the waters—if everything is cool, you move to the next stage.

All along, like "hooking up" is related to getting married, you, the vendor, are looking for an exclusive relationship—that is, repeat business from a client who considers you the only vendor. This is the rarest form of client-vendor trust and is called being a *sole source vendor*. The client only uses you. Even when hundreds of other vendors come looking for business, the client tells them, "I'm happy with my current vendor. Don't bother calling me again." Being a sole source vendor to a client is like going to heaven, because no one expects you to be exclusively loyal in return. (Although you may be expected not to work for the vendor's competitors!)

In-between "cruising" for clients and becoming a sole source vendor, there are a lot of other levels of hooking up, each of which has an analogy in the dating scene. For instance, if a client is the biggest company in your town, trying to get them as a client is like trying to hook up with the homecoming queen. Screwing up an animation assignment because you didn't listen to instructions is like getting dumped because you stood up your date on Saturday night. I hope you get the point.

So how do you get some action? Where do you go to hang out? How do you hit on a client?

When I was single, I'd go to a bar or some other joint and spend a good amount of time sizing up the place. I didn't make a move until I had considered every prospect. (During which time I also allowed myself to be sized up, because, hey, sometimes somebody hits on *you* first.) The same goes with starting an animation business (or looking for your first job) and scoping out your first clients.

If you already know something about the company you are going to pitch, it is likely you will be more successful. Even better, if you already have some animations on your reel that are similar to what your target client does, you can use that to get a foot into the door. For instance, if you are down with the *C.S.I.* series and have made some animations that feature human organs being violated by death-dealing devices, you might have a chance at pitching your capabilities to the companies that vend to TV crime dramas. You might also pitch your work to pharmaceutical or medical device companies.

You've no doubt heard the phrase, "You are what you eat." Well, in pitching, you could say something similar: "You are what you show." Whatever you have on your showreel will have a great influence on the kind of work you get in the future. So follow that path to selecting potential clients.

But your reel is not the only influence on the clients you hunt. Your own hobbies, interests, experiences, and avocations play a large role too. For instance, if you spent a summer teaching children how to swim, perhaps you might pitch yourself to physical education projects, outdoor and youth-oriented TV programs, or even a feature film that takes place at a summer camp. Employers are always trying to "score" their job applicants. With so many similar resumes and showreels, the slightest advantage might place you on top.

You are now going to start a sales campaign. Your goal is to obtain 10 clients in one year. Is that goal too long-term? Okay, make it five clients in six months. Lazy? Reduce it to three clients. Just get it started. Here's what you do.

Let's begin by listing the subjects that turn you on. Think of the things you like to do or have done in your life that make you a little different from anybody else. List these things on a sheet of notebook paper. When you get several of them down, consider your showreel. How many of your interests are represented in some way on the showreel you have created? If you already have a pretty full showreel, my guess is that the list and the reel have some significant match-ups. This is natural, because what we do for fun and what we want to do for work (that is, the spec content of our reels) are much the same thing. Surfer animators like to animate waves. Gear head animators like to animate machines. The list you just made is the first step in *exploiting* your enjoyment as a career.

Selling yourself is hard. It helps if you start out selling something you already enjoy and know from your heart. Maybe the surfing animator really hates staying home and making sales calls, but if those calls are to all the best surfboard manufacturers and he's calling about something he really knows, the morning doesn't exactly drag by, right?

So, like the surfer dude, look at the list of your interests and try to think of companies, TV shows, or feature films that express the same interests. For instance, if your interests include skydiving, your sales direction should be toward companies that make parachutes, the producers of extreme sports TV shows, and the producers of films like *Point Break*. Get on the Internet and start Googling the names and addresses of companies that fit these categories.

Then, you can cast your net a bit wider. For instance, skydiving is a dangerous sport. It requires a lot of safety devices. There is an entire business category built around manufacturing safety devices. The same goes for aviation. Skydivers have to get up into the sky. So, add safety and aviation companies to your Google list. Add producers of flying shows and reality programs that deal with the results of unsafe practices. You get the idea? In a few hours, you should have pages and pages of potential clients and their addresses.

In addition to Google searches, there is a more sophisticated method of finding potential clients in your areas of interest. This method uses a system developed by the U.S. government to categorize every job that a human could do. In an effort to categorize every professional task known to humankind, the *Occupational Safety & Health Administration (OSHA)* division of the U.S. Department of Labor has devised a system that assigns a specific code number to every occupation. This list is the *Standard Industrial Classification (SIC)* system. Sounds amazing, but the list is pretty complete. You can access it at http://www.osha.gov/pls/imis/sicsearch.html. You simply type in your interest, such as "parachute," click Submit, and you'll get the following list:

> 2221 Broadwoven Fabric Mills, Manmade Fiber and Silk
>
> 3429 Hardware, Not Elsewhere Classified
>
> 7999 Amusement and Recreation Services, Not Elsewhere Classified

Click on SIC code 2221, and you'll get this:

2221 Broadwoven Fabric Mills, Manmade Fiber and Silk

Establishments primarily engaged in weaving fabrics more than 12 inches (30.48 centimeters) in width, wholly or chiefly by weight of silk and manmade fibers including glass. Establishments primarily engaged in weaving or tufting carpets and rugs from these fibers are classified in Industry 2273; those manufacturing tire cord and fabrics are classified in Industry 2296; and those engaged in finishing manmade fiber and silk broadwoven goods are classified in Industry 2262.

- Acetate broadwoven fabrics
- Acrylic broadwoven fabrics
- Automotive fabrics, manmade fiber
- Bedspreads, silk and manmade fiber-mitse
- Blanketings, manmade fiber
- Canton crepes
- Crepe satins
- Draperies and drapery fabrics, manmade fiber and silk-mitse
- Dress fabrics, manmade fiber and silk
- Duvetyn, manmade fiber and silk
- Elastic fabrics, manmade fiber and silk: more than 12 inches in width
- Failles
- Fiberglass fabrics
- Flat crepes
- French crepes
- Fur-type fabrics, manmade fiber
- Georgettes
- Glass broadwoven fabrics
- Jacquard woven Fabrics, manmade fiber and silk
- Leno fabrics, manmade fiber and silk
- Lining fabrics, manmade fiber and silk: except glove lining fabrics
- Linings, rayon or silk-mitse
- Marquisettes, manmade fiber
- Modacrylic broadwoven fabrics
- Necktie fabrics, manmade fiber and silk: broadwoven

- Nylon broadwoven fabrics
- Nytril broadwoven fabrics
- Paper broadwoven fabrics
- Parachute fabrics
- Pile fabrics, manmade fiber and silk
- Plushes, manmade fiber and silk
- Polyester broadwoven fabrics
- Polyethylene broadwoven fabrics
- Polypropylene broadwoven fabrics
- Pongee, manmade fiber and silk
- Poplin, manmade fiber
- Quilts, manmade fiber and silk-mitse
- Rayon broadwoven fabrics
- Saran broadwoven fabrics
- Satins
- Serges, manmade fiber
- Shantungs, manmade fiber and silk
- Shirting fabrics, manmade fiber and silk
- Silk broadwoven fabrics
- Slipcover fabrics, manmade fiber and silk
- Spandex broadwoven fabrics
- Suiting fabrics, manmade fiber and silk
- Taffetas
- Tapestry fabrics, manmade fiber and silk
- Textile mills, broadwoven: silk, and manmade fiber including glass
- Textile warping, on a contract basis
- Twills, manmade fiber
- Typewriter ribbon cloth, manmade fiber
- Upholstery fabrics, manmade fiber and silk
- Velvets, manmade fiber and silk
- Vinal broadwoven fabrics
- Vinyon broadwoven fabrics
- Voiles, manmade fiber and silk

Even if you are a monomaniacal psychopath who polishes Lincoln head pennies 18 hours a day, you can still build a handy list of potential clients from that one special interest. The trick is pursuing the list. Here's how you do that.

The Parameters of a High-Potential Client

Okay, let's assume you have a client category picked out—you want to make Paramount Pictures your client. Why? What made you choose Paramount? You've heard of them? They distributed the latest *War of the Worlds* movie? You have a contact there? These reasons are valid, but three specific questions produce the most immediate and successful results. Not only will the results be faster than with any other method of selecting potential clients, but also the clients you select will have a high potential of responding to your call. We call these *high-potential clients*. Here are the questions you need to ask:

- How big is the company?
- Where is the company located?
- What is the cost of sale?

How Big Is the Company?

When you want to hook up with a client, it helps if the client is the same size in the entire business world as you and your company are in the animation world. If you are a seasoned pro with two or three animators working for you, you could be considered a medium-small operation. You can go after companies that are medium-small in their category. Hence, Paramount, one of the largest feature film distribution production empires, might not be a good match for your company.

Or, let's say you are just a freelancer with a home-based animation station. Would you try to get work from ILM? Not unless your reel already had some blockbuster feature films on it.

When you go beyond your own size category, you could be wasting a lot of time and energy. True, you might luck out and get an interview, maybe even a job, but your chances are so small in comparison to the work you will invest that you might as well buy a lottery ticket and do something else for a living. Go ahead, dream, give it a shot, but don't expect much.

On the other hand, don't pitch yourself to companies that are too small or whose work does not match your reel's quality. You aren't likely to get a $40,000 animated commercial project from the local car dealer. Their budgets are more like $1,000 to $3,000 for a commercial.

You can easily find out a company's size by searching its Web site, or consulting a book in the library called the *Standard Directory of Advertisers*, also called "The Red Book." It lists every major company in the U.S. that does any kind of advertising, and shows the number of employees, revenues, how much the company spends on advertising, the names, addresses, and phone numbers of key employees (the ones you want to call), and even the names of the company's advertising agencies.

Using the Red Book, you can select from a category of business (publishing companies, for instance), pick the companies with the right size, find the person in the company who hires animators (the director of advertising, for instance, or the VP of Training), and make your first call! Bingo. No time wasted.

Similar directories exist just for the entertainment world. For instance, the *Hollywood Creative Directory* (www.hcdonline.com) lists production companies, television shows, and studio/network executives by title. Find the guy who hires CGI people for your favorite show, and call him up.

Where Is the Company Located?

Although we live in an Internet-connected global community, where it is entirely possible to sell your creative services to any individual anywhere on the planet, it's still difficult to achieve. Perhaps when you are a world-class animator and your work is familiar to producers from Bollywood to Hollywood, you can live in Tahiti and telecommute by email. People really do this. But for a newbie, the chances of making a long-distance sale is pretty bleak. Your best bet is to pitch locally. If you want to sell into the L.A. market, you're just going to have to move to Southern California—at least as close as Santa Barbara.

Therefore, it is wise to trim your list of potential client contacts to people with whom you can set an appointment for a face-to-face meeting. In the beginning stages of starting a business, you really have to build in-person trust, and the only way to do that is if the potential client is within a 60-mile radius of your place of business. Farther away than that, the client can usually find someone else, equally talented as you, who's closer.

What Is the Cost of Sale?

When you pitch a client, you incur a cost to yourself. In addition to the phone call, making a showreel and mailing it, and so on, there is the cost of your time. It takes time to get customers, and as you know, time is money. This cost is known as the *cost of sale*.

For example, in New York, where I work, there is a large pharmaceutical company that I have been pitching as a client for something like 10 years! I've made calls, identified and spoken to people who can "greenlight" a project, sent my brochure and showreel, had meetings, even sent proposals. After 10 years, I closed a large deal—an $80,000 animation. In the last month, I've also identified a new client, made one call, had one meeting, and closed a deal for $8,000. Assuming my profit margin on both company's projects were equal, on which project did I make the most profit?

The $8,000 one! After 10 years of pitching the pharmaceutical company, my cost of sale was already way over the $80,000 total gross budget. I was a fool to pursue the pharma company so long, and should have given up after a year! Yes, you can say that now that I am in with the larger company. I may get more work. But how long would they have to keep using me before I break even? Well, there is a calculation for this, but it's too complex. Let's just say it would be a very, very long time. And large companies hardly ever use one vendor consistently for a long time. Their greenlight guys change jobs too often, they change vendor policies, and too much goes on that cuts into your profit.

Always keep an eye on your cost of sale as you choose potential clients and manage your call list.

Going for Broke

Regardless of everything I say and write about how to choose a company to pitch, there are those who will go after the largest, most remote, highest cost-of-sale company, because it is their dream to do so. You grew up with *Star Wars*, and you won't rest until the HR department at ILM sees your showreel. I can understand that. So if you want to grab your lance and go charging at the big windmill, here are some basic cautions and few helpful tips. As they say in the NY Lotto ads, "Hey, you never know."

■ **Time-consuming:** You are going to spend more time going after a large company than a small one. Large companies are complex, and it takes longer to find the right person to call. Once you find the right person, they will have an attitude. After all, you aren't the first one who's called this person today, looking for work. Most of your targets will hide behind voicemail and never return your call.

To counter these drawbacks, prepare in advance. Find the name of the right person from a directory or online database. Use your talents to pre-record a snappy voicemail message that you can play into your phone. Maybe the person will think you are clever enough to return the call.

- **Competitors:** You aren't the only person with a dream to crack the big walnut. Seasoned pros with better reels than yours will be knocking on the same door. Once you get in the door, your offering may be small potatoes, and this bad first impression will reduce your chances of ever getting in the door again.

  Before you knock on the door, be sure you have your best presentation all ready. But don't let the challenge of making a great presentation become procrastination. You will never have a perfect reel or a perfect pitch. Sooner or later, you are going to have to say, "This is the best I can show at this point in time." If you honestly think that, and the presentation is at least as good as an entry-level worker can expect to show at the "big company," go for it. Honest effort is never ridiculed, and you will certainly learn something.

- **Slow payment:** Once you get work from a big company, expect to wait longer to get paid than you would with a small company. Big companies often delay paying their bills in order to earn interest on what *should* be your cash. This is called "floating the payables." Obviously, it would be useless for a small company to float payables, because the amount and interest rate are so small. But 0.3% a month on $10 million (which is a common level of float for a big firm) is $30,000. That's worth making a small vendor like you wait. Among the worst floaters are advertising agencies (who will often expect to be paid by their client before they pay you, which is unethical, because you aren't a bank) and large pharmaceutical companies. These firms commonly make you wait more than 90 days to be paid. If you finish your project in a month and add 90 days to that, you could be into the next season before you get dollar uno.

  To combat slow payment, bill your projects in halves or thirds, with a payment "up-front" before you start working. Consider offering a discount as a reward for early payment. Most companies will pay in as soon as 10 days for as little as a 2% discount.

Fish the Children

I, too, sometimes get suckered into going after a big fish. But I use a different strategy than most fishermen. I fish the children. Here's an example: You want to pitch a really big company that you admire. Instead of going to the company's Web site, looking up the headquarters, and beating down the front door, you look for the back door.

The "back door" is often a smaller subsidiary of the big company. For instance, a large pharmaceutical company in my neighborhood is a classic, vendor-hating, time-wasting, slow-paying monster that eats up my competitors like ranch-flavored Doritos. But this same company has a veterinary medicine subsidiary. It also has a division that specializes in agricultural "medicine." Instead of going after the big daddy, I go for the children. The decision-makers in these smaller units often answer their phones on the first try, and many are happy to hear from a vendor.

For many years, a major Hollywood animation company maintained a secret little development studio at the eastern tip of Long Island in New York. If you could find the phone number, they'd answer it cheerfully, and a friend of mine got in the door!

Once you land one of the children as a client, you can add the name of the big company to your resume—it's no lie! Not only that, but you can now start knocking at the headquarters' front door, claiming you are already a trusted vendor. In fact, your happy clients in the child company will often recommend you up the ladder.

But here again, my point about going after small companies, where you get your calls answered in fewer than three tries, is still the working rule. Fishing the children simply makes going after a big fish the same as going after a small fish—with added benefits.

Use Directories

My first directory, back when we started our company in 1982, was the Yellow Pages (there was only one Yellow Pages back then), and I would look under the heading "Motion Picture Producers." Out of the 50 or so listed, I made good with about 20. Today, there are dozens of "yellow books" coming to your doorstep every year. Use them all. Each one has a different collection of clients, and there are many more headings you can use: "Web Site Designers," "Video Producers," "Educational Media Producers," and so on.

Later, I learned about directories that are specifically designed for creative people—even animators. One is the *Motion Picture, TV, and Theatre Directory* (about $15.00), published by Motion Picture Enterprises in New York and available on their Web site (www.mpe.net) and in bookstores that specialize in film and theatre. While you're at the bookstore, you can also look for *The Hollywood Creative Directory* (hcdonline.com), which lists many potential clients in the feature film business.

Then, long after I was set up in business—so long it embarrasses me to say—I discovered the bible of directories for people who want to sell creative media. This is the *Standard Directory of Advertisers*, also called the Red Book, published by National Register Publishing (800-836-7766 or http://www.bowker-saur.co.uk). The Red Book is available by paid subscription, and is published once a year. A yearly subscription entitles you to their quarterly updates, which are extremely useful. Unfortunately, the subscription is about $1,000 including shipping and tax, but Amazon.com has new and used single copies, without updates, for about $250. A CD-ROM of the data is also available, with updates, for a bit more than the print subscription. This is handy, because you can transfer data from the CD directly into your computer's database. You can also subscribe to an online service at www.redbooks.com.

The prices seem expensive at first, but the time you save doing research to find the right name to call is worth the price. If you make just one good contract from this directory, you have easily paid for several years of subscriptions.

The Red Book contains nearly every company that advertises in print, TV, or e-media. Each entry includes the main phone numbers and addresses of significant people to contact. Usually these significant people, like the VP of Marketing, won't take your call, but their administrative assistants will often give you the name of a subordinate whose job it is to take your call. Thus, the directory narrows down your search from a dozen calls to two. And don't forget, when a VP's assistant tells you to call his subordinate, you can tell the subordinate that "So-and-so's assistant *referred* me to you." And if you can *name* the assistant, like you *know* her, that helps—so get the assistant's name, duh.

In addition to the Standard Directory of Advertisers, Bowker also offers *The Standard Directory of Advertising Agencies.* This directory lists all the advertising agencies in the U.S. that are large enough to do the kind of work you like to do best. If you are interested in animating commercials, this book is your second big investment (after your workstation).

The Internet is full of useful, often free directories of possible clients, many of them localized to your hometown (or the biggest city near it). Simply use one of the popular search engines and enter words like "animation," "bid," "RFP" (request for proposal), "directory of employees," or any other phrase that relates to what you want—client leads. Hey, how about "client leads?"

Building Your Hit List

Before you can start selling, you need to build a "hit list" of companies, or even names of people who work for companies that you want to make into clients. To make this list, you need a nice, clean, lined notepad, at least 8" × 10". Don't use one of those little notebooks they give you at the bank. You will be writing here fast and furiously, and you'll need lots of space to write.

On the top line, write the name of the first company you are going to call today. Add the phone number, the address, and the names and titles of people you already know, if any. These instructions may sound obvious, but trust me. They are not. For example, if you actually get someone on the phone and he says, "Send me a letter," are you going to be stupid enough to waste his time by asking for the address? No! You will already have it on your pad, next to his name. But are you going to be stupid enough to trust the source of information from which you got the address? No! You are going to ask the person, "That's 410 Sphinctre Street, correct?" And even if the address is wrong, the guy will be impressed that at least you got something.

Good. So now you've got the first company listed. Skip down the page a bit and write down another company. Keep listing companies until you have at least 10. Do this instead of calling the first company, because the act of listing is not the act of selling. Once you get into the act of selling, you don't want to stop. If you stop, even for a minute, the child in you will want to play. You will stop selling and start playing. You will not complete your sales mission. You must finish your sales mission! You must make 10 calls before you get to play. Is this clear, Private?

Oops. I slipped into R. Lee Ermey mode there. Forgive me. I have often been asked to run a "sales boot camp," but when I agree to do it, no one signs up. Yeah, selling is like doing push-ups and marching to cadence. But freelancing isn't free. I think there's a bumper sticker that says that.

Okay, you've got your client hit list. By the way, this is not intended to be a permanent record of your clients. It is just a worksheet. As soon as you get the first person on the phone, you should be making furious notes. Even a voicemail announcement is full of useful information, such as the recipient's name and sometimes title. They will often list other people and their extensions to call. You have to write all this stuff down. Put it on your hit list. If you actually get someone on the line, even if it's just the janitor, *get the person to give you another name.* The words "I was referred to you by . . ." are worth their weight in Snickers.

Later, I will show you two ways to organize the information from your hit list into a system that will ensure your success. But for now, the hit list will simply serve as your record of all human contact while selling. Use it to record every useful bit of information you can glean from your calls.

Your Pitch Script

Eventually, in selling, you have to talk. But because you are going to talk on the phone, no one will see if you are using a script. Once you have 10 or more clients on your hit list, it's time to make a script. Even seasoned, professional salespeople begin with a script—even when they know what they want to say. Unlike just speaking off the top of your head, when you make a script, you can write out every single thing you want to say. After you are done, you won't be saying, "Darn, I wish I said that," or, "Shoot, I forgot to mention my Porky animation!"

So what are you going to say?

One thing to keep in mind: Your script shouldn't be more than 10 seconds long. You think that's easy? Try saying everything you want to say in 10 seconds. It's going to take some hard work. Think. What are the key attributes that you can offer as an animator to your target customer?

Look over your hit list. Imagine these people answering the phone—or imagine their voicemail recorder going, "Beep!" And here's a tip: You can make a different script for different kinds of customers. If you anticipate a feature film producer, make a "feature film animator" script. If you have a car dealer who might want an animated commercial, make a "car dealer" script. I have dozens of scripts—but of course, after 20 years of selling, I know them all by heart. You will learn yours by heart too, after only a few weeks of selling. And as the Hollywood saying goes, "When you can imitate sincerity, you've got it made."

Now it's time for you to relax, sit down, and write a script that you can use to sell your skills. Never start out by saying, "Hi. I'm [YOUR NAME]. How are you today?" Already, you've wasted four seconds. Every beginning salesperson uses that tired old opening, so, by using this opening, you've told your prospect that *you're* a salesperson. Find an opening for your script that pitches your strongest suit first. Read each version of your script at a normal, easygoing pace. Even stick a few "ums" and "ahs" in there for authenticity. Nothing is worse when reading a script than sounding like you're reading a script.

Here are some samples to start with:

Sample 1: "Hi. I'm the animator who saved the XYZ Company $40,000 last month by animating their product launch in a way that no photographer could capture. Are you the person who contracts for TV commercial productions?"

Sample 2: "If you're the person who's looking for an animator on [TITLE OF NEW LOW-BUDGET FEATURE FILM], I'd like to show you how I can create things like explosions, flying monsters, and people whose heads turn into runny mush. Would you have a minute to let me show you my reel?"

Sample 3: "I make 3D animation that turns your printed logo into a flying, spinning, sparkling object of beauty. Companies like yours use animated logos for commercials, Internet sites, and trade shows. Would you be interested in seeing a few of mine?"

Sample 4: "Hi, [CLIENT'S FIRST NAME]. Would you be interested in knowing how you can obtain the best-quality 3D animations for your video productions? In a short meeting, I can show you how to add thousands of dollars of profit to every production you make. What about next Wednesday?"

Notice that each of these samples does away with introducing yourself and gets down to the important job of addressing your client's need. There's always a "you" implied in each script and very little "me"—unless the "me" is talking about what "me" can do for "you."

Also notice that each script asks for a meeting or at least a viewing of your showreel, which under the best circumstances you want to show in person. Every script ends with a question that encourages the client to give you information or make an appointment. After 10 seconds of you talking, you have to gauge the client's response profile. Are you talking to the right person? Is the person interested? Does the person have time to see you?

Unless it's the wrong person entirely (in which case, you should use this person to find out who the right one is), you are going to get an answer that is somewhere between "I'm happy with my current supplier" and "Can we set an appointment to talk about my project?"

Of course, millions of possible responses can come between these two extremes. Now is the time for you to start hearing them. Put this book down. Get that script written. Dial the numbers. Make 20 sales calls. Take notes. I'll see you in a few hours.

How Clients Respond to Your Script

Welcome back.

Let's explore the responses you got back from your 20 calls. How many voicemail recordings did you get? Did you run through your script for the voicemail? Why not? It's free advertising, and if it's just 10 seconds, the person usually hears the whole thing before she erases it!

Okay, on the hit list pad, you should have written the name of each person you called. If you left a message, you should have noted that. I usually write LMCB for "left message to call back," and I make a note of the date and time of the call. For every LMCB, try to find the person's email and then send a printed version of your script. Eventually, you can use Adobe Acrobat or a similar facility in your word processor to create a mini-brochure of your work. Mine is a PDF that's about 7 megabytes, with photos, clickable links—the works.

For every LMCB, you have to decide when you are going to call that person back. A week is a good time to wait for the next call, but add one day and change the time of day you make the call (that's why it's important to note the date and time of your calls). Your first attempt might have been when the client was out for a daily coffee break. If you call again at the same time, he may be on that break once again.

Rarely, the person will call you back. That's a golden opportunity, because the person was so motivated by your call that he wants to talk to you. Most of the time, it means a job is brewing! Good luck.

Out of 20 calls, if you got voicemail on 10, that's average. Of the remaining 10, you might have reached a person whose job is to "filter" phone calls. You know you're being filtered when someone other than the person you're trying to call answers the phone and says, "Mr. X's line." You identify yourself and then you hear, "I think he's in a meeting. Let me see." And after a moment, guess what? Mr. X is in a meeting and you're leaving a message. This person who's filtering the calls is called a *gatekeeper*.

Gatekeepers

Your very first and most important job when dealing with a gatekeeper is to get information about the boss. The most important information to find out is *if her boss is the right person to be calling*. Often you will find out that he isn't! In that case, you've saved yourself tons of time and effort, and hey—another recommendation!

But let's say the gatekeeper's boss is precisely the right person. Then you have to figure out a way past the gatekeeper, or meet her criteria for getting through the gate.

Assuming the gate is closed, I have several techniques you can use to handle gatekeepers. Try calling really early in the morning, or just after 5 p.m. Most likely, the gatekeeper will not be on duty, but the boss might be there. Or call during lunch hour, for the same reason. Gate keeping makes people hungry, while being a boss is such a breeze that they often sleep at the desk!

Perhaps the best way to handle a gatekeeper is to befriend her. Pretend that you're more interested in talking to the gatekeeper than to her boss.

"No, Melinda, I'm calling *you*. You're the more interesting one to talk to. What do you do on weekends?"

Find out what makes the gatekeeper's day, how he or she thinks. Hobbies, kids, and so on. Then, in a subtle way, try to find out what her instructions are regarding calls from vendors.

Use charm on a gatekeeper. This may or may not work, depending on how savvy the gatekeeper is. Being a gatekeeper is a really numbing job that could turn Mr. Rogers into a curse-spitting maniac. Try a distraction, like telling a joke or sharing a recipe. Hey, you're a creative whiz kid—do I need to tell you tricks to win someone's interest?

Never forget, today's gatekeeper eventually might end up being the one whose gate is being kept. Not a few gatekeeper friends of mine have moved up to being clients—and have issued explicit directions to *their* gatekeepers to pass my calls right through. Take care of your gatekeepers today. They may be your clients tomorrow.

Always remember to take notes on what your gatekeeper talks about. Often, important names will be mentioned. Don't be shy about asking for the spelling of a name, and a phone number. Ask what job the named person does. Consider yourself a keen detective, always searching for valuable clues.

Close Encounters

Of the 10 calls that were not voicemails, perhaps one or two were answered by real live prospects; people who need your services, or at least people who want to meet you. Don't get nervous. Just take a deep breath and calmly deliver your script. If a prospect thinks you're reading a script, you're toast, man. Try to sound natural.

If you complete your script well, the client might ask for more information. Be ready to give it. How do you get ready? Try rehearsing with a friend. Have the friend give you every possible response you can imagine. Make it a game, where your friend tries to trip you up. Friends know you better than a customer, so these rehearsals can be fun and informative.

Winning the game ultimately results in getting an appointment to show your reel or portfolio to a client. It's a wonderful game. Sometimes you have to talk fast, other times slow. And you always have to know when to shut your mouth, take notes, and wait for magic. Magic sounds like this:

"You know, I'm not the right person to talk to, but I heard that Bob in Vertical Markets was looking to do a series of animations about . . ."

Obviously, if you don't have your pad and pencil ready, it will be very embarrassing.

More often than magic, however, you get objections. Objections from a potential client are not death. They are more like hurdles or tests of your ingenuity. Here are some common objections, and an appropriate response for each, to prepare you for the challenge:

Objection	Response
"We have an in-house capability."	"Great. Can you tell me who runs it, so I can offer my services?"
"Do you have any literature you can send me?"	"Of course, but would you prefer I email it?"
"We can't afford animation."	"We should meet. You'd be pleasantly surprised how cost-effective *my* work is."
"I'd have to consult my boss on that."	"Would my assistance in that consultation be appropriate?"

Objections, as you can see, are clever little verbal devices whose objective is to exhaust your efforts. Looked at in a different way, they challenge you to see if you have the right stuff to be of service to a client. An objection might make you angry, but consider this: If you and five competitors call the same client, and the other five give up after the first or second objection, you—persuasive and patient—will be the vendor who gets the work. Objections, therefore, are your friends.

If you stop and consider that even the worst objections ("Our company has no use for animation." "Nick? He died.") are but dust in the winds of time (Response: Call back again next year), you'll realize that anything less is an opportunity waiting to pay you money.

What to Do with Your Notes

After your first day of calls, say 20, your notepad should have enough information on it that you'll be wondering what to do with it. You have two choices: paper or electronic databases. The two purposes of a database are to record vital information about your clients and potential clients, and to remind you when you should contact them.

If you have a few hundred dollars to spend, you can buy a "contact management" software product (Act! and Goldmine are the two most popular), or you can do the same thing with a simple loose-leaf notebook combined with a daily calendar pad.

Here's what you do if you don't want to spend the money on the software: Take a sheet of loose-leaf notebook paper (the kind that has three holes punched along the left margin and light blue horizontal lines). With a dark, soft pencil, draw the following design on the page as a blank form. Then photocopy as many blank forms as you need. You can also copy this design into your favorite word processor as a table, and print out as many copies as you want. All the copies go into one of those handy three-ring binders.

Company Name _____ HQ Phone _____

Address _____ City_____ Zip _____

Web Site _____ Principal Business _____

Name A: _____ Title A: _____

Phone A: _____ Email A: _____

Name B: _____ Title B: _____

Phone B: _____ Email B: _____

Name C: _____ Title C: _____

Phone C: _____ Email C: _____

_____

_____

_____

_____

_____

Using this form is simple. You transfer all of the useful information from your notepad to the form. The useless information—a dead end, a bankrupt client, whatever—is left on the notepad. One page will hold all the information necessary to keep track of three employees of the same company. The company data goes at the top of the page, and then you list the names of three employees of that company under Names A, B, and C. To the right of the names, you fill in the title, phone number, and email address of each employee. If there are more employees in the same company who you wish to follow, add another page with the same company name, and put that page behind the first in your loose-leaf holder.

Once you have the basic data on the top part of the page, you use the blank lines to log every call you make to the people named above. Using a line for each person, start the first line with a letter that represents the person's name, then continue to use that line for that person. When you run out of space on a line, go to the next empty line below and enter the letter again.

I like to use a code that reduces the number of words I have to write. For instance, if I call person A and leave a message for her to call me back, I write "LMCB." Then I jot the date, such as 3/9/06, and then I write my next task for that person: "CB (call back) 3/21/06." If you speak to the person, write "spk" and a short comment on what was said: "Has project for Fall. CB 10/1/06."

Once you've transferred all the data from the notepad page to the database page, you throw the notepad page into a file folder. Never throw anything away. Even data about dead ends can be useful one day. If you ever start down that dead end again, you'll be able to save a lot of time by referring to your old notes. Now that you've evaluated a potential client as being worthy of the loose-leaf page, you can continue to work from the loose-leaf to keep in contact and record your efforts.

The loose-leaf is your source of data, but it is not your schedule. When you wake up in the morning, you need to have a tool that tells you who to call or visit. This is done with a companion to the loose-leaf database.

This companion is a simple calendar notepad, like a DayTimer or a Week-At-A-Glance that you can buy in any Staples or similar office supply store. Yes, you can also use your personal data assistant (PDA), but I prefer the paper versions because you can store them indefinitely for future reference. Now, whenever you write the results of a phone call into your loose-leaf notebook sheet, you go to your daybook and enter an "order" to yourself regarding what you want to do next with the client.

For instance, if your loose-leaf note said "spk, call in three weeks," you would go into your day book, flip over three weeks into the future, and write in an order: "Call Joe at Comzoc." Three weeks from now, when you get up to make your daily calls, you'll see the note to call Joe at Comzoc. You'll open your loose-leaf notebook and read your last note and know what you have to do.

The routine then boils down to this:

Make 20 calls a day. For the new calls, use a regular notebook to gather information. Transfer the new information to new pages in your loose-leaf data sheets. For follow-up calls, simply follow your orders in the day book and update the information on your loose-leaf data sheets. The only difficulty is maintaining the discipline of making the calls and taking good notes.

Eventually, the clients will start responding with appointments. You'll show your reel. You'll get bids. You'll win some bids. You'll make money. How much money will depend on how many calls you make.

Electronic Databases

Electronic databases, also known as contact management software, are far superior to the paper-based system I described above. The only drawback to electronic systems is that they do not produce a permanent paper record of everything you do. I like paper. I like being able to go back to my 1984 data sheets and look up old targets. Why? Because life is long. Even people who would never talk to you in 2006 might finally give you a shot after 20 years of nagging. It's nice to know that after 20 years, when you can't remember the guy's name anymore (in fact, you're lucky if you can remember your *own* name!), you can go into the closet and dig up your call notes from early in your career. But aside from that, the computer systems are better.

Here's how they work: Instead of sheets of paper, you get a screen for each client. The screen has all the information you could ever want, even places to enter the client's kids' names and their birthdays if you want. Just like the lines at the bottom of your paper data pages, the program has infinite space to write notes. Instead of using a date book, you simply click an icon that symbolizes the type of order you want to make—a phone to remind you to make a phone call, for instance. Click it to open a calendar, click the date and time, and presto, the computer stores the date and will even ring an alarm when it's time to call the client.

If the client asks you to send her a letter, you click one icon and a mail merge letter is opened, complete with the name and address at the top, on your personal letterhead. You can use existing boilerplate business letters, or, if you are imaginative, you can make your own boilerplates, one for each type of animation or client. I have about 50, from "architecture" to "youth-oriented."

Let's say you forget a client's name and the client's company, but remember that her office is in Connecticut. You can do a search for "Connecticut," and in seconds, you'll have all the clients with offices in CT listed on your screen. The same goes for any other parameter, from kid's names to ZIP codes. You can even set up the computer to dial your calls, send faxes, and so on.

If you have $200 to spare, I would highly recommend looking into contact management software. Changing from a paper-based to computer-based system doubled my overall contact rate (calls, letters, appointments, and RFPs) and had a similar effect on my income.

The Sales Pyramid

Okay, if you've stuck with me this far, you deserve to know what kinds of rewards you can harvest if you stick to a plan of making a set amount of sales calls every day (or at least whenever you aren't working on a paid animation job). So, let's stick with the 20-call challenge and do what I call the Sales Pyramid.

Imagine, if you can (but of course you can, because you're a graphics professional), an Egyptian pyramid.

Using your mind's eye's "laser," cut the pyramid horizontally into six slices of equal height. Now, each slice should appear to have a lot less mass than the slice below it.

Mentally label the bottom layer "All Possible Contacts." This layer represents all the contacts you could possibly call. When you make 20 new client calls, this is the layer from which you extract the leads.

On the average, 20 calls will produce about 15 voicemail or no-answer results and about six contacts with a live person. As you make these calls and take notes on each of these contacts, you convert the people from "all possible contacts" to "entered contacts." In other words, you've taken them from the world at large and placed them in your database of possible clients. Entered contacts is level two of the pyramid.

I distinguish entered contacts from a smaller group, namely the people with whom you have actually had words. The words might be as few as "Call me back in a few months." Those words convert the entered contact to a "contacted" contact. Any words from the contact that lead you to make further communication qualify that person as a contacted lead. Of course, if the person says something that shuts the door, like, "I never need your services," he drops back down to the first level—maybe even below that level—because you don't want to waste time calling this person again.

Contacted people make up the third level of the pyramid. Of the people you call, the ones you actually speak to move up to the next level of the pyramid. So after your first day of calling, your pyramid should have 20 in the first layer and five in the second.

Out of these five contacted people, one in three will ask for a brochure, a letter, or the address of your Web site. They want some form of document to read about you. Each person who reads your letter, brochure, or site (and gets their name added to your schedule, so you make a call back to that person within a week) becomes one more person in the fourth level of the pyramid, "Documented People."

For every three documented people, my experience tells me that one of these, if properly called back, will set up an appointment to meet you and see your work. The fifth layer of the pyramid, the "people I've met" layer, only starts getting filled up after you spend more than one day of making calls. Statistically, therefore, you need to put 36 names into the first layer of the pyramid (that's less than two days of phone calling, dude) before you can expect to get one appointment. That's not so bad, is it? But wait—there's more calling! But now it starts getting interesting. Here's where you start to make money.

For every three meetings, if you properly follow up with these contacts over, say, six months, three will give you a bid. That means three clients consider your talents impressive enough to ask you for a plan of action that could lead to contract work! One out of three—think about it. Not such bad odds. But you have to get three people up to the "people I've met" level. To do that, you have to put 108 people into the first level. You have to make 108 calls. But if you do 20 original client calls a day, that's fewer than six days of work and maybe clients for your pyramid's first level. You're down with that, no? But keep in mind, you also have to keep making calls to all the other people on each level of the pyramid, trying to push *them* up to the next level.

I can't tell you how many calls this will take, because it depends on how often you want to call somebody a second and third time. But let's say you limit each person to three calls—that would give you a total of less than 400 calls, or about 20 days of work. Now, you ask, "When do I get to see some cash? Show me the money!" I will.

Let's say you take a vacation after 60 straight days of hard-selling work, making 20 original client calls a day and minimal follow-up on the various levels of the pyramid. You might have 324 people in the "all possible clients" level, 71 in the "contacted people" level, 27 in the "people I've met" level, and nine in the "bidded clients" level. You've got three bids out there, and you can reasonably expect that one of them will close. Yes, that's the average rate. Because most companies bid three companies for every project, you have a statistical probability of winning one out of three. Winning a bid places a contact on the top level of the pyramid, the "clients" level, and when you win that one bid, the average project bill is $20,000.

This average includes every kind of animation project under the sun, from a Flash logo to a feature film project. I know this because as the head of a small animation production company, from my first day to the day I sit writing this 22 years later, that has been my average. It also checks out with several animation guys I know in the New York and L.A. areas. These are small companies—not ILM, for Pete's sake. You could do better if you're located in Hollywood and specialize in features, but I'm a generalist of average talent, so I think you can rely on my average being a fair benchmark of all the U.S.-based dudes and dudettes out there who might get into animation on a regular basis.

So, after about 1,000 calls total, you've got one lousy $20,000 project under your belt. That ain't much, right? But wait—there's more. More money. Let's say you quit, right there. No more calls. Will you make any more money? Sure you will. If you did a good job on that $20,000 project, the client will probably call you back and give you more work. What's more, the client, if really pleased, might not bid out the next job. She might give it to you "sole source." On top of that, the two other clients, the ones you bid but lost, may call you in again for another bid. Your chances on those bids are still 1 in 3. So even if you stop making calls (which would be dumb), you still make money. Let's continue to see what would happen if you keep making calls.

Let's say you go on to make calls for a solid year—that's five days a week for 50 weeks. (You can take a two-week vacation—I'll go easy on you with that.) Assuming that a minimum of 2/3rds of your calls are going to be follow-ups, you might have to do upwards of 60 calls a day to put 20 new names a day into the first level of the pyramid, but most of these calls will be quickies. You just dial a number from your records and either chat for a moment or two or leave a voicemail.

When this year is over, you will have about 5,000 names in the first level of the pyramid. At the top of the pyramid, on the "clients" level, you will have 15! Their gross billings for just the first-time projects, averaged at $20,000 each, have brought you $300,000. That's not so bad. In fact, with that kind of money, you could start paying somebody else to make the phone calls, right? But the goodies get better. Remember that the $300,000 is only the *first* job you get from a client. What about repeat business? What about word of mouth recommendations, where a happy client tells a friend about you, and that friend calls you out of the blue to give you work?

And consider this: The average client, if kept satisfied, lasts an average of 10 years. That's 10 years before the client loses his/her job, croaks, gets bored with your work, whatever. One solid year of hard calling, and with some regular maintenance, you can count on making $300,000 a year for 10 years. That's $3 million.

Now, if you divide that $3 million by all the calls you've made, what would you end up making for each fricking call? I figure 15,000 calls per year, over 10 years, that's 150,000 calls. Divided that into 3 million bucks and it comes out to $20 per call!

So, in your spare time, between doing the animation work that you love to do, if you knew you could get paid $20 per phone call on the side, would you make 20-60 calls per day? I hope you answered something like, "Oh, yeah."

Now let me give you some pointers on how to move clients quickly and efficiently up the pyramid.

The First Contact

Whenever you manage to get a live person on the phone and deliver your pitch, try to set an appointment. If you can set an appointment, you effectively jump the person over the "documented people" level of the pyramid and save yourself lots of phone calling.

Usually, a first contact call will not set an appointment unless there is a job brewing, so if you're lucky and skillful, an appointment can result in a bid pretty quickly.

If you don't manage to set an appointment, the contact will likely impose some kind of hurdle for you to jump. The hurdle can be a request for literature (the letter or brochure), which obviously takes you money to print and time to mail. You can cut this time and cost by offering to send the required materials by email, or you can direct the client to your Web site. The trip to the Web site is good, but you won't have any evidence that the client went there. If you send an email, at least you know that the client had to delete it.

Either way, you must follow up the request for documents with another call. This call should go out no later than five working days after you expect the contact to have received the documentation. For a letter, that means two weeks (one week to get the mail, one week before they read it). For an email, the clock starts ticking the moment you click Send.

Don't automatically offer to send documentation. That's like asking to be brushed off. Pursue the appointment. That way, if the contact makes it a condition that you send documentation, you have a reasonable position upon which to request something in return, like the right to call the contact back to set that appointment. You can say, "Fine, I'll send you my PDF brochure with clickable samples of my work. May I call you back in a week or so to follow up?"

When you make that follow-up call, once again, you are going to pursue that appointment. If you get voicemail on the follow-up call, log an LMCB into your database. If you get more than three LMCBs in a reasonable amount of time (like over two months), something is wrong.

When Something Is Wrong

All of the people on your pyramid have one thing in common: They are contractors who are looking for an animator like you to do work for them. If they are not, they do not belong on your pyramid or in your database, and they must be removed as soon as possible. If they're not removed, they continue to suck up your available time and money, demanding calls and documents that they have no right to get.

Sadly, people will often avoid telling you that they are not valid contractors. Maybe they want to feel important. Maybe they are about to be fired and want to make everyone around them (including their boss) believe that they are doing some work—like taking your call or meeting. Maybe they are just plain stupid.

Whatever the case, it is your obligation to filter out these bozos, the same way they try to filter out vendors who don't know what they are doing.

The best way of filtering out an invalid contact is by imposing a strict limit on the number of calls you will make that are not returned, or LMCBs. More than three LMCBs in a two-month period (meaning you didn't make all three calls in one week) is a sign that the contact is not valid. You must test the validity.

Start by going back to the original reference source. Did you make a cold call to a receptionist to get that contact? If so, call the receptionist again and make sure the contact is still in the same job as before, or better yet, verify the job title of the contact. If you find out that the contact is a secretary or powerless assistant, find out who the boss is and substitute the boss's name in your database. Another possibility is the seasonal nature of our business. Sometimes work only gets bid out in the fall, or the bids depend on your client's company getting a big assignment. Before you mark a contact as invalid, you have to determine if your entire timing is off, and then reassign the calls to that client in the right general time period.

If, after diligently verifying the contact is valid, you still don't get a call back, there are only two possibilities: The contact is too busy to return your call, or the client is not doing his/her job. If the contact is too busy, you can't waste time calling—it won't help. Sure, the person could become less busy by employing you, because you, a great animator, can save time and money, but the contact doesn't know this yet. And not knowing this is a sign that the contact isn't a top-notch contact. In other words, possibly the contact isn't doing his/her job.

If a person is a valid contractor, *their job is to meet vendors!* You might say, "Like, duh, that's understood." But you would be surprised to know how many people get paid good money these days to do incompetent work, or no work at all.

What happens when someone doesn't do his or her job, or does it lousy? *They get fired!*

Now, here's a great little secret: Whenever I pile up three LMCBs on a contact and then I verify them as a valid contact, I do one thing. I enter their name in my schedule *one year into the future.* One year. And in the reference window of my contact management software, I write, "Fired yet?"

Would you believe that, for every 10 people I log in as "Fired yet?", fully *nine* end up having been fired when I call after a year? It's true. And what's more, they are fired just a little while before I call. Probably a coincidence . . . maybe because it takes most American companies a year to find out someone is a jerk and fire them. This is great news. It's great because the very best time to call a newly hired contractor is about a month after they've taken over the job. You can say, "My previous contact was your predecessor, who never returned my phone calls. You can see where _that_ got her." Delivered with the proper dose of good nature, you will usually get a laugh—and an appointment.

Here's another thing you can do. When you leave that last LMCB, you can suggest the person buy a copy of this book and refer him/her to this page. I once did that, and the contact called me back and set an appointment. She should have called me sooner, though, because she still got fired the next week.

The Appointment

Always be on time to an appointment—which means 15 minutes early. Be clean, be well-groomed, and wear good-quality clothing. Notice I didn't say, "Wear a suit and tie, remove your face jewelry, and cover up the tats." All these accouterments of the animator's lifestyle are attractive to most contractors. I say "most" because you have to be careful when you set appointments with people who know nothing about animation.

If you go to meet the president of a pizza chain or the director of a private school for girls, and you assume they want some animation for a commercial or Web site, you'd better ask your parents how to dress.

When you meet the client, spend about five minutes on small talk. Try to find something in common with the contact. Decorations in the office are a clue— kids, a boat, a fancy car—and a polite comment like "Nice car" or "Cute baby" can start a nice conversation. After the small talk, start to move the conversation around to the person's work and the reason for the meeting.

You can say, "So tell me about your work here and how I might fit in." This is an invitation for the person to talk about himself. Sometimes, the person can get carried away. This is a sign of trouble. Gently move yourself into the picture with comments like, "I think I can help you out with that," or "How do you go about selecting your vendors?"

The next step is to transition the conversation to your work. You can do this by presenting some paper documentation—a resume or brochure—and letting the host take a glance at it. Before he/she gets too deep into the text, offer to set up your demonstration while the person reads the document. Ask the person how they would like to see it—on their desk if you brought a laptop DVD, or on the conference room media wall—and start unpacking the reel or portfolio.

After your document has been read and you're ready to show your work, do so. I like to look at the eyes of the host while my reel plays (or during the showing of a print portfolio). Whenever the eyes show interest, I add some more details verbally. When they look away, I note that this was something the client may have disliked, and sometimes I will ask about that.

After the presentation is over, start to pack up your things. If the client slows you down, this is a sign that there is a bid waiting. Slow down. If the client says something like, "I wonder if you could look at a project we have planned," or "How are you at doing XYZ?", stop everything. Shut up and listen. The best response to any question like this is to ask for details—as many details as the person can give you. Never offer a price at this meeting. Always say you will examine the details and get back to the person later, either by phone or in writing. Writing is best, because this becomes a proposal.

If there are no leading questions or an invitation to stay longer, pack your bags and head for the door. Just before you leave, it is fair to ask how you did: "How did you like my work?" or "What is your honest appraisal of my capabilities to help you?" If you get trashed, take it like an adult and promise to do better. If you get praised, ask the person when they would like to be contacted in the future.

If your presentation went well, the assumption is that you would be welcome to call periodically to see if there are any jobs on the horizon. Ask the person how soon and how often they expect to be called. Getting a bid request is mostly being in the right place at the right time. You've found a right place. The contact has to tell you when is the right time. Ask for that and expect to get an honest answer. If the answer is three months, call in three months. If the answer is vague, maybe you didn't do such a good job after all, or maybe the contact is not valid.

After the Presentation

A client on your "people I've met" level of the pyramid requires a different schedule of calling and maintenance from the contacts who are lower on the pyramid. You should establish a regular routine with such a client, based on their stated needs and the yearly timeline of their work. They might request that you call them as often as once a month (which is high maintenance), or not at all. In order to be of service, you must know how many projects a year this contact is generating and when those projects begin. If there are no projects, or the projects come up sporadically, you can set aside this client for a call every six months or every year. If you're unlucky and miss the right time to call, and the client calls another vendor, don't sweat it. Either the client didn't feel loyal to you anyway, or the job wasn't worth the calls. It's better to keep searching for new clients than to try to make a busy client out of a client with little or no work. It's the same story as the three LMCBs: A non-busy client isn't really a client.

A client who is busy, however, and has established routines for bidding out work should get frequent and careful attention. Learn everything you can about this person, their likes and dislikes, their favorite vendors and why they are favored, their budget limitations, their time frames and deadlines, the names of their kids, birthdays, anniversaries, and the names of their staff and boss.

Keep careful notes whenever you call such clients, building your knowledge base and their trust in you. Sooner or later, this client is going to call you for a bid. Your existing knowledge will determine how you handle the bid, what you write, how much you charge, and what your chances of success will be.

You're Asked to Bid

If you do your job, sooner or later you are going to be asked to bid on a project. Sometimes the client will want to give you the bid quickly, over the phone. Other times, the client will want a meeting, perhaps at your place of business, to see what kind of facility you operate and who is working there.

Either way, there are four questions you must answer before you can make a successful bid:

- Who is the audience?
- What is the message?
- What is the budget?
- When is the deadline?

In Chapter 11, we will get into these questions in further detail as I teach you how to make a budget and proposal. But just in case, if you get asked to do a bid *before* you read Chapter 11, you should ask these questions and take careful notes. If you get the answers, I can help you make a winning bid.

Another thing you should find out when you are asked for a bid is how many other companies are bidding against you. This is a tough question to ask, but knowing the answer will help you enormously. Even the way the client tells you the answer is useful. If the answer is two other bidders, that's normal. If there are three or more bidders besides you, you have to figure out why there are so many and if you're just a tack-on at the end of the list. Being the tack-on isn't a bad thing—sometimes that's a part of getting your foot in the door.

If the client tells you boldly and quickly that there are X number of other bidders, that's a good thing. It means your client is confident, and that's the way things are done. If the client equivocates, doesn't answer, or hems and haws before telling you, that's a sign of a weak client who may not be in control of the selection. Perhaps the client is just gathering information, or gathering bids that his boss will decide on, or making the bid process look legitimate when there is already someone selected to do the job.

There's nothing you can do about a bid process that is suspect. Oh, if you have four other bids to do that week and you want to select which one to do first, it's useful to know which one can be left for last. Otherwise, you just have to do each bid as if you have a fair chance of winning. But if you know you don't have a fair chance, it gives you room to get innovative. Maybe you want to shoot a real low-ball bid, just to make the guy sweat who's already got the job but not the price. Maybe you want to try out some unusual creative idea that you wouldn't risk on a solid-bid client. Either way, knowledge is power. Maybe not *much* power, but in any amount, power is useful.

Okay—enough about the boring topic of selling. How about we get back to the exciting business of animating? In the next tutorial, you are going to explore the creation of a character. I know, you're thinking of that famous *Frankenstein* scene: "It's alive!" Yes. It is alive, and you, dear reader, are now going to play God.

Chapter 8

Bones and Skeletons: Imparting Objects with the Ability to Move and Deform

Character rigging and weighting is a very deep topic, and we will only cover the tip of the iceberg in this tutorial. However, the concepts and techniques discussed here are fairly universal, and they should serve as a good base for understanding the steps necessary to prepare a character for animation. For the sake of clarity, we will first do a quick setup, using a stock character and a matching skeleton that ships with XSI. Then we will repeat the process using some special tools designed to help you in more unique circumstances.

1. Open a new scene and select Get > Primitive > Model > Body-Man (or Woman). This places a simple polygonal human figure in your scene with the feet positioned at the origin.

2. If you open an Explorer window (set the filter to Objects Only), you will see that the actual polygon object is the child of a *model* null that is also at the scene's origin.

3. Press Shift+A to center the body in all of the views.

   The term *model* in XSI refers to a special type of null object that helps you to organize objects, cameras, and lights in your scene. A model contains a full set of object properties, as well as a mixer for the actions and shapes belonging to its children. You can create a model by selecting the objects that you want to be a part of it and choosing Create > Model >

New Model. Models may be renamed without affecting the names of their children, which makes them ideal for naming characters that need to have identical bones, controls, and so on. The symbol for a model null is a tiny character in a "T" pose.

4. Now repeat the same steps, except choose Get > Primitive > Model > Skeleton-Man-Basic (or Woman).

   You will notice that the stock body and the stock skeleton are built so that they fit correctly. If you want to change the size of your characters(s), you should scale the model nulls rather than the polygons or the bones. If you change the scale of these objects before enveloping them (sometimes called *binding*), they will not function correctly. In addition, before performing the actual enveloping, it is a good idea to put all of the bones that will influence the skin into a group for easy selection.

5. Simply select the bones and click the Edit > Group button at the bottom of the Master Control Panel. This has already been done for you on the skeleton model.

6. Switch to the Animation module (press 2 on the keyboard).

7. On the menu bar, select Animation Construction Mode from the center menu.

8. Open an Explorer window and expand the skeleton model so that you can access the group containing the bones (called *enveloping* in this case).

9. To bind the skin to the bones, select the figure, choose Deform > Envelope > Set Envelope, and pick the group containing the bones.

10. Right-click to end the picking session and accept defaults, and close the envelope assignment window.

    You will notice that the bones have changed to different colors, and the vertices on the body now reflect which bones are influencing them (see Figure 8.1). By default, each vertex (point) is influenced by the two bones that are closest to it. The color on the vertices reflects which of the two is exerting a greater amount of influence (weight) on that point.

11. To test the enveloping, select a bone (for instance, a forearm) and rotate it. The skin should now move with it.

    If you distort the body too badly, use Deform > Envelope > Reset Actor. This is a pretty awkward way to animate, but don't worry. Later you will use control objects to manipulate your skeleton in a more natural way.

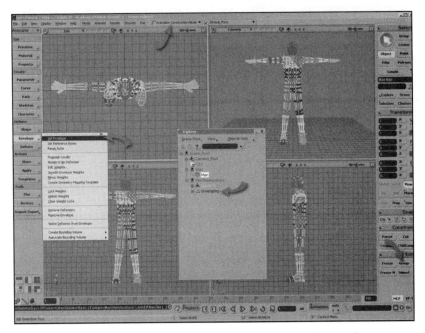

Figure 8.1 *The vertices on the body reflect which bones influence them.*

Learning the Character Designer

There are a multitude of tools in this program that will allow you to build characters from scratch, but to get you up and running with the creative tools, we will use a built-in feature called the *character designer*. The character designer is really a model that contains scripted operators for adjusting parameters such as head size, features, body dimensions, and so on. We will use this to create something that would not possibly conform to one of the stock human skeletons, and then create a custom skeletal rig to control its movements.

Using the Character Designer

In this exercise, you learn how to use the character designer:

1. Begin by opening a new scene and selecting Get > Primitive > Model > Character. A Character Designer Property Page (PPG) opens, which has tabbed pages and adjustment sliders for all of the different body parts.

2. Have some fun by experimenting with the different body types and proportions. See Figure 8.2.

3. When you are done, reset the character with the button on the first tab of the PPG.

   If you accidentally close the PPG, you can reopen it by selecting the body, clicking the selection button on the MCP, and clicking the orange gradient labeled Character_Designer.

4. Make a character that is somewhat distorted. Create longer, beefier arms, a large head, thick legs, and so on.

   The important thing, for the sake of this tutorial, is that you make a character that does not fit the exact proportions of the default skeleton. This is a situation that will arise when you are building unique characters for your own projects. Next, we will use the biped guide to create a rig that is correctly proportioned to your character.

   A *character rig* is a combination of the bones that move the skin and a set of control objects that allow you to conveniently manipulate the bones.

5. Select the polygon body of your character.

6. Click the KP/L button at the bottom of the Master Control Panel to reveal the Keying and Layers panel.

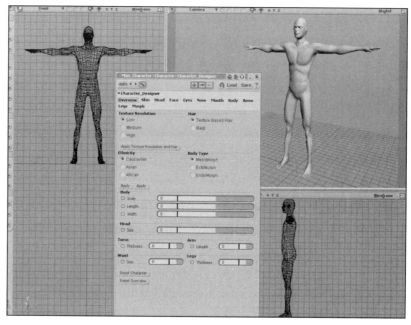

Figure 8.2 *Character Designer Property Page (PPG).*

7. Click the Layers button and select New Layer from Selection.

8. Name it Body, and uncheck the switch for selectivity. Now you will be able to adjust the guide without accidentally selecting the body.

9. Choose Create > Character > Biped Guide and accept the default settings.

   You will see what looks like a red skeleton with white cubes between the bones and yellow lines around the edges. The white boxes allow you to move the joints of the skeleton so that you can apportion it any way you want.

10. Starting at the center of the rig, work your way toward the extremities, moving one cube at a time to line up the bones inside your custom character.

   If you accepted the default setup, everything is proportional so that if you move a joint on one side of the body, the opposite side will be updated as well.

11. Use multiple views to ensure that you keep the bones inside the body. The cubes on the ends of the yellow lines can be lined up along the outside of the body (see Figure 8.3).

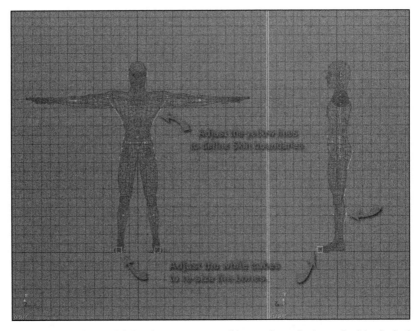

Figure 8.3 *Use multiple views to ensure that you keep the bones inside the body.*

12. When you are satisfied with your work, select the guide and choose Create > Character > Rig from Biped Guide. You will see a tabbed PPG with many choices for how to set up the control system for your rig. These include foot roll, spine structure, skin deformers, and more.

13. You will accept the default setup for this example, so click OK. And before your very eyes, a custom character rig is created.

14. You can now delete the guide (or simply hide it if you think you may need it again).

    If you open an Explorer window, you will find that there are prebuilt groups contained in your rig for hidden items and the bones that you will need to envelope.

Increasing Control of the Rig

Begin by making your body layer selectable again.

1. Check that you are in Animation Construction mode (top menu bar).

2. Select the body, choose Deform > Envelope > Set Envelope, and click on the envelope group in the Explorer window.

3. Accept the default settings and close the envelope assignment window. You can now manipulate the skeleton with the various control objects that are attached to the rig.

4. The cubes on the feet can be moved to position them, or rotated to create a rolling of the foot and ankle.

5. The squares at the waist control hip and upper body placement.

6. The cubes at the wrists can be used to position the arms and so forth.

7. Take a little time to experiment with the controllers.

    For an even easier selection, pick any part of the control rig and press F3. This opens the synoptic page, an HTML page that allows you to easily select your controls by clicking on an image of the character. We will talk more about this later when you are setting up actions.

8. When you are done playing around with this, reset the rig from the synoptic page.

9. You apply envelope weights in the Animation Construction mode so that the calculations are not confused with those in the modeling stack. They are calculated after the modeling, so that you can go back and make

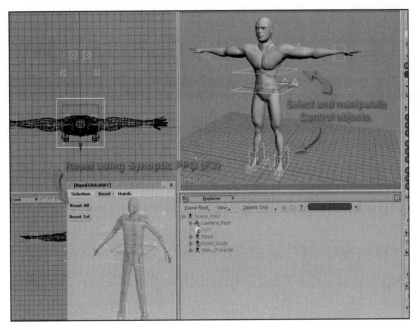

Figure 8.4 *Resetting the rig.*

adjustments in the model mode without destroying what you have done
with the weighting.

The biggest problem with this type of automated weighting is that the
weights are assigned to the two nearest bones based strictly on distance.
That means sometimes the wrong bones or the wrong weight balance is
selected, and you have to repair the errors manually.

This is the reason that we use a "T" pose or a modified version with
the arms slightly lower (sometimes called a "Y" pose) to help with the
tension in the shoulder region. These extreme poses keep the bones
separated so that the envelope doesn't have too many confusing choices
to make.

It is also possible to add additional bones, nulls, or geometry deformers
that directly affect the areas in question. In this case, notice that when
you lift the leg of the character, the stomach caves in. And when you
rotate the forearm, the skin is quite distorted. The first problem (stomach) is quite common and also occurs frequently in the armpit area. You
will repair it with a few strokes from your weight brush. The second

problem (forearm deformation) is quite extreme and is due to the exaggerated arms of this character. You will need to use a more precise method of adjustment for this situation.

Fixing Common Weight Problems

Let's continue using the rig you created and proceed to fix the weight problems that arose from deforming the standard body design.

1. Weight adjustments are interactive, so you want to pose the character so that you can see some of the unwanted deformation (see Figure 8.5).

2. For the stomach, apply a smoothing brush to the weight map that was created during the automatic assignment. Press the W key to enter weight-viewing mode. Your character's skin should turn into a brightly colored map of the bone influence.

3. Click the small brush icon at the bottom-left corner of your screen to open the weight brush controls.

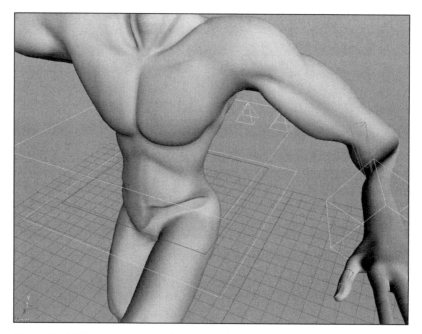

Figure 8.5 *Viewing unwanted deformations.*

With this panel, you can add or subtract influence from selected bones, or apply a smoothing effect that will spread the influence between several bones in the vicinity of the area that you are painting.

4. Make sure to check the box that says Interactive Refresh.

5. Click on the smooth button under the Paint tools, and turn the opacity down to a smaller number. I use about 20 percent so that each stroke adds a bit more influence to the skin.

6. The middle mouse button will allow you to change the brush size interactively.

7. If you turn on Sym (symmetry) in the MCP, you can paint both sides of the body at once (see Figure 8.6).

8. Paint a few strokes where the "denting" of the stomach is occurring to see the effect.

9. In addition to the smoothing, you might try selecting Hip Plate from the list of bones and painting a bit of influence in Add mode (also turn the opacity down for this).

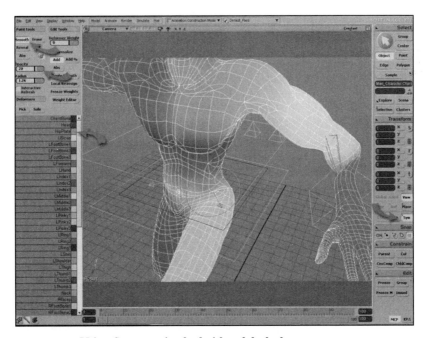

Figure 8.6 *Using Sym to paint both sides of the body at once.*

10. For the arm, you will need to directly manipulate the weight on specific points using the weight editor.

11. With the body selected, press the minus key on the number pad to turn down the number of subdivisions on the polygon character.

12. Next, press T to enter point selection mode. Pick a single point on the forearm where it begins to distort badly.

13. Then, hold down the Alt key and middle-click on another point in the same ring to select the whole loop around the forearm (see Figure 8.7).

13. Press Ctrl+E to open the weight editor. You will see a list of all the selected points and the influence of the two bones.

14. Click on the name above the forearm weights.

15. Make sure you are in ABS mode (in the weight editor) and push the slider up to 100%. The loop of points moves to encircle the forearm bone.

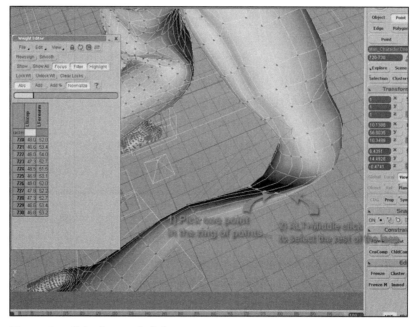

Figure 8.7 *Selecting a whole loop.*

16. Go to the Select menu and choose Select Adjacent > Points. As of version 5.0, you can tear off this little panel and leave it on your screen.

17. Selecting Adjacent picks the loops on both sides of the original, so deselect the one closest to the wrist by holding down Shift+Ctrl and dragging a marquis around the points (see Figure 8.8).

    If the weight editor is not still open, open it and adjust these points to 100% forearm as well.

18. Repeat one or two more loops (see Figures 8.9 and 8.10). You can adjust the weights to less than 100% depending on what looks best for your model.

19. You should save frequently under unique names as you work on weighting, in case you need to go back to a previous version and start over. Figure 8.11 shows a "before" and "after" of these areas.

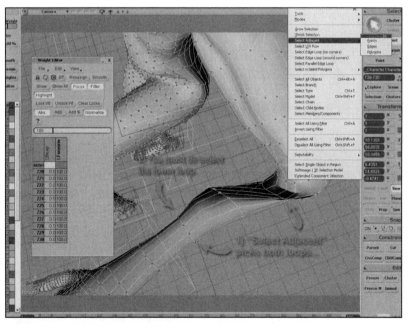

Figure 8.8 *Using Select Adjacent.*

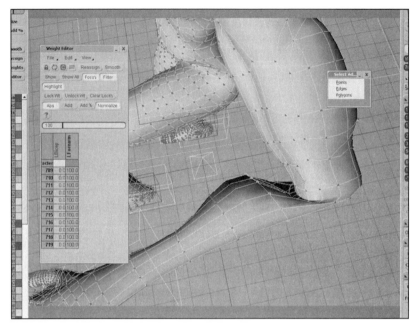

Figure 8.9 *Repeating the loop process.*

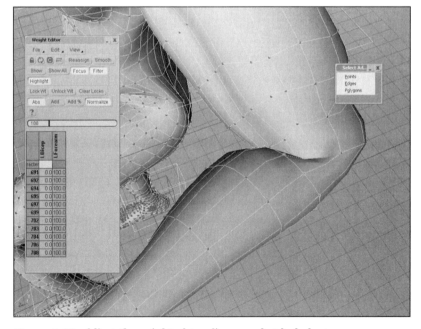

Figure 8.10 *Adjust the weights depending on what looks best.*

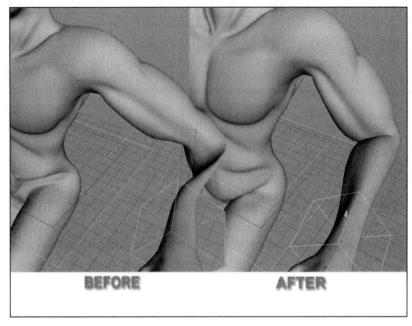

Figure 8.11 *Before and after.*

20. Continue using these techniques on the other trouble spots until you can move the control objects into reasonable positions without distorting the character too badly.

21. Press the plus sign on the number pad to smooth the finished model, and reset the rig using the synoptic page if you want.

22. Save your scene!

Creating a Library of Actions

Open your weighted character scene, if necessary. You could animate your character by simply selecting the individual bones or control objects and saving keyframes for translation (position) and rotation, much the same way that you did back in Chapter 6 when you flew the parts of your logo around on the screen. Indeed, if the movements are simple enough, this might be the most economical way of proceeding.

However, in cases where you need repetitive or reusable motions, it is often easier to create and store a library of *actions* that can be applied over and over to any model with similarly named components. This is perfect for character rigs that retain the same names on all of their bones and control objects, with only the model name at the top of the hierarchy being unique.

You may have noticed that there were a few hand poses stored for the generated rig when you were playing around in the synoptic view. These still poses, as well as any animation sequences and shape targets, are stored in the mixer that is part of your model. If you save actions or shapes on an object that is not part of a specific model, they are stored in the mixer under the scene root, which is also a model. Therefore, if you want a unique set of actions to be associated with a specific character, make sure that the components of that character, its rig, and its controls are all part of a model. See Figure 8.12.

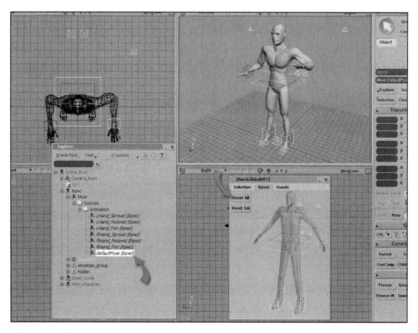

Figure 8.12 *Making the components of a rig part of the model.*

Building a Library of Actions

1. Open an Explorer window.

2. Change the filter to Objects Only, and then open the filter menu again to add Mixers.

3. Open the mixer for the biped rig and navigate to the animation folder. Inside you will find the hand positions, as well as the default (reset) position for the rig.

4. Try selecting one of these actions in the Explorer, and then choose Actions > Apply > Actions in the Animation module.

   You will see the action applied to the rig. This is a bit clumsy, so you will use the Animation Mixer to apply your actions on specific frames and blend between them as necessary. Using the Animation Mixer is somewhat like using a non-linear editing system. You can lay tracks of animation or stills on top of each other and fade or cut between them. This ability to reuse actions also means that you only need to create the animation or the pose once. So take your time. Do it right the first time and you will be rewarded.

5. Let's start by simply saving some poses of your own. You already have a default pose (the reset), so save one of your own for practice.

6. Reset the rig in its default "T" position, branch-select the biped rig, and choose Actions > Store > Transformations Current Values. Since this was a static pose, there was no reason to save F-curves.

7. Just to make sure it worked, open the mixer for Biped Rig and look under Animations. Sure enough, you have added your first action clip.

8. Repeat this procedure a few more times to save a few more interesting poses, like head turn, hands down, or leg lift. It's totally up to you. Just move the control objects until you have the pose that you want, and select Save > Transformations Current Values.

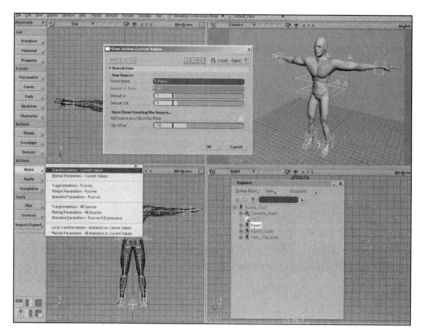

Figure 8.13 *Storing the current values.*

9. Reset the character, and you will now create an animated action clip.

   One nice thing about the default rig is that it constrains the feet separately from the hips. This allows you to move the body up in the air while the feet and toes continue to point down, as they do when someone is actually hopping.

10. Press the V key to enter translation mode.

11. Select the larger of the two squares at the character's waist (biped upper body). Make sure that you are on frame 1, and press K or click the keyframe icon in the timeline to set a key.

12. Move to frame 10, and pull the upper body control down in y so that the character is crouching.

13. Save a key.

14. Move to frame 15. Pull the upper body control up in y so that the feet are off the floor (you decide how high).

15. With the key on frame 20, position the character back in a knees-bent posture.

16. Save a key.

17. Finally, duplicate Frame 1 at Frame 30 (middle-mouse drag from 1 to 30) and save a key.

    Now that you have a 30-frame animation of your character hopping up in the air from a neutral start position, you will turn it into an animated action.

18. Return to Frame 1 if you are not already there. Choose Action > Store > Transformations F-Curves.

19. In the PPG that appears, make sure that *Remove original animation* is checked and *Add source as clip in mixer* is unchecked.

20. Give it a clever name and click OK.

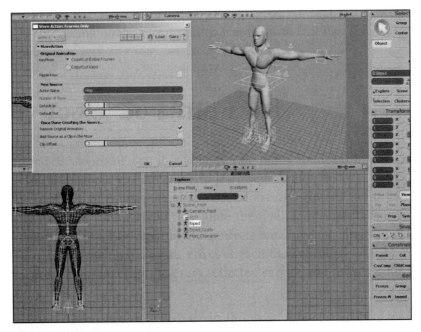

Figure 8.14 *Storing the F-Curves.*

Now for the fun part . . .

21. Press Alt+0 (zero) to open the animation editor. Make sure that the mixer says Biped Mixer in the title bar.

If you don't have anything selected when you open a mixer, you might open the scene root mixer by accident. You should see two empty green animation tracks.

If you want to add more tracks, you can press Shift+A.

22. To insert one of the action clips that you just saved, right-click in one of the animation tracks, choose Insert Source, and pick an action. Once an action is on an animation track, it can be scaled or cycled.

23. For even more control, right-click over your clip and choose Clip Properties. Here you can precisely control the trimming and offset, or you can specify the interpolation before and after the clip begins. The handles appear at the top, middle, and bottom of the clip ends.

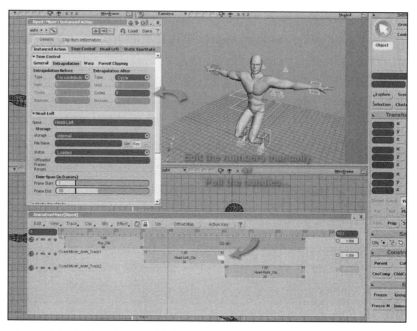

Figure 8.15 *Using the Biped Mixer.*

If you push or pull on the middle handle, you will cause the clip to scale.

If you pull on the top handles, the default behavior is to hold.

If you pull on the bottom handles, the clip will cycle. These default behaviors can be overridden in the Clip Property PPG.

It is important to remember that each clip in the animation editor is an instance of the original. When you change the behavior of one of these clips, you are not affecting the original source.

If, however, you right-click on a clip and select Animation Editor, you will open the F-Curve editor for the original source clip, and any changes you make will be permanent. See Figure 8.16.

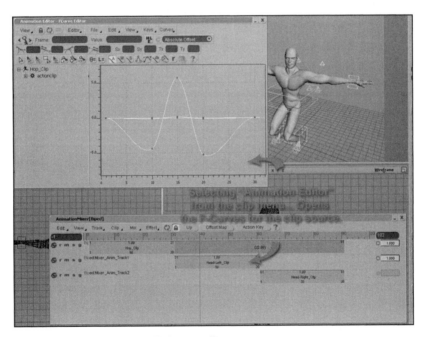

Figure 8.16 *Viewing the F-Curve editor.*

What's Next?

You've now completed all the exercises on bones and skeletons. You now have enough information and experience to try more things on your own, or to search the Internet for new tutorials using this powerful set of character manipulation tools.

As you complete these learning exercises, you should be assembling some of the best examples of your work into a showreel, duplicating your resume, and making lots of sales calls. If so, you should now be pretty close to getting an appointment with a person who can change your future.

Therefore, it's now time for this book to turn your attention back to the business of animation, specifically how to handle that all-important, face-to-face meeting with an employer or client.

If you thought bones and skeletons was challenging, you will now learn how to keep your own knees from knocking as you master the art of "making a pitch."

Chapter 9

Showtime! Presentations to Employers and Clients

In this chapter, you learn how to make an effective presentation of your work to a prospective employer or client.

Up until now in this book, your goals as an animator have been along two tracks: building your animation skills and building your business. Both of these tracks come together when you are called upon to present your capabilities to an employer or client.

In such a meeting, complete strangers try to decide how appropriate you are to their needs. Such meetings last 10 to 30 minutes, sometimes longer. The result of such a meeting could be a full-time job that may last you several years, or a contract that could involve many thousands of dollars. When you think about it, 10 to 30 minutes is not a fair amount of time for someone to make a decision of such magnitude.

A lot of criteria must be included in the decision-making process. These criteria include your animation skills, as demonstrated on your reel; the rarity of the skills you offer in your geographic area, as compared to other vendors the interviewer knows; your likeability, as demonstrated by your speech and manners; your exploitability, as demonstrated by your sophistication and eagerness; your loyalty, as demonstrated by the tales you tell and other subtle hints; and finally, the level of trust you generate, as demonstrated by all of the above.

Out of all these criteria, the most critical is trust. After a client has reviewed dozens of candidates for a project, your skills, rarity, likeability, exploitability, and loyalty might be second-rate, but if the first-rated animator is not considered trustworthy, you could get the job. Likeability is the second most important trait, because everyone wants to enjoy their work. Given a choice, a boss would rather surround herself with people she likes and trusts than with people who are skillful, pliable, and loyal.

Your goal in any meeting, therefore, is to convince the interviewer that you are an individual who can be trusted. You can be trusted to deliver what you promise, trusted not to get yourself or anyone else into trouble, and trusted not to steal software, equipment, money, or worst of all, a client. The most obvious method of generating trust, as you might guess, is being trustworthy. But, as rare as the pure attainment of this attribute may be, being trustworthy may not be enough. The interviewer has to *see* your trustworthiness in the brief span of 10-30 minutes.

You might think what I am going to say next is extremely cynical, but read carefully for a moment. As a beginner to the business, what does the adjective "trustworthiness" actually mean? Have you been around long enough to have your boss's client offer you a job? Has a client proposed that you pay him some cash in order to win a bid (also known as a *kickback*)? Have you had to decide between going hungry and doing something unethical to earn money to survive? Have you worked at a facility long enough to be tempted to copy a costly plug-in and install it on your computer at home? Probably not.

You have not been seriously tempted by the Devil, so can you truly say that you are trustworthy? No. That's why it's relatively easy for a novice to *appear* trustworthy. In fact, the very essence of being a novice—your fresh naïve charm, your youth, the sparkle in your eyes—give the strongest evidence of your trustworthiness, but that's the problem. No one can really rely on a novice's trust, because a novice hasn't been tested! Consequently, a really savvy interviewer will be looking for subtle ways to test your honesty. For instance, nearly everyone lies about their height, and even more lie about their weight. Ever notice how so many job applications have Height and Weight blanks to fill in? That's why.

Other subtle questions that will come up in a job interview, questions about your sports activities, current events, animation technology, even the act of filling out the "time you arrived" blank at the reception desk, all provide valuable clues to your integrity. These are the first and often the most important tests in the evaluation process.

Later, when you are a seasoned pro, you will be able to demonstrate your honesty in many sincere and powerful ways. In New York City, for instance, there was an advertising executive who was famous for only giving projects to people who paid him significant bribes. Every savvy employer in New York knew this man's reputation. So in a job interview, if anyone asked you if you'd worked for this man, the honest applicant's answer was, "I never seemed to win any of his bids." But, being a novice, you haven't yet gained such experience, so proving your trustworthiness depends on your basic instincts. Examine your instincts long before you make your first appointment. If they are not inbred in you, if you need to keep them in mind in order not to give the wrong impression, by all means, keep them in mind. Stay truthful at all costs.

Making the Appointment

Sooner or later, your diligent telephone sales efforts are going to pay off, and you will be granted an appointment to show your work. An appointment consists of six agreements that you must make with your prospect. These agreements are person, location, agenda, time, equipment, and date (PLATED).

You may find yourself making an appointment with a secretary or administrative assistant. Although most artists avoid the grievous mistake of assuming the appointment is with the assistant, many do not ask for the full names of the people who will be attending the meeting. If you are not speaking with the person with whom you will be meeting, it is polite to ask, "Can you please give me the full names and titles of the people with whom I will be meeting?"

Many times you will set up an appointment with one person, not knowing that two or more people will be attending the meeting. Other times, the other people will be implied, such as when someone says, "Let's meet with my team on Tuesday." It's your duty to find out how many people are on the team and what their names are. This is important for many reasons. You may be planning on showing your reel using a laptop, which would be impractical for six people to watch at once. You may wish to bring a brochure for each individual. If you are really smart, you may want to memorize the name and title of each person who will be attending so that when you are introduced, you can address each person appropriately. This makes a powerfully professional impression.

Before the Appointment

Hey, I'm curious here. When you read this heading, "Before the Appointment," what was your immediate impression of the word "Before?" To you, does this mean the time between parking your car and entering the client's building? Or maybe an hour before? No, no, my friend. I mean the *night* before.

The "morning of" is too late to prepare for a meeting—even if the meeting is after noon. Too many things happen the day of a meeting that it's too late to prepare effectively. These are the things you should do the night before you have an important meeting:

1. Confirm the meeting the night before, or, failing that, just before you leave to go to the meeting:

   Date, time, and place

   Names and titles of people who will attend

   What you are expected to present (based on the host's needs)

2. Set aside what you will wear.

3. Gather everything you will need in one place:

   Brochures and business cards

   Datebook, notebook, and two pens or pencils (one to give to your host if needed)

   Showreel, DVD, videocassette, portfolio

   Method of presentation (computer, DVD player, monitor)

   Directions to the location (dictated by a representative of the host *and* verified with Mapquest)

   Car keys, tokens, tickets, eyeglasses, breath fresheners

4. Assemble any notes or files you already have on the contact (from previous phone calls and research).

5. Rehearse your performance.

In the Sam Peckinpah movie *The Killer Elite*, the CIA freelancer George Hansen (Robert Duvall) proclaims, "Proper preparation prevents piss-poor performance." By following this credo, Hansen stays alive in the people-killing business. You should follow it to stay alive in the animation business, because even animators die a thousand ugly deaths after bombing a job opportunity that otherwise would have been in the bag. Believe me, I know.

One other thing before the meeting: Plan on arriving 15 minutes early. If you plan on that and arrive late, you might be just in time. If you show up 30 minutes early, it will look like you're too eager and don't have anywhere else to be. (And you do, because you are a very busy animator, right?) Go get a soda or something to use up 15 minutes.

If you're really going to be late, call ahead and warn your host. (This is one of the only good reasons I know to own a cell phone. It doesn't have to have a fancy ring-tone or video camera built in.) Offer to postpone the meeting. If the host says it's okay to come late, be sure to apologize as soon as you arrive and say something like, "I hope I didn't ruin your whole day's schedule." By making your error sound worse than it could be, your host will be prompted to make it sound like less than it is. This is halfway to your host *believing* that it's less of a problem than it really is, but this only gets you off the hook one time. Try never to be late, even though it's fashionable for creative people to screw up the normal, everyday parts of life. Like going to meetings on time.

Matters of Respect

In this age, when respect is frequently forced out of someone through the barrel of a loaded pistol, it is difficult to describe how it used to be "back in the day." Real respect is something that someone earns through a combination of hard work and humility. Anyone worth meeting at a job or client interview can be assumed to be worthy of your respect. Even if they have not truly earned it, you can best assume that giving it will be appreciated.

In a professional encounter, one shows respect through actions and appearances. As I write this, these suggestions read like utterly simple kinds of things, but I fear that many people entering the professional marketplace today may not have been exposed to them. I'm embarrassed to say that in my own middle class, professional family, I meet nephews and nieces in their teens and twenties who appear never to have been instructed in the simple common courtesies of respectful social interaction. Their parents, well-bred and respectful, seem never to have introduced their children to the skills that so effectively underscored their own rise to success.

I don't know how this came to be. I have noticed that hip-hop culture is full of behavioral codes that are directly opposite what I suggest here. "Giving eyeball," never smiling, and maintaining a tough exterior are all traits of the streets. But in seeking employment and contracts, we are departing the streets for a more cultured and polite environment. There's nothing wrong with being street-smart and surviving, but many of the survival necessities of the street work just the opposite in business. Therefore, I will impart a few simple instructions and the theory of respect behind them, hoping that it will make the difference between your success and failure. If you find these comments redundant due to your fine upbringing, I offer my apologies in advance.

Maintain Eye Contact

When you meet someone new, look him or her directly in the eyes and maintain eye contact. There is a powerful cultural assumption that the eyes are the windows to the soul. Many people claim to be able to determine whether they like people by looking them directly in the eyes. If you look away from a person when you are supposed to be communicating with them, you are making a powerful statement that you are not to be trusted. You are also denying yourself the opportunity of looking into your future employer's or client's eyes and seeing if they are willing to be open to you.

Smile

First, smiling makes you look happy. If you are a happy person, others may surmise that you are successful. If you are successful, you are not desperately looking for work or contracts, but instead are assumed to be offering your service as a courtesy. This is precisely the right image for getting work at the highest possible price.

Second, smiling makes other people happy. If the person you're meeting feels happier when you enter the room, you and what you offer will be more desirable.

Shake Hands Firmly

Always seek opportunities to shake hands, and do so with a firm conviction that you are enjoying the physical contact. Don't try to squeeze the life out of the person's hand, but offer as you receive. Any kind of socially accepted physical touch, skin-to-skin, creates a favorable impression.

An interesting experiment was done once. People were placed in situations where they appeared to need help—a flat tire, needing a quarter to make a call, and so on. When the requester touched the person while asking for the favor, it was granted 50% more often than when the person was not touched. And the research showed that almost any kind of touch, from a tap on the shoulder to a full handshake, was enough to make the difference.

The custom of shaking hands (and the custom is to use the right hand only) derives from ancient warriors showing their trust for one another by sheathing their swords and extending their naked sword hands in greeting. Today, the custom survives as a sign of trust, friendship, and mutual respect.

Make Introductions

If you come to a meeting with other people in your group, introduce them to your prospect in order of respect. This means that women are introduced before men, and older people are introduced before younger ones (a younger woman before an older man, by the way). No meeting should begin without everyone being introduced. If your host fails to show this courtesy, you may politely ask to be introduced by extending your right hand to the person and saying, "I'm sorry, we haven't met. My name is . . ."

Excuse Yourself

Anytime something accidental happens that may be embarrassing to you or another person, two simple words work wonders: "Excuse me." You might need to squeeze past another person in a small meeting place. You might spill a bit of coffee. You might even let a small burp slip past your lips. Simply excuse yourself and move on. No big deal. Everyone is human, but acknowledging your mistake with a simple request to be excused is expected and appreciated.

There are many more of these simple courtesies that you can learn about in any book on etiquette. Take the time to learn them, especially if you plan to have lunch with a boss or client or spend more than a few minutes with them.

Dressing to Show Respect

As strange as it may seem to you, the way you dress for a meeting can show or deny respect, and can have a great deal to do with the success of the meeting. Back in the day, it used to be easy to dress correctly: a simple dark suit, white shirt, and plain tie for men, and a dark dress, low heels, and string of pearls for women. You would never show up at a job interview in athletic shoes, a t-shirt, jeans, or with uncombed hair! Tattoos were strictly low-class, and anything but pierced earlobes for a woman were unheard of. If a person didn't dress according to these customs, the host would be very offended! Imagine not getting a job because you wore flip-flop sandals to the interview? I hate to tell you this, but even today, it happens sometimes.

The reason that appearance is important in an interview is that a lot of decisions have to be made about you in a small amount of time, with very little evidence. Let's say you have to meet 50 people this week and decide which one you are going to trust with your future success. And each meeting is going to take 20 minutes, tops. Assuming you have to choose one person to hire out of the 50 you meet, you could say that your task requires you to identify 25 important traits and rank them for each individual. That would mean that you'd have about a minute per trait in each interview. That's mind-boggling, but interviewers do this all the time. They do it by—may I use the word—*profiling*.

The first level of profiling is based on your appearance. *Do you look like me?*, thinks the interviewer. If so, that's good. *Do you look like I expect you to look?* That's good too. If you don't fit either of these criteria, you start to drop down the ladder. Old-looking clothes? One rung down. Sloppy dresser? Two rungs down. No deodorant? Ten rungs down.

Animators, however, belong to a special class of job and contract seekers. We combine nerdiness and hipness into a new social class that defies both convention and courtesy when it comes to clothing and hygiene. As long as you don't actually smell bad, you can get away with pretty much anything—and sometimes you can even get a job *because* you wear a tongue stud. This is because most interviewers are expecting weird-looking people when they open the door to creative types. Often, the interviewers are animators or creative people themselves, in which case *Do you look like me?* is a no-brainer. One animator told me he recently won a contract because the client liked his eyebrow stud.

Me? I get squeamish at the sight of a nostril stud. I can't bear to watch a person's reel if I'm consumed by thoughts of how excruciating it would be to get my tongue split in two. Tip: If you come to Avekta to pitch me your work, think about what it was like back in the day, and be kind. You may find yourself interviewing with guys older than 40. Dig it. They usually have the most money to spend, and the button for the green light is close at hand. Guys over 40 have different rules for being hip. Find them out, and do what's expected of you if you want to pitch winning deals.

And how about us old guys? What do we do when we go out to interview for a job? Well, we come from a time when there were only two kinds of people: straights and freaks. Creatives were usually freaks. I'm definitely a freak, but I dress straight, which today is the freakiest of all: a $2,000 custom-tailored suit. Sometimes I drive my vintage Ferrari to the meeting (the ultimate freak-straight twist). I pull out a Mont Blanc pen and a leather-bound notebook, and I carefully listen to the parameters. Then I pitch the weirdest concepts the client has ever heard, and watch the slow burn of recognition as they think, "A-ha, he's a super freak down *inside*."

If you want to flaunt your creative nature, do so by all means, but just be sure that the person you are meeting is in the loop on what creative people are like today. For example, if you are an animator from Tribeca in New York City, and you're going out to meet a client in Sweetwater, Texas, chances are your client is going to have radically different expectations than a client in a Madison Avenue ad agency.

Showing respect in your appearance and behavior means, very simply, looking and acting like your host expects you to look and act. A little weirdness, a bit of surprise is fine, but too much will make the host uncomfortable. This is disrespectful on your part, and you, not the host, will pay the price eventually.

The Meeting

As noted earlier, the typical animator/employer or animator/client meeting will last 10 to 30 minutes. The basic, underlying purpose of the meeting is so that the prospective employer or client will get to know and like you. However, as you gain more experience, you will also begin to use such meetings to get to know your potential employer or client. Consequently, you will appear to have more experience, and hence more value, if you give the impression that you are indeed politely examining the other person while he is examining you! After all, the best, most in-demand creative people are highly selective. Often the initial meeting is as much "Do I want to work for you?" as "Do I want you working for me?"

If you feel comfortable with it, feel free to ask questions of the host and make the information exchange a two-way street. Under such conditions, the interaction will be more of a meeting of respectful equals than peon-to-king.

Here is the agenda for a typical meeting. (Typical for the United States, that is. If you're an international reader, you may find a U.S. business meeting to be a very aggressive, impolite, and invasive encounter. Meetings like this would never take place in Japan or the Middle East, and might even be considered far too aggressive for the UK and most of Europe. Americans are foremost in the world for getting down to business and making money as fast as possible. Elsewhere, much more time is taken, and each minute of the typical U.S. meeting might represent weeks, months, or years in other cultures.)

Light, Introductory Chit-Chat (3-5 Minutes)

You meet in the lobby and are led to the meeting room. Perhaps you set up your computer or the conference room's VCR. During this time, you engage the host in some pleasant conversation. Most commonly, the opening regards the weather, your drive to the location, the nice office. But you can also delve deeper.

If you are in a personal space, like an office, look at the decorations. Often a host will decorate the office with cues for conversation. A painting of a sailboat might invite an inquiry about weekend activities. A photo of children is always an invitation to talk about family. A trophy prompts game details. You get the point. Pick up on these cues, and engage the client in some light personal conversation that highlights the similarities between your lives.

If you sail or have kids or have competed in trophy sports, you are on your way to bonding with the host and forming a lasting relationship built on common interests. If, however, nothing in the room corresponds with something from your own life, let these cues be an opportunity to learn. Never been sailing? Say, "Wow, you sail? I've always wanted to do that. What's it like?" The interest you will fire up in your host might form a stronger bond than if you'd skippered a win in last year's SORC race. You might even get invited to a fun weekend outing.

The purpose of this initial chit-chat is to lay the foundation for a warehouse of knowledge in which we hope to do business with your contact. If that foundation is built carefully and mutually, the rest of the building—the meeting—will be built with little effort.

Keep in mind that the cues you find in the meeting place may be of little or great importance. You might be meeting in a very sterile room, designed specifically to deprive you of cues. You might be meeting in someone else's office, where the cues will be totally wrong for your host! On the other hand, on rare occasions, you might be meeting in the virtual "house of worship" for your host, where every object opens up vast caverns of profound concern.

I once commented on a cute child's photo, only to be told that the child had recently died of cancer. Another time, my reel, which features a clip from one of the first documentaries on Alzheimer's disease, left my client in tears, remembering her recently deceased mother.

On such occasions, you have to apply the right degree of empathy, direct from your heart, and hope your efforts are received in kind. The people you will meet are living, breathing individuals, as complex and engaged in life as you. Sometimes, touching the deepest part of someone else during something as mundane as a job interview can truly mess up an otherwise successful meeting. Other times, it can be the start of a wonderful friendship. That's the risk we Americans take when we jump into business as quickly and deeply as we do. That's why this part of the agenda is called "light chit-chat." It's not a shrink's encounter session.

Needs-Capabilities Discussion (5-10 Minutes)

Once you've warmed up the relationship a bit, it's customary to start moving the conversation around to the task at hand, reviewing your capabilities as an employee or vendor. Usually, your host will initiate this change in topic, and you can sit back and learn how good an interviewer your host is by how smooth she segues into it. If she is skillful, the segue will probe your capabilities. This puts you at a slight disadvantage but allows the host to run the show, which is the polite thing to do.

If the host doesn't make a segue to the needs-capabilities discussion after 3-5 minutes of chit-chat, or if the host sits back and waits for you to drive the agenda, you need to make a move.

I prefer to see if the host will open up with her needs first. If I already know what those needs are, I can structure my presentation specifically to address them. You might follow the same path, once your presentation develops to the point where you can modify it on a moment's notice. But if all you have is one presentation, it doesn't matter who goes first, as long as you get a chance to demonstrate your capabilities. Don't expect this to happen automatically. I've gone to meetings where the client talked for an hour and never asked to see my work!

If you're going to take the lead, you might ask something like, "So how long have you been working here at XYZ Company?" Don't ask, "Would you like to see my brochure/resume?" That will move the discussion into your capabilities before you know what the host's needs are. I like to ask, "So what is your mission or goal here at XYZ Company?" This moves the conversation to the host's priorities and needs. My brother, a major client, likes his vendors to ask, "What keeps you up at night?" Not that my brother has a hard time sleeping, but he wants vendors who are passionate about solving his production problems. So you might also ask, "What are you currently missing in the capabilities of your vendors?"

Such questions may cause your contact to sit back and hesitate for a moment. These questions are very professional and get to the heart of the matter in a way that not too many novices use. You can tell you've hit the professional sweet spot when the employer or client adjusts his posture, moves some things on the desk out of the way, or leans forward and starts to get really serious and says something like, "Let me tell you what I need."

You'd be very surprised to learn how few of your competitors know how to use the word "you" in a pitch meeting. Instead, they dwell too long on the "me" things. No one really wants to know about *you*. They really want to tell you about *themselves*. The sooner you can get them to do this, the better. And as long as they talk, listen.

So here's the key: Concentrate on the "you." "What are *your* problems? What is *your* mission? What do *you* want from a vendor? How can I help *you*?"

Once your host has spent 5-10 minutes talking about his needs, he should wind down a bit and look to you for a response. That's your opening to start matching what you have heard with what you are going to say; what he needs with what you can deliver.

Then it's your turn to talk. You have about 5-10 minutes, not including your showreel or portfolio. If the host has gone first and listed needs, be sure to summarize those needs. If you can, match each need to a capability you offer. For instance, if the host says, "I really need someone who can do high-definition animation," and you've done that, you can say, "You mentioned needing HD animation capability, and I'm happy to say that I spent two years at Hodgepodge Lodge doing tons of HD production." Don't say more unless prompted, because the less you say and the more you show, the better. That is, you want to *demonstrate* your HD samples on the reel. The reel is truth. Talk is cheap.

If you don't have much experience yet—and what novice does—review the needs that the host has enumerated and express a sincere interest in helping out with them. You might say something like, "I really appreciate that you want to have better-looking characters in your films, and that has always been my direction in animation school. Great characters are the most important part of a successful production." Most of the time, you can make a great impression just by demonstrating that you listen and understand what you're told. This alone may mark you as a leading intern or assistant animator, which will get you in the door.

Whether the host's needs come first or your capabilities come first, remember that unless you match the two, you have not completed your mission. All too often, a candidate simply shows his reel and says goodbye, never inquiring what the host is looking for. Maybe your reel is totally inappropriate to the client's needs. If so, you'll never know unless you ask.

The Showreel (or Portfolio) Presentation

Now that you've discussed both the needs of the client and your own capabilities, it's time for you to prove you've got what you say you've got. We've already discussed the theory and method of assembling the best examples and arranging them for the most effective results, but there is also an art to presenting the reel or portfolio in an interesting way.

Obviously, a portfolio is going to require a bit more showmanship than a motion picture reel, since the portfolio doesn't come with a soundtrack. For portfolio presentations, I like to create a little story for each significant piece of work. These stories are flexible, always designed to match the artistic capability with an anticipated need of the client. After a few presentations, you will get a feel for what needs come up most frequently, and you can script a story to match.

For instance, "meeting a tight deadline" is one need that is often mentioned, so I have at least one superb work example that was done on an incredibly short deadline. I even ask the clients how long they think the job took, and when they say 2 or 3 months, I tell them the job took 15 working days and came in under budget. That fills one need really neatly.

If you can prepare three or four little 30-second tales that demonstrate your humble ability to make a client look good (notice the "you" quality in this challenge), and you can match the stories up with a specific work piece, you are having steak for dinner tonight.

With showreels, it can be tricky to tell stories while the video is playing. Animation reels are tight little constructions that are best left alone to do their work. However, a client may go so far as to pause a reel, or pose questions after the reel has shown. In such cases, it pays to have your responses ready. If a short introduction is followed by longer examples of work, and the client takes the time to watch these with you, stories can work wonders. However, you must watch your host's eyes when you begin. If the host's eyes move away from the screen to look into your eyes (women seem to do this more than men), you've either got to pause the show or stop the story. You don't want the client looking away from the reel!

Now you need to consider some of the differences between showreels and portfolios:

Portfolio

If you're a picture artist and you show your work in a portfolio, be sure to ask permission to use your host's desk or table space before you start unfolding your work. A portfolio requires considerable verbal presentation. Don't just open the book and expect the pictures to do all the work.

Be sure you rehearse your presentation with a friend who knows how to ask tough questions. Rehearse your responses to such common questions as, "How much did you charge for these storyboards?", "How long did it take for you to do this?", and "What did you do on this project?"

If these questions are not forthcoming, you might worry that the host is not properly engaged or sufficiently impressed with your work. That could be her fault or yours. Time will tell. If every client or employer you meet looks at your portfolio and doesn't ask a question, something is definitely wrong.

Make sure that your work examples are firmly attached to their respective pages. Nothing says "amateur" more than a portfolio that starts coming apart and spilling all over the floor.

Sometimes a client or employer will ask you to leave your portfolio, ostensibly to present it to someone else—a boss or client. This is a tough choice. It deprives you of making another presentation, and you are never sure just what is going to be done with your portfolio while you aren't around. I've been at meetings where other people's portfolios were used to show me what I was expected to produce. That's not fair, but it happens.

On the other hand, leaving a portfolio could lead to getting a job or big contract. You have to decide based on what you sense from the host. One way to make this decision easier is to create more than one portfolio. I have four. Of course, you can politely refuse to leave the portfolio, and offer instead to bring it by again at any time.

Either way, make sure you have your name, address, Web site, and phone number featured prominently on the portfolio's face and spine, and on every page if you can manage it. That way, when your portfolio is shown to anyone (or if you misplace it!), your name will always be seen.

And if you decide to leave the portfolio with someone, make sure you know when and how you will get it back. And then, at the agreed time, get it back.

Showreel

Back in the day when VHS tapes were the best way to show your work, the worst part of a presentation was when you had to put the tape into your host's VCR and adjust the monitor. I am convinced that the Japanese have never designed two VCRs with the same controls. I think they actually have machines that randomly insert the Play and Eject buttons in a different place on each and every VCR. After 10,000 presentations, finally I learned to give my host my brochure just before I went to set up the playback. This way, when I had to go on my hands and knees searching for a jack or plug, the host was looking elsewhere!

Now that most presentations are made on a laptop or DVD player that you bring to the meeting, there is very little time wasted on setup. Maybe if your battery is low, you have to take a moment to find an AC socket, or you have to wait for the operating system to initiate. If so, this is always a good time to hand over your resume or company literature. When you're ready to start the show, look up and wait for eye contact.

Another trick I like to use employs a really clean and shiny computer screen. Angle the screen so that you can see the host's reflection in it. While the host is watching the show, you can pretend to be doing the same thing, but actually you're watching the host's expression. You can learn a lot by noticing at what precise moment the eyes look away (and how often). This is where your reel might need tightening.

Always rehearse a reel with a tough, honest friend before you take it on the road. Spouses especially—that is, your own spouse—have an uncanny ability to spot weaknesses in your reel and ask questions that make you stutter. Be sure to practice putting the showreel on pause, jogging it back and forth to specific scenes. Do this at home, long before you are tempted to do this for a stranger. I have never seen a computer DVD utility that worked with me while pausing and shuttling through a presentation. This skill takes considerable practice, or you end up crashing and needing to reboot. (Yes, Mac fans, this is a chance to rub it in, but don't cast the first stone unless you're free of guilt.) Also know where the volume control is on your machine and how to adjust it quickly.

Often, hosts will offer you their own presentation hardware to show your reel, especially if the presentation is for two or more people. It's hard to show a reel to five people on a 15" laptop screen! If this is the case, it pays to prepare the equipment ahead of time. The best way is to speak to the host's administrative assistant and arrange to get into the presentation room about 15 minutes ahead of the appointed time (that is, 30 minutes before the meeting is scheduled to begin).

You also have the option of hooking up your own laptop to the host's projector. Be sure to bring the appropriate monitor cables and an assortment of adapters, especially for the audio output of your laptop. I have yet to walk into a host presentation and manage to get the audio working through the host's amplifier and speakers! Luckily, my laptop has a pretty loud internal playback, but it's never quite as good as having the stereo coming out of the house speakers.

You can put all these wires and adapters into a pouch of your computer's carrying case and take them wherever you go. All you need to do is practice the setup once on your home entertainment system, and you'll have all the experience you need. Take two of everything, and make sure you have both RCA and 1/4" male output adapters to fit into whatever the host system has.

As a courtesy, don't forget to restore the host's playback system the way you found it. (Most likely tuned to a popular soap opera channel.)

After the Showreel (or Portfolio)

Once the presentation of your work is over, your host will most likely wind down the meeting and make motions to get you out the door. This is normal. Expect no more than five minutes of summation time, during which you should accomplish three major tasks. I call these the *wrap-up tasks*:

1. Ask how the host liked your work.
2. Ask what projects the host has planned, or what jobs the host is trying to staff.
3. Ask how often and by what means you should continue to make contact.

"How Did You Like My Work?"

Once upon a time, there was a very popular mayor of New York City named Ed Koch. (I never thought he was a good mayor. I nearly killed him once in Forest Hills when he stepped from his campaign RV right in front of my truck, but that's another story.) Mayor Koch was famous for standing up in front of crowds and yelling, "How am I doin'?" Maybe no one had anything good to say, but they appreciated the humility of this guy. At least he took an interest in getting a fair appraisal of his performance.

You can learn something from Ed Koch. After all, he was reelected three times and retired by choice. If the mayor of America's greatest city can ask, "How am I doin'?", so can you. When the reel is over, simply turn to your host and ask. Just be prepared for honest answer. You may get BS, but you may also get some valuable input. And sometimes, the guileless humility of asking this can endear you to a client or employer who might not think much of you otherwise.

Not too long ago, I asked a potential client what he thought of my reel, and he told me with a straight face that it stank! I asked him why. He said that all my graphics sucked. Now, I make no claim to be a graphic designer. In fact, I do stink in this category, but until that individual made his appraisal, I never gave the graphics on my reel that much thought. After all, I'm a motion picture guy. Who gives a Cracker Jack engagement ring what the graphics look like? Well, this guy did.

So I went home and polished up the graphics. Then I sent the reel back to the guy and asked him what he thought. He still hated the graphics. But he gave me an assignment. He liked the results, too, because he recommended me to others in his company. Today, I get a good, steady income from this firm. However, the original client won't let me do any graphics on any of the company's projects! He insists on me sending the video and animations to his office, where his staff adds the graphics and sends the master back to me.

Now, this is a pretty radical example of the principle I am trying to teach here, but heck, I've had my share of interesting experiences in my 25 years on the path to pixel perfection, and this one teaches a good lesson. Ask for an honest opinion, and if you can't measure up after giving it your best effort, be honest about it. Often, your client will go more than halfway to meet you and help you along. And that effort on your client's part, while not motivated by your excellence, is sometimes the very human touch that builds a long-term, mutually respectful relationship.

"What Kind of Work Do You Have Coming Up?"

This is the question to ask if you are an independent animator looking for a production contract. If the response to "How did you like my work?" was favorable, you might ask what sort of production work the host has planned in the next 3 to 6 months. Maybe this will sound a bit presumptuous, as if you've already passed through the "vendor filter" into the sweet water from which bid proposals bubble. Oh, what the heck, *be* presumptuous. After all, the host likes your work. Unless that's a lie (and lots of times it is), it's logical to assume you are now on the "bidder's list." You've done all the client/employer research work, made the calls, got the appointment, showed up on time, and displayed your work, so it's fair to presume that your host has something coming up and that you might be considered for the next assignment. If you don't ask, the host has no obligation to offer, although it's nice to be told you're on the A-list without having to ask. Who knows? Sometimes asking actually gets you considered. That's my feeling, anyway.

If the host has no work coming up, or if your work was not quite up to par, you might be told something vague like, "We're going through a lot of transitions now. The future is a bit unclear, but if we have a need, we'll give you a call." This is a nicer way of saying, "Don't call us, we'll call you."

Don't let that discourage you, however. There are two courses of action based on this response. The first is to wait a few months, and then call the person and say, "I'm just touching base." Listen for the response. Is it encouraging or still vague? Often, when you meet a person, they are not in their best form, and even a perfect presentation will elicit a cool response. If the response is still vague, mark the contact for a one-year delay.

The second course of action is to move on to other clients on your call list. After all, there are hundreds of people to call on any one day, and many, many more people with whom to set appointments. Why waste time on one who didn't like your work?

Sometimes, your presentation is perfect and the host indicates that he would like to engage your services, but that there is no need at the present time. You must ascertain how often the host expects you to stay in touch. Just because you've made a good impression does *not* mean that the host will remember you six months later when he needs an animator just like you. Your job is to call that host at the right time. How will you know what the right time is?

"Will You Have Any Positions Opening Up in the Near Future?"

This is the question to ask if you are looking for a full-time or freelance assignment. Notice that you do not ask if there are any jobs open now. *That* would be presumptuous to the extreme. By placing your inquiry in the future, you are giving your host a way to say "No" without being rude.

Even if the person hated your presentation, he could say, "Yes, probably in about ten years." (As he thinks, *When your reel may have improved to my satisfaction.*) But if the host likes your work, she could say, "Yes, and I would suggest you call me back next week to get you in to see the Human Resources department."

It's often as simple as that. Getting a job is simply a matter of being the right person showing up at the right time. Do your best to become the right person for every employer, and then make lots and lots of appointment calls. Your chances of being there at the right time will increase significantly over all the other "right people" who are competing for the job.

If you get a response somewhere in-between these extremes, don't be discouraged. The host may not have an immediate need, but may be shopping to fill an anticipated need. Good employers, by virtue of their job description, have to be constantly aware of all the available talent in their neighborhood. They do this by frequently making appointments to see people just like you.

Your presentation may be absolutely perfect, and the host may even say so, but that doesn't mean there is an immediate need for you in the company. You may hear something like, "I really like your work, but right now we have no need." In that case, you must establish a comfortable frequency of contact between you and the host. If you are a talent who the host wants to hire someday, you won't be of any service if you call that host before he needs you.

"How Often and By What Means Should I Continue to Make Contact?"

Remember, once you've met with a potential client, that client is now just one short row on the sales pyramid away from giving you a job or a bid. This contact may be one out of hundreds you have called. Unless the person has told you, "Never call me, ever," you have a better chance of making him a client than anyone lower on the pyramid.

Just before you say your thanks and goodbye, you must establish the rules for future contact. I like to say, "I know it's a thin line between being of service and being a pest. So tell me, how often would you like me to call to stay in touch and see if you have any immediate needs?"

This question acknowledges that you are accepting the responsibility of being there at the right time by calling as seldom or as frequently as the contact would like. Some clients are pretty busy and scatterbrained, and they'll forget a good vendor or potential employee like you. These people might want you to call as often as once a month (which is pretty frequent). On the other hand, some people are meticulous record-keepers and remember a meeting with a vendor from 10 years ago as if it happened the day before. Such people may request that you never call them, but sincerely intend to call you when you are needed.

Most clients or employers will give you a schedule that will not annoy them. If you call a few times on that schedule, they will be most impressed with your professionalism.

Other times, the host will hesitate. This is your opportunity to gauge the host's general level of need. The trick is to suggest a time for the next follow-up call, and make it about twice the time you expect to hear. If you think the person will want you to call in two months, say, "How about if I call you in four months?" This may prompt the person to react with a shorter time, sometimes much shorter. I have often said, "How about six months?", and the prospect answers, "Heavens, no. Call me next month! We have annual marketing videos to do then."

Somehow, the host is psychologically motivated to correct your estimation in your favor. It's like when you make a small mistake on the job and apologize with a statement like, "Boy, I bet I ruined the whole job," and the boss says, "Ah, it was nothing. Forget about it." Psychology. It's a wonderful thing.

One way or another, you need to learn when the person would like you to call and how often to call again. Make note of this in your data sheets and day book. Be sure to follow up with each prospect as frequently as required. Eventually, you will extract from this person a job offer or a bid request.

Often, the host may refer you to other people. If this happens in the meeting, do not be shy about asking the host to spell the names fully and to give you their titles and phone numbers. You may think this is an imposition, but the very act of filling in the details helps your host to confirm her trust in you. In many cases, going the extra mile to get the details will propel the host to call the referral herself and say a few nice words on your behalf. Other impediments come from the clients themselves.

Of course, you should always have a pad and pen handy to take down these very valuable bits of information. Imagine how bad it would look if you had to ask the host for a pad or pencil to write down her references? Yes, but not as bad as struggling to remember this information because you forgot your tools. If you forget a pad and pen, just ask. Everybody's human, and if you're suitably humble, the host will help you out with a smile.

Ending the Meeting

By all means, it is your obligation to know when the meeting should be brought to a close and to start closing it. Do not linger so long that your host starts to give you signals, such as an obvious examination of the wristwatch. You have an agenda that should last between 10 and 20 minutes. Stick to it. Once you have shown your reel or portfolio and accomplished the three wrap-up tasks, it's time for you to get back on the road.

There may be impediments to getting out the door. One is your own ego. You may think you've botched up some part of the presentation, so you linger and attempt to undo the damage. No. If you've mangled your hand, put it in your pocket to hide the blood and get out of there.

Another ego issue arises if you think you did a fantastic job, and you want to stick around to bathe in the glow of admiration. Again, no. Leave them wanting more. They will call you.

Making a great presentation is a tricky balance between ego and necessity. You obviously have to activate and demonstrate your ego, or you would not have what it takes to make the presentation in the first place! And yet, during the whole ordeal, you cannot appear to be so full of yourself that the host will hate you. This is why many successful artists have representatives. A representative can say, "Joe is a genius." *You* cannot say, "I am a genius." A famous actor once got the best of both worlds by calling clients and pretending he was his own agent. "This guy is brilliant. Meet him tomorrow." And then he'd go to the meeting and act very shy and humble. It worked, but now the guy spends a lot on therapy to glue the parts of himself back together!

The best way to control your ego, without going nuts, is to set a strict limit to the amount of time you spend with a prospect and adhere to a performance agenda that gets you out the door while the host still wants more of you.

The way to do this is to start initiating your "departure activities"—packing up your laptop and other presentation tools as you continue to talk with the host. You can ask the questions that complete your wrap-up tasks while you do this. It tells your host that you are getting ready to leave. You can also simply start thanking the host for his or her time and "kind consideration of your efforts." If your thanks is appropriately humble, the host may offer some helpful criticism of your work or even compliment you, if no criticism is required. Both kinds of response are good, because they bond the host to you socially in a way the host will remember. Being remembered is important when work or bids are to be distributed by the host.

An aware host will complement your departure activities with similar actions like rising from behind the desk to help you out, or opening up a date book to jot down some notes about when you will call again, things like that. In a few moments you will have everything packed up, and you can extend your hand for a goodbye shake. Sometimes the host will see you out to the exit door, and once again, you can reinforce some of the sales points you made in the meeting. Don't forget to once again thank the host, not only for having you visit, but for the extra courtesy of seeing you out.

Don't forget to thank the host for his or her time. Be gracious. Often, the dona-
tion of time is of significant value, and you should make an effort to acknowledge
this. If it's a Friday, wish your host a good weekend. If you've talked about something significant in the host's personal life, make mention of it to reinforce the
connection. Then get out the door.

Once you are out of there and in a private place, don't forget to make notes on the
meeting. These notes will often capture some valuable piece of information that
you will probably forget if you wait until you get home. Fresh impressions are very
valuable. Write them down and take them home with you for entry into your
database.

When You Hit a Homer

Sometimes, things go so well in a presentation that you can't believe your good
luck. The best of all is when the host comes right out and makes an offer. "Well,
how would you like to come and work for us?" Or, "I have a project that I'd like
you to work on."

This can happen at any time in the meeting. When it does, say, "I really appreciate your offer. Tell me more." Then, shut right up. *Don't talk.* Pull out a pen and
paper, and listen. Take profuse notes. Don't leave anything to memory. Above all
else, don't do any more selling. Selling time is over. You've made the sale—now
you just have to close the deal. This is the home run you've been praying for. Don't
bungle it by continuing to sell.

Once, while I was making a presentation to a potential client, after I'd showed her
my brochure and chatted for a few moments before showing my reel, out of the
blue she said, "You know, we have this video we want to make. The budget is
$50,000, and it has to be 10 minutes long." She went on to tell me other things
about the project: how many days of shooting, where we would have to travel, who
we'd have to interview, the whole nine yards. She all but wrote the check. After
she was finished, she asked if I could write a contract/proposal and have it on her
desk by the end of the week. I said, "Yes. Of course." Satisfied that she had found
her favorite producer and that her deal was closed, she stood up to say goodbye.

Then I said, "Would you like to see my showreel?"

She replied, "Well, yes. I guess so."

And then I showed my reel, which was good. I regaled her with stories about how each production had been made, how we were held in such high regard by our clients, how we had saved everyone money and made the world a safer place for democracy.

When it was all over, I asked her what she thought.

She said, "Feel free to call on me from time to time." We shook hands and I left.

In the parking lot, I thought a lot about the last thing she said: "Feel free to call me from time to time?" That didn't sound like my new client talking to me. It sounded like I'd just made a normal sales call, and the client could now be put in my "Contacted" category. What happened? All the way home I wondered, "Did I screw up the deal?"

Boy, did I rush to finish that contract/proposal before the end of the week. I sent it to the client two days early and followed up with a call to make sure she got it. I got voicemail. Two weeks later, I still got voicemail. I never got the contract. I never spoke with the client again.

The lesson here is simple. The woman had accepted my credentials from the moment I showed her my brochure. She handed me the job. That should have been enough, but no, I had to continue selling her. That's a fatal mistake. It immediately tells the client that you don't know what you are doing. Overselling shows fear instead of generating confidence. It kills deals faster than bad breath. Remember my mistake. When the client opens up the deal, quit selling and close the deal.

In Chapter 11, "RFPs and Bids," I'll show you how to put together a formal proposal. For now, if a client opens up a deal during your presentation, just concentrate on what the host is saying. All the rules of the presentation—the agenda, the schedule, showing the reel—all of them go out the window if you are offered a deal. Just go with the flow. Let the host drive the agenda.

When a Meeting Doesn't End

Here's another interesting true story. I once made a sales call along with an old friend, Dennis, who was a principal in a public relations firm. The prospective client wanted both a PR firm and a production company to handle some new business. Dennis and I often teamed up to offer a combination of services. (You might think of doing this if you have potential clients who could use, say, both animation and Web site design. Keep your eyes open for potential "joint venture" partners who you can trust and with whom you can work to jointly satisfy a customer's needs.)

Dennis and I met with this client, and we made the 20-minute presentation we'd rehearsed. At the end, the client wanted to show us the work *he* had done. This is unusual, but not uncommon. A client may drag out his own showreel of sorts, just to show you what you are expected to create. Sometimes, the client will even tell you who did the work, and what he liked or didn't like about it.

Dennis and I are too nice and too savvy in the business to ever say anything bad about another producer's work. Even if the work we are shown is total crap, we'll say, "That's nice." Then there's the famous, "There's more there than meets the eye," which is a filmmaker's secret code for, "I can't see anything here worth anything."

There are many reasons a client will drag out something to show you and ask your opinion. Sometimes it's the work of his child. Sometimes it's the work of a favorite vendor who someone in the company criticized. Sometimes, as in this case, it's the work of the host! That's why it's good to say nothing unkind.

Then, after the client showed Dennis and me three or four videos, he dragged out some press releases, photographs, press kits, brochures, and whatnot. For each piece, he methodically recounted the production procedures, the original objectives of the project, and how happy everyone in the company was to see the work accomplished. After a while, I began to wonder what this was all about.

I waited for a pause in the client's banter to ask a very important question: "Tell me, Joe, do you have any projects like these ready to go into production in the next month or so?"

The client (his name wasn't really Joe) looked at me a bit strangely and shook his head. "Not right now, but you never know. Things come up all the time here." And then, he continued to show Dennis another brochure his "creative team" had designed. I let the man talk a bit more.

The meeting was now well over one hour. I glanced surreptitiously at my watch, which said 2:30 p.m., and realized the meeting would go until 5:00 if I didn't call it to a close. To Dennis's chagrin, I looked at my watch rather obviously and said, "Geez. Dennis! We have to get over to IBM and meet with Smithers." (Honestly,

I actually made up the name "Smithers," and I'll bet in the entire IBM roster of some 140,000 employees, there isn't a single Smithers.) Dennis, being young but very cool, understood I was concocting an excuse to call the meeting to an end. He nodded, and with apologetic reluctance, he started helping me pack up our goods.

Later, out in the parking lot, Dennis and I had a little conference:

"Why did you call that meeting to an end?", asked Dennis, seriously concerned that he had done something wrong. "Did I mess up?"

"No, you were great," I replied. "We're never going to get any work from that guy."

"How do you know?"

"I don't know exactly how I know," I replied. "But I know."

"Did we do something wrong?"

"No. I don't think so. But the guy was wrong."

"What do you mean?"

"I mean, no meeting with a potential client should ever go beyond an hour, unless there is a bona fide job to be bid."

"There was no bid, George. You asked, and he said there wasn't."

"So why was he wasting over an hour to show us all his work?", I asked.

Dennis nodded. "He wanted to make someone look like he was busy." Dennis was nobody's fool. He quickly figured out one reason a meeting could go on over an hour with no immediate business at hand.

Think about what Dennis figured out. Let's say you're an employee of a large corporation. Part of your job is to interview new vendors. But there have been rumors that a downsizing is coming down the pike. Efficiency experts have been hired to find ways to cut the budgets. Rumors of layoffs are in the wind. As an employee who's fearful of being sacked, you want to look busy. You want to look like you're the center of activity. So what do you do? You wait until the boss or the efficiency experts are due to arrive, and you book a meeting with a couple of vendors. You keep them in your office, talking and showing brochures to each other, and hope that the boss says, "Look at ol' Joe there! Isn't he one fireball of a worker. Let's keep Joe and fire somebody else."

There are many other reasons a client will keep you in a presentation beyond the customary time. Sometimes he's just lonely. Sometimes he wants someone to tell him what a great job he's doing. Sometimes, he's just plain certifiably insane. Don't laugh! I've had clients who went from $100,000 contracts with major vendors straight to the Academy of Laughter. It's sad, and quite honestly, many times you'll humor such people out of the kindness of your heart. (Because what's an hour or two of meeting time, really?) And sometimes, well before the commitment date, such clients will repay your kindness with a juicy contract. But be forewarned. Long presentation meetings rarely—*very* rarely—end in a bid.

If you don't have anything better to do, let the meeting roll on. But don't delude yourself into thinking that the client has suddenly decided to make you a bosom buddy. If a meeting goes over 45 minutes with no immediate bid being offered, something just ain't right. Get your bones out of there and on the road to something real.

What's Next?

Now you know how to show your work, get a job, and pitch a client for freelance work. If you've read this chapter carefully, you should be ready to take that next meeting and convince an employer or client that you are the best person to hire. I sincerely believe that if you have a half-decent reel or portfolio, and you follow my recommendations, you will get your foot in the door and perhaps even close your first big deal. It's not magic. Underneath it all, people who agree to meet with you want you to succeed. Secretly, perhaps without them even realizing it, they're rooting for you.

You can test this truth very easily. Do you remember the last time you watched someone make a presentation? Perhaps you went to a comedy club and saw a rank beginner get up onstage and tell jokes. Maybe you watched a play or a speech in some live venue. Or maybe someone you didn't particularly like got up in front of an audience to say something. How did you feel when the person stepped on the stage? Were you hoping he'd fall and smash his nose? Were you praying he'd bungle the bollard? No, you were secretly hoping he'd be a smashing success and make you laugh, or entertain you, or give you some useful information. You were secretly rooting for the presenter to succeed! This is a very, very common human expectation.

All audiences want to see the presenter win. When you stand up in front of any-one to make a presentation, you start off with a win. Only by sabotaging your own performance can you lose. If you see this simple truth, trust it, and rely on it, you will never fail a performance. Even if you arrive late, look down at your feet and see that you're wearing different socks, open your backpack and realize you forgot your laptop, show your reel and realize you only brought your copy of *Napoleon Dynamite*, spill your coffee all over the host's desk and designer clothes, or have bad breath and a funky odor on your clothes, the client wants to see you succeed. Don't ask me why this is so. I don't know why, but it is. Trust me.

I'm not telling you this just to fill you with false confidence, or so you can scorn proper preparation and think you can just wing it. I'm telling you this because it is true, and it is proof that we live in a nice world where things usually turn out for the best. If you can believe that, and you have a kick-ass showreel, in the long run you cannot fail. You just have to get out there and try your best to show people your hard work.

In Chapter 10, "Let There Be Light: Adding Light and Atmospheric Effects to Your Productions," you're moving back to the Softimage workstation. You are now moving into the more esoteric aspects of animation, where subtle enhancements produce startling differences in production value. Let this hands-on tutorial work act as a psychological break from the tedium of business and client-chasing. In Chapter 11, you'll return to the business side and discuss what happens when a client finally asks you to submit a bid and contract for an animation production. Boy, that's when this all comes together and you start to make money doing what you love!

Chapter 10

Let There Be Light: Adding Light and Atmospheric Effects to Your Productions

In this chapter, we're back to working in Softimage, this time on lighting techniques. If you have any experience in photographic, cinematic, or video lighting, you'll find many of the terms and concepts quite familiar. Except in this chapter, nothing is real!

So Many Tools, So Little Time

Softimage has a great number of tools, and at about this point in the book and your personal development, you should be getting pretty confident in using many of them. In this chapter, you are going to learn several more toolsets concerning lighting. There are, of course, many more for creating light and atmosphere in your scenes, and I encourage you to explore them all. It is important to know, however, that many sophisticated lighting effects entail render-intensive mathematics, such as raytracing, where the effect of each theoretical ray of light in the scene is plotted from its origin to every reflected surface and refracted medium until the ray ends.

It is important to remember that raytraced lighting contributes heavily to the time that your scene takes to render. If you are experimenting for your own education, or working on a project for which there is no deadline, you might not be too concerned with the time it takes to render. But when time is of the essence, or when you are just plain impatient, you should always be aware that most scenes can be illuminated sufficiently with very few lights if they are placed correctly. Such correct placement leaves you free to add "effects lighting" without driving up the time of your renders to the point where you miss your deadline.

So, although you have a whole arsenal of tools at your disposal, a little bit of planning and forethought may save you a lot of time in the long run.

Three-Point Lighting

Three-point lighting has been used for years in theatrical and photographic lighting, and it serves us very well as a jumping-off point for any discussion of general scene illumination. In three-point lighting, three lights surround each subject. These three lights are the *key light*, the *fill light*, and the *rim* or *back light*.

The *key light* defines the direction and intensity of the primary light source in your scene. This could be the sun, or a table lamp, or even the brightest reflected source of light if there is no direct lighting.

The *fill light* represents secondary light coming from other direct sources that are farther away, or a reflection of the primary source (such as bounced sunlight). The fill light fills in the dark shadows caused by the primary or key light, and makes the general lighting less harsh.

The *rim light* or *back light* comes from behind or above and creates a halo (or rim) of light around your objects or characters.

If all of your objects are lit only from the front, especially if they're in front of a backdrop, the scene will render very flat and two-dimensional. Backlight serves to pull the subject away from a background or separate it from other characters or objects in the scene, which may be in front of or behind the subject. The back light, therefore, gives the scene a sense of depth.

Figure 10.1 is the top view of a simple scene where a human figure is lit with a three-point lighting array composed of fill, back, and key lights.

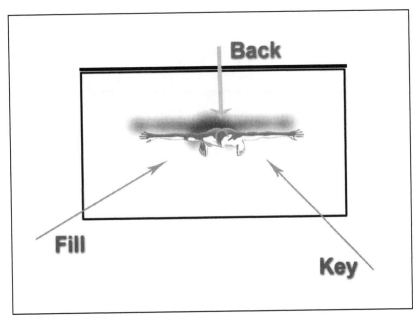

Figure 10.1 *A three-point lighting array.*

So, enough with the theory. Now let's look at some examples of lighting in XSI. I have created a simple scene consisting of a floor, a rear wall, a primitive man model, a primitive woman model, and a colored sphere. (See Figure 10.2.) All of these can be found in the Get > Primitive menu in XSI. For the floor and wall, you could use two grids. I deleted four sides of a cube and then used Modify > Polymesh > Invert. This is not necessary for rendering. Figure 10.2 shows the XSI interface with the three objects loaded and ready for your three-point lighting tutorial.

Make sure to use unique materials for each object. My wall and floor are gray *Phong*, the people are white *Lambert*, and the sphere is blue *Phong*. This simple scene gives us enough variation in shape, color, and space to be able to discuss the basic lighting principles in XSI. If you have created this scene, save it at this point in case you need to reload it later.

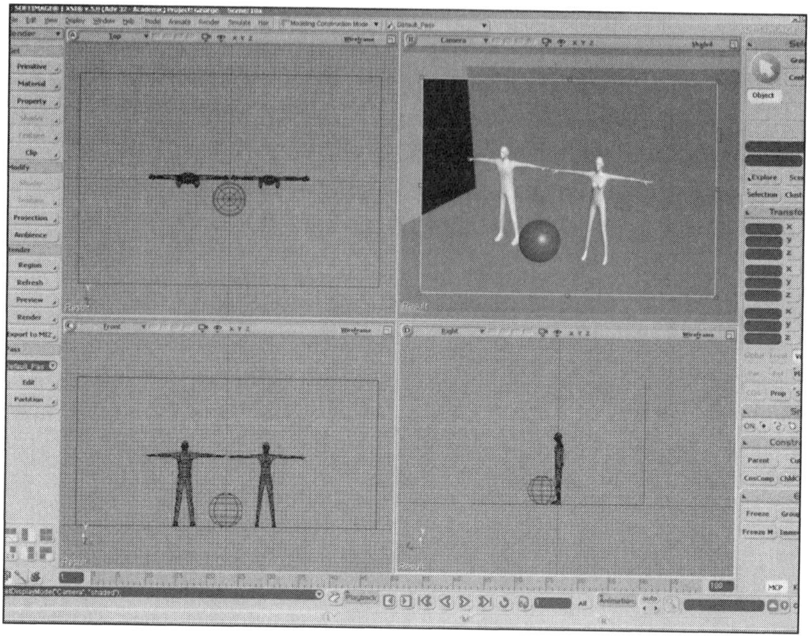

Figure 10.2 *The XSI interface with three objects loaded.*

It is worth mentioning how Softimage approaches its default general illumination before we go ahead and alter it. When you add objects to a new scene (as in this example), they are illuminated and appear three-dimensional. This is a quick fake for what eventually will be your key and fill lights. In this default setup, there is just one *infinite* light source, which is hidden by default. There is also an ambient light component applied to your scene, which washes out the shadows.

Scene ambience is controlled with Modify > Ambience in the Render toolbar. In the real world, ambient light is the sum of all indirect light. Ambient light essentially determines how dark the darkest shadows will be, but objects still appear three-dimensional when lit by ambient light.

In XSI, the *Ambience* slider creates a constant fill from *inside* each solid object, based on its ambient material color. If you remove the direct light source and turn the ambience up, the objects become flat-colored silhouettes. (See Figure 10.3.) This is why the ambient material color is slightly darker than the diffuse color. It helps the illusion of darker shadowing on objects that get too washed out by the scene's ambience. Figure 10.3 shows the XSI interface, showing controls for determining the characteristics of ambient and direct lights.

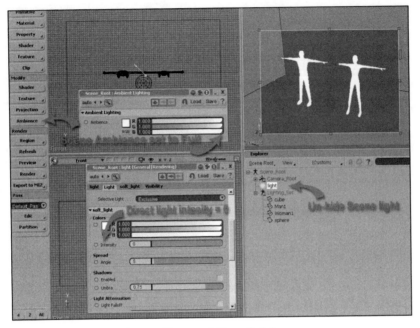

Figure 10.3 *Controlling ambient and direct lighting.*

This basic setup is provided so that average animators can build and animate their scenes without getting caught up in the complexities of light placement. However, if you want to be aggressively creative and create more realism, you will have to do a little more work. As a rule of thumb when setting up your own lighting, you should turn the scene ambience off (or very low) to begin with.

Let's take a minute to look at the types of light sources available. If you select the Get > Primitive > Light menu, you will see that there are five types of lights available in XSI: Infinite, Point, Spot, Light Box, and Neon.

The *Infinite* light is like the sun. It has parallel rays that come from very far away, regardless of where the light icon is placed in your scene. You may therefore place the icon wherever it is convenient for you, but the only thing you can adjust with the icon is the direction of the rays. If shadows are enabled, they will be cast by all objects in the scene, because the rays are coming from very far away. The default scene light is a hidden infinite light.

The *Point* light is the simplest of the light sources. It behaves like a naked light bulb, casting light spherically in all directions.

The *Spot* light produces a cone of light that can be adjusted for angle (size of the light pool) and spread (the softness at the edge of the pool). It has three components: a master null called the *root*, the spot light itself, and an *interest* null. The light is directionally constrained so that it will always point at the interest. The light and the interest may be moved together by manipulating the root. You can create a *free spot* by cutting the light from the root and deleting the interest.

The *Light Box* is a diffuse light source, much like a spot light with a piece of frosted gel placed over it. The quality of the diffusion can be controlled by adjusting the U and V samples in the Area tab of the light's PPG.

The *Neon* light produces a diffuse point source that can be scaled to create a long hotspot when it is near a surface, much like a neon tube. The precision of the diffusion is controlled by the area sampling, like the light box.

So, let's get back to our three-point lighting setup. If you have been playing with the lights during this discussion, reload the basic set and turn the scene ambience to zero now. The scene light is an infinite light, and it will serve us well for our key light in this example.

TONY'S TIP

For general illumination, a single infinite light can replace a number of other lights that would need to be placed side-by-side in order to cover a large area (because the source is infinitely wide). So, a single infinite key, a single infinite fill, and a single infinite backlight could replace a bank of evenly spaced spot lights for each of the three directions. Unless of course you are trying to create the look of light pools that occur, for example, on a stage.

Three-Point Lighting Set Up

1. Select the scene light in an Explorer window, and press the H key to unhide the light icon.

2. Press F2 and rename the light *Key*.

3. Press Enter to open the PPG for the key light. Check the box for shadows enabled, and drag the umbra slider to 0. *Umbra* defines the amount

of light that can pass through objects in your scene. Therefore, 0 in the umbra equals 100% shadow, and 1 (or 100%) in the umbra equals 0 shadow. If you turn your ambience to 0 as well, you now have totally black shadows everywhere outside of the key light.

4. With the key light selected, press Ctrl+D to duplicate the light.

5. Press the C key to activate rotation, and rotate this duplicate so that it's illuminated from the opposite side of the stage (see Figure 10.4). I like to use Global rotation in the Top view to set the initial direction of the light, and then switch to local rotation to adjust the steepness of the light angle.

   Because the fill light should fill and not compete with the key, you will make some adjustments to this light.

6. First, rename the key light (using the Explorer or in the key light's PPG).

7. Press Enter to open the PPG, if it isn't already open, and uncheck the boxes for Specular and Enable Shadows. Then set the intensity to around .25. Unchecking the specular contribution of this light removes the second hot spot on the surface of the sphere. Removing the shadows creates the impression that there is one primary light direction, and that the shadows are being filled by secondary light.

8. To further enhance this look, open the PPG for the key light and change the umbra setting to about .25 as well.

Now for the third component...

1. Select the Fill light and duplicate it.

2. Rotate it so that it points down and from the rear. If you had duplicated the key light, you would have to remove the shadows and the specular again.

3. Name this light Rim, and turn its intensity up to 1. This pops the characters away from the back wall.

   You can balance these lights a bit more in terms of intensity and angle to create the illumination that you desire, but this is now a good example of basic three-point lighting.

4. Save your scene.

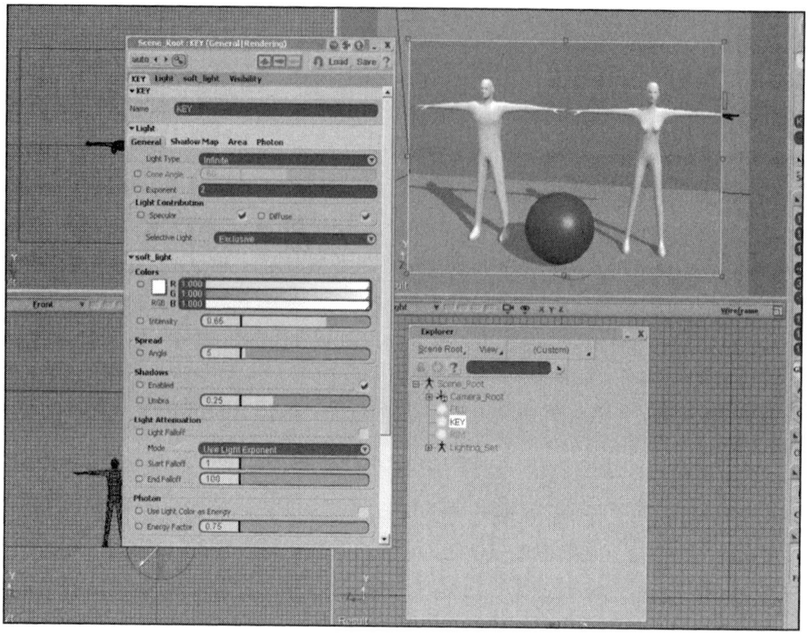

Figure 10.4 *Illuminating the duplicate.*

Here are another few adjustments that you might want to experiment with before we move on. If the stage appears too washed out with the addition of the third light, you can exclude it from the rim light.

Unlike real-world lights, in Softimage, each lighting instrument can be set to include or exclude certain objects. This is very useful when you want to add a bit more light to a certain hero character, or in this case, to remove a bit of light from a certain source without affecting the rest of the scene.

1. Open the PPG for the rim light.
2. Make sure that the Selective light property (at the top of the PPG) is set to Exclusive. Now you can associate certain objects to this light and they will be excluded from its illumination.
3. If your Explorer is set to a higher filter level than Objects Only, you can expand the light to expose a group called Associated Models. Simply drag the objects you wish to exclude into this group.

4. Otherwise, select the object(s), in this case the stage, choose Get > Primitive > Light > Associate Light, and pick the light(s) that you want to associate, in this case rim.

Voilà! The stage is no longer illuminated by the rim light, but everything else continues to be.

Adding Color to Lighting

Now let's add some color. Color can affect the mood of a scene; it can imply daylight or moonlight, fantasy or realism. If you add a bit of warm color into your key light, it is a good idea to use a bit of cool complement in your fill. You do not need to be exactly 180 degrees away on the color wheel, but using a color that is in the same family as the compliment will cause the objects themselves to remain smoothly lit while adding a bit more color to the shadows. If you just add a light tint of color, the scene will have more of a realistic feel. However, if you want to simulate a more dramatic time of day, such as sunrise or sunset, using more saturated colors and lower light angles will do the trick. Try some combinations on the simple scene we have set up.

TONY'S TIP

Musical comedy lighting frequently employs pink and blue combinations that leave the characters in white light where the lights overlap, but lend a festive look overall. Try activating all of the shadows to emphasize the stage lighting effect. For rich evening colors, try an amber or straw (yellow) key with a lavender fill. For moonlight, try leaving the key white and reducing the intensity. Then use a deep blue shade for the fill, and adjust its intensity according to taste. In each instance, you may wish to adjust the rim light to suit the intended mood.

The humans in your scene are matte white (Lambert) and will most accurately display the color choices that you make for your lights. When choosing colors for the sphere object, for instance, notice that its saturated surface color will combine with the light to produce a different surface color. This effect is more noticeable as you begin to choose more saturated colors for your lights. It is an effect that brings a high degree of real-world realism to your work.

Remember, the three-point lighting setup is for general illumination and for establishing the mood of the scene. You can add selective lights (as described earlier) that add light to the protagonists or subtract light from areas of the scene that need to be darkened. Later in this chapter, we will also discuss some basic effect lights that can be added as well.

One more element that will contribute to the general feel of your scene is the type of shadows that you choose. By default, you are using hard-edged raytraced shadows. Because these shadows interact with the surfaces of each object in your scene, they react to properties like transparency. If you add an incidence node to the transparency property of the colored sphere (see Figure 10.5), the edges of the transparent object will be thicker than the center. Because raytraced shadows are being used, this variation in transparency is reflected in the shadow as well. Figure 10.5 shows how you adding an incidence node to the transparency property of the colored sphere produces a shadow with properties that mimic the density of the sphere.

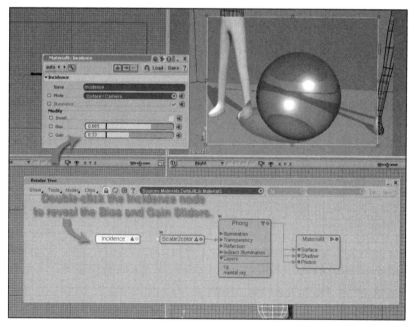

Figure 10.5 *Using the incidence node.*

Adding an Incidence Node

To access the incidence node, select the sphere and change to the Render Tree combination view by clicking on the icon at the bottom left of the screen.

1. Choose Nodes > Illumination > Incidence, drag the green dot on the Incidence node over the Phong node, and release.

2. Choose Transparency from the list. (Don't worry about the converter node that automatically appears between the two nodes.) You should see the surface and the shadow update.

3. If you wish, double-click on the incidence node and adjust the bias and gain settings.

4. For another touch of realism, open the Phong node, select the Transparency and Refraction tab, and tweak the refraction slider (set it slightly above 1.0) and the reflection slider (Ctrl+drag any of the RGB sliders slightly to increase the overall reflection).

You can adjust the general opacity of the shadows by changing the Umbra setting. You can also turn off the shadows and specular highlights for everything but the key source, in an attempt to maintain a sense of directionality despite the fact that you are using multiple light angles.

This is all fine, but in many cases you may wish to have soft shadows from several of the lights in your scene. This occurs in nature as well, depending on the distance and diffusion of the various lights.

As stated earlier, some of the stock light sources automatically create soft shadows (light box and neon). This is done via the area sampling tab in the PPG of these lights. You can enable area light properties for other light sources as well, but this results in long render times and frequent adjustments.

For a faster "cheat," you can enable the check box on the Shadow Map tab of the Light PPG. Make sure to click Use Shadow Map in Region in order to see the results. The shadow map replaces the raytraced shadow with an image map of the approximate shadow in your scene, and it has sliders for resolution, sampling (precision), and softness. This will frequently give you a faster "soft-shadow" than the raytraced area samples.

You should be aware that if you turn up the samples and the resolution high enough, you will end up with a very long rendering time with this technique as well. The other downside to shadow maps is that you lose the nifty transparent shadow calculations that you were getting with the raytraced light. A combination of these sources will probably do the trick. Figure 10.6 shows an attempt to employ various forms of lighting, carefully tweaked to create a balanced effect of light and shadow, without driving up the render time.

Figure 10.6 *Adding lighting without increasing render time.*

Basic Effect Lighting

So far, we've explored the default lighting that Softimage provides for the average animator who is not interested in aggressively pursuing a creative approach, as well as the basic lighting techniques involved in building your own three-point lighting setup.

Now that you are familiar with the rather simple aspects of lighting a scene, let's learn the basics of *effect lighting*. This is the creative effort of imparting specific artistic intentions upon a scene, or elements within it. Here, you get to play the role of a feature film lighting director, the person who gets to insert an individual *auteur* style into the production, second only to the director.

Building a Basic Scene

Let's begin by building a basic scene with a couple of primitive characters and a grid for the floor.

1. Open an Explorer window, delete any lights, and turn the Ambience slider to zero.

2. For now, hide the sphere and reposition your characters if you wish. If you have a render region open, you should see pure black because there are no direct light sources and no ambient light from unseen sources.

3. Begin by adding a spot light (Get > Primitive > Lights > Spot). The spot light has three components: the spot root (master null), the spot interest (where it points), and the spot itself.

4. Raise the spot and move it toward you slightly (positive z-axis).

5. Move the interest so that it is located between the two figures.

6. You can view and adjust the cone of a spotlight by pressing the B key and dragging the edges of the two cones with your mouse (see Figure 10.7). The outer cone is the cone angle (widest part of the light pool), and the inner cone is the spread control. If the spread angle is zero, there is no difference between the two cones, and the light pool has a sharp edge to it. As you increase the spread angle by adjusting the number in the Spot PPG, or by dragging the inner cone away from the outer cone, the edge of the light pool becomes softer.

7. Turn the shadows on full (umbra to 0) and turn the intensity to 1 (full).

8. For a little more control, check the box for Light Falloff, and set the start distance to around 60 and the mode to Linear. You will see two colored rings appear in the cone. The light will fall off linearly between these two rings.

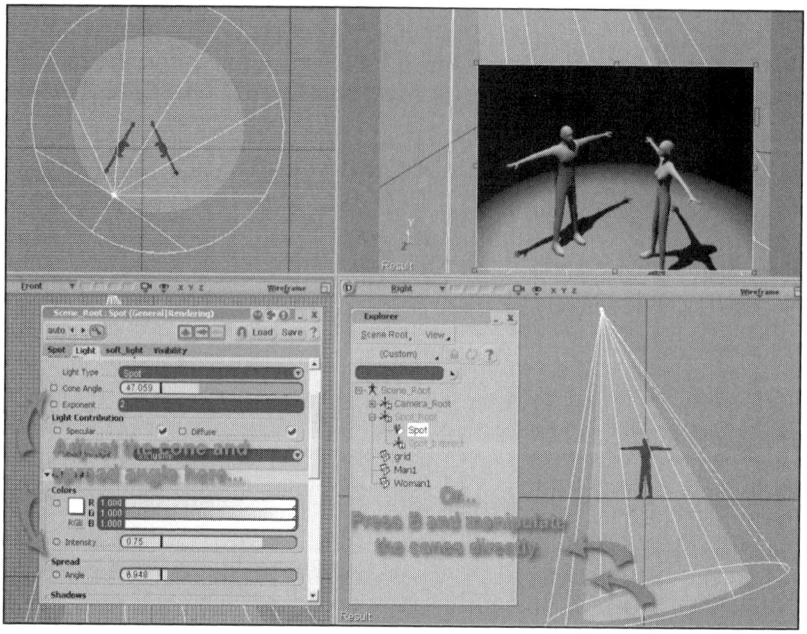

Figure 10.7 *You can adjust the cone in two ways.*

TONY'S TIP

If the mode is set to Use Light Exponent, you can adjust the bias of the falloff by changing the number at the top of the page. This is set to 2 by default, which causes the light to fall off based on the inverse square law.

Now for your first effect!

1. Make sure that you are in the Render Module and that your spot is selected.

2. Press the 7 key to open the Render Tree.

3. From the Node menu, select Light > More > Sib_Slide_Projector.

4. Connect the output of this node to the intensity input of the Soft Light node. This uses this image's luminance to control the light intensity, creating shadow patterns in the light.

5. You can create your own patterns in a program like Adobe Photoshop to give the impression of leaves, window panes, logos, and so on. For our purposes, get an image out of the XSI Samples database that ships with the software.

6. Navigate to the Pictures directory in XSI Samples, and choose Ripples64_tga (or you can certainly create your own). This creates a nice mottled light across our characters.

7. Play with the position of the spotlight and its falloff until you have something that you like.

8. For extra credit, try inserting an intensity node (Node > Image Processing > Intensity) between the projector node and the converter node. You can use this to control the overall intensity of your pattern light. Your XSI Spot Light PPG should look something like Figure 10.8, showing the source of your projected effect (Ripples65_tga) and the graphic representation of your insertion of the intensity node between the projector node and the converter node.

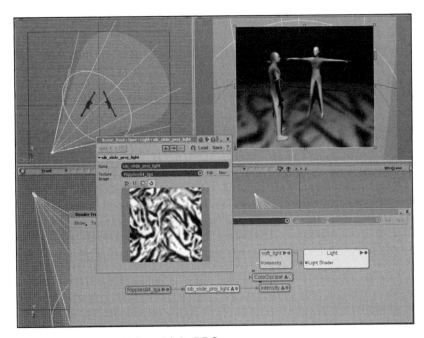

Figure 10.8 *The XSI Spot Light PPG.*

Now let's add another spot with a different effect.

1. Set up a second spot light pointing at our characters from the same side, but also slightly from the rear.

2. This time, select the light and choose Get > Property > Volumic, and you will see the beam of light in the render region. Volumic simulates a beam of light passing through dust or smoke so that it becomes visible. The PPG that pops up has controls for Map Size, Reflectance, and Min Distance.

3. Map Size is the size of the effect in the beam, Reflectance is the brightness of the smoke or dust, and Min Distance is how far from the light the effect begins (a value of 0 creates a sharp point at the top of the light cone).

4. Check the box for Force Volume Shadows to see shadows inside the beam. The Transparency setting is used when the light is passing through objects that have transparency values (we will look at this in a moment). The Shards tab allows you to create streaks in the light beam. This will help it look like it belongs in the scene, with the pattern projected from the other spot. You will need to adjust the balance between the different spots to get just the effect that you want. As with everything else, it is not a bad idea to name your lights so that you can tell which one has a certain effect applied. See Figure 10.9.

TONY'S TIP

This PPG can be accessed through the Selection button on the MCP. In addition, there is a scene Volumic PPG that you will see in the Explorer if your focus is set to Properties. This controls some additional properties, such as step (precision) and fractal smoke generation (dust appears in the beam by default). There is also a tab that applies the fill to the entire scene and allows you to adjust the particulate color.

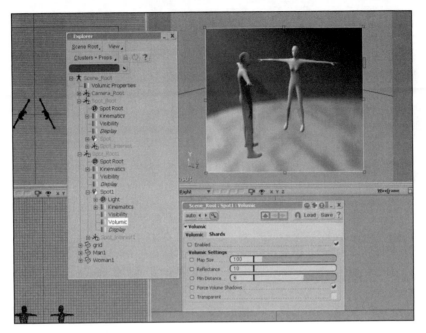

Figure 10.9 *Adding another spot.*

"Light Through a Window" Effect

So far we have looked at putting a projection in one light and creating volumic rays in another. This time we will do both by shining a volumic light through a window (or a slide, if you prefer) with a colored pattern in the window.

1. Duplicate the second spot, and move it around to shine from the other side of your scene. You could create a new spot from scratch, but this way the volumic property is already applied.

2. Temporarily hide the other two spots so that you can focus on this new effect.

3. Create a primitive grid, name it Window, and apply a Black Lambert material.

4. Frame up the grid in the top view and raise it off the floor slightly so that you can see it in the render region of the camera view (see Figure 10.10).

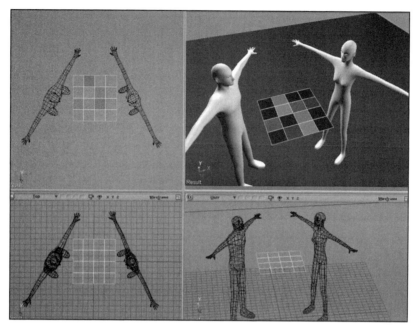

Figure 10.10 *Viewing the render region.*

5. Press the U key to enter raycast polygon mode.

6. Click on a couple of the polygon squares and apply a new material.

7. Pick a nice bright color and change the material's transparency to about 50%.

8. Repeat the process a few more times so that some squares are opaque black, and the rest are various colors and semitransparent.

9. When you are satisfied with the pattern, translate and rotate the grid so that it is positioned near the spot and is in the beam of light.

10. Select the spot, making sure that shadows are enabled on the main light PPG (umbra = 0).

11. Open its volumetric PPG and enable the transparency and force shadows options.

    As shown in Figure 10.11, the visible rays now take on the color and opacity of the colored grid.

Figure 10.11 *The rays now take on the color and opacity of the grid.*

Lighting with a Flare

Rather than start a new scene, we will add a few new lights to this scene in order to demonstrate how flares work. In the real world, lens flares occur when the lens of your camera points directly at an exposed light source. The same effect occurs in Softimage. Replicating the real world, you won't see a Softimage lens flare that is applied to a spot light unless you are actually inside the cone of light and looking back at the light source.

Lens flare works well for creating realistic effects of cinematography. Even though lens flare is considered an unfortunate side effect of lens design, many cinematographers have employed lens flare over the years as an artistic touch! For instance, when the beam of a lighthouse sweeps over a movie camera, it produces a lens flare as a kind of visual grace note.

The lens flare, if applied to the rotating spot in Softimage, will be visible only during the frames where your camera is looking directly into the path of the light, and it will disappear again as soon as the cone rotates away from the camera. However, applying what I like to call, "creative aggression," (that attitude that stops at nothing to be as creative as possible), we'll be a bit subtler by placing the effect on a couple of point sources that we will place in the background of our scene.

The starting point in our lens flare exercise is a scene like the one in Figure 10.12, with two figures facing a horizon.

Creating a Romantic Scene

Let's prepare for this next exercise by creating a romantic scene with two really stiff people.

1. Orbit the camera around until you have a view of the scene that you like.

2. Turn down or turn off some of the other effects until you have the two characters illuminated by a couple of the spots, but not blown out. Be sure there is some empty space visible behind them.

3. Choose Get > Primitive > Light > Point, and position a couple of point sources behind the current scene objects so that they are still visible to the camera (see Figure 10.12).

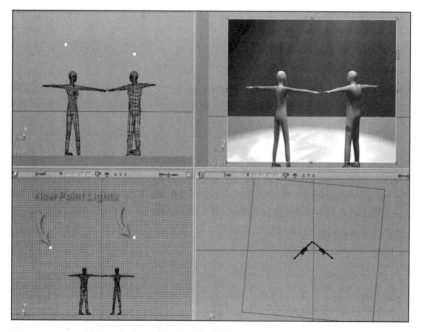

Figure 10.12 *Point lights added behind the current scene objects.*

4. Give them pretty colors.

5. Select one of the new lights and choose Get > Property > Lens Flare. Initially, the Flare and Glow properties are disabled, but the Star property makes the source visible.

6. Click the Star tab and experiment with the number of rays and their length. Alternatively, you could enable the Glow tab and turn off the star.

7. Using a combination of these two settings allows you to create visible light sources, the filament of a light bulb, distant planets and stars, and so on. Try changing the intensity and color of the light itself as well.

8. Check the box on the Flare tab and use the drop-down menu to select from a range of distinctive lens flares.

9. Access the scene Volumic Properties from an Explorer window, and add a bit of depth fog to give the scene some color and to soften the edge of the floor grid (see Figure 10.13).

Figure 10.13 *Adding fog.*

Indirect Illumination

There is an alternative method of illuminating your scene that bears mentioning, even in this basic discussion of lighting concepts: Final Gathering (FG). If you've ever been on a film or video set, you've probably seen the cameraperson using white or metal foil panels to bounce available light from the sun onto a scene. Final Gathering is akin to this real-world technique, which provides an attractive, diffuse light source that softens the shadowing.

When Final Gathering is initialized, every surface in your scene contributes to the illumination of every other surface of your scene within a certain radius. This is not a true raytraced calculation like Global Illumination (or Radiosity), but rather an approximation that takes a sample from each surface (diffuse color and intensity) and carries that information to nearby surfaces. Consequently, Final Gathering takes a lot less time to render than Global Illumination.

How far the sampled surface information travels is the result of a number of factors, but the simple concept is this: A red sphere on a white grid will transfer some of its color to the grid, and the grid will wash out some of the shadows under the ball. You don't need any direct illumination in your scene in order for Final Gathering to be applied. However, you do need at least one light source that is not hidden even if its intensity is set to 0.

It is usually desirable to set up your FG separately from the direct lighting and then combine them. If you are simulating lots of diffuse sources (such as a large showroom with many bounced lights or a cloudy day where the sun is not visible), but everything is still evenly lit, you may not need any direct light at all, but you will need a big bounce surface.

Setting Up a Test Scene

To set up a test scene, get several brightly colored primitive objects. Distribute them around a white or pale gray grid, and add a large sphere that surrounds the entire scene (see Figure 10.14).

1. Make the surrounding sphere's material Constant white. Get>Material>Constant.

2. Open the Explorer and select the scene light.

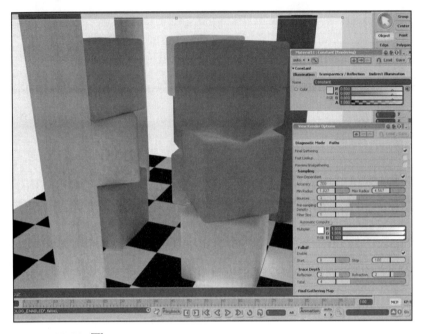

Figure 10.14 *The test scene.*

3. Press Enter to view the light PPG.

4. Drag the Intensity slider to 0 so that there is no direct light contribution in your scene.

5. Draw a render region in the camera view. If you can still see the outlines of the objects, you may also want to lower the scene ambience.

6. Now for the fun part. Select Render > Region > Options and click the Final Gathering tab.

7. Check the box next to Final Gathering to turn it on. When the render refreshes, you can now see the scene illuminated by the constant material on the sphere.

8. Press the Automatic Compute button. This sets up the minimum and maximum radius values for the bounce calculations. You can play with these values manually, but it is a good idea to let the computer set a good starting point. Using incorrect radius values can greatly increase your render times and degrade the look of your scene.

9. You can now select the background sphere and select Modify > Shader to access the illumination setting of the constant material (press the lock icon in the upper-right corner to keep it from recycling).

10. Play with the color and luminance values to affect the overall illumination and color of the light in your scene.

11. You can even put a texture on the sphere or add color to individual polygons to vary the bounced light. With no direct light rays in your scene, you probably don't see any color transference yet.

12. Without closing the locked shader PPG, select Render > Option > FG PPG and lock it as well.

13. You can turn up the number of bounces and enable falloff to make the color of the various objects carry to nearby surfaces (see Figure 10.15).

As a final example, I have included a rendering of a simple portrait using FG and direct light blending (see Figure 10.16). Our stock character is illuminated using only the single standard scene light set to a low intensity value (approximately .25), with shadows enabled. Here, there is no scene ambience, but there is an FG sphere with areas of color created by adding multiple constant shaders to selected polygon groups. This simulates multiple soft-colored fill lights.

Sphere illumination color = .75   Sphere illumination color = 1.0

Figure 10.15 *Color carries to nearby surfaces.*

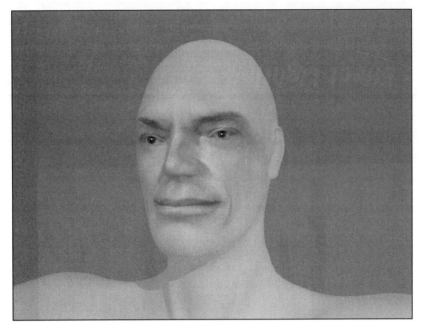

Figure 10.16 *A rendering of a simple portrait.*

You are now so close to being a practicing professional animator that it is high time you learned how to write and present a bid to produce animation for a client. Don't be scared. This client can be a friend, a family member, or the owner of a small business in your neighborhood. In the previous business-oriented chapters, you've been learning how to identify and court such a client. If you are successful, one of these clients is going to ask you for a proposal. The next chapter introduces you to the business of responding to a request for proposal, or RFP. This is essential knowledge in order for you to start your own business, or at least to know how to best serve an employer who already has one.

Chapter 11

RFPs and Bids

This chapter is for freelancers and new studio bosses who are ready to start making money on their own. Here, you will learn how to respond to a Request for Proposal (or RFP) with a bid that presents your ideas and pricing in the most compelling manner.

If you've followed my guidance thus far, done the tutorials, created a decent showreel, made some presentations, and worked hard at building an independent business, you are probably about to receive or have already received an RFP from a client.

Don't get too excited. An RFP is not an offer for work, and it is not a contract. Sometimes it is only a request for information and nothing more. Other times it is your ticket to independent wealth. Basically, it is a request for your ideas, your plan, and your prices.

The RFP

An RFP can take many forms. In the simplest form, it can be a phone call where the client says, "Hey. I need a 30-second animated spot with two characters in a bar, drinking two brands of beer. A few close-ups of the labels, some titles, and we'll supply the audio track. Can you give me a rough ballpark price?"

In its most complicated form, usually from some governmental body, an RFP can be 200 pages of legal language that will take you a week to digest, much less reply to.

Verbal RFPs

Frequently, a client will call you into her office and describe the project. Sometimes, you may find other animators at the meeting who are also receiving the RFP. At such meetings, in groups or by yourself, it is your task to acquire as much information as you can about what the client wants. Often, clients are not very savvy about the technology of animation. You might have to spend some time educating the client so that she can accurately describe what she wants. It's a good idea to mention famous animated films and commercials in order to establish a common understanding of style, complexity, and content.

Once you have an understanding, you must establish a list of things you will deliver, as well as a mutual understanding of the work that will go into making those things. This is called the *scope* of the project. For instance, if the RFP requires you to make a storyboard, design a virtual set, create two characters, and import camera-ready art for the labels on the beer bottles, all of these items are part of the scope and must be listed somewhere in your proposal. If you do not have a complete understanding of what the client wants, you can't make an accurate scope.

Typically, you will have to ask a lot of questions:

- How long is the animation?
- Who will supply the soundtrack, and will it consist of dialog, music, and effects?
- What is the style? 3D or 2D? Cartoonish or realistic? Raytraced or flat-rendered?
- How will the final work be delivered? As a sequence, tape, or film?

And so on.

The Four Most Important Questions

However, amongst all the questions you will ask, there are four that are the most essential:

1. What is the message?
2. Who is the audience?
3. When is the deadline?
4. What is the budget?

What Is the Message?

Many people, especially fine artists, get a bit riled when someone suggests their work might have a message. Sorry, we are not talking about fine art here, and the message to which I am referring is not an artistic or philosophical message—for the most part.

By "message," I'm referring to the reason someone is paying you to make the animation. If no one is paying you, there might not be a message. You might be making an animation for your own personal happiness . . . great. But if you want to eat, chances are you will be making animation for someone else. The reason they're paying you to make the animation is to convey their message.

It is very important to know what the message is. However, sometimes it may be very difficult to extract the message from a client. The client may not be very bright, or may not be the person who came up with the message or thought about conveying that message with animation. You might be having an RFP meeting with an administrative assistant who, not wishing to admit his ignorance, may give you a completely erroneous idea of what the message is!

Let me give you an example: Joe, a Senior Marketing VP at Exit Soap, wants to sell a new type of soap to Scandinavians. The soap contains layers of deodorant embedded within the bar. Joe comes up with an idea to create a Viking character who cuts the bar of soap with his sword to reveal the layers of deodorant, while a Brunhilde gal, with a horned iron helmet, leans in and sniffs the Viking's armpits.

The message of this animation is that sometimes Scandinavian guys don't use deodorant. (Actually, they do, but this is a hypothetical commercial, okay?) In order to make sure these guys don't go out smelling like dead cod, their gals should buy this soap.

Knowing the message, you can be sure to spend sufficient time on the parts of the animation that convey the message. What are these parts? To begin with, you want a burly, potentially smelly Viking. Then you need to show the soap's contents. And finally, you need a really cute Brunhilde, doing a convincingly efficacious sniff and showing a convincingly satisfied smile.

But Joe's administrative assistant just moved into his position from the hair care products side of the company. He picks up the specifications for the job while Joe is on vacation. Reading the specifications, all the admin knows is that there are two characters and a bar of soap. What message do you get? Maybe that the Viking's hair should be frizzy and the gal's nice and soft . . . who knows? To get the message, you may have to ask a lot of questions, read the specifications—especially the storyboard, if there is one—and try to think like the client.

Thinking like a client is a big deal. Doing it right sends you quickly to the top of whatever professional hierarchy you, as an animator, want to climb. Quite honestly, it's the hardest attribute to obtain and requires the most perceptive form of imagination. A whole book can be written about how to think like a client, but it all boils down to answering one simple question: "How is this animation going to make me money?"

Of course, the answer can get very complex indeed. For instance, what do you do if the client doesn't realize his animation is going to lose him money? Should you act in his interest and modify or kill the project? Or should you execute it as ordered? This example is classic, and there are many such situations that refine the art of thinking like a client. Incidentally, the answer to the above question is to politely warn the client—*once*.

Of course, it might be very easy getting the answer to "What is the message?" Your client might be quite adept at giving vendors adequate information. In such a case, make sure you copy the answer down exactly as dictated, and adhere to the message as you execute all the creative requirements of the project. In other words, don't go off and spend weeks designing the best sword ever animated, even if you get off on swords. A great sword might distract attention from the soap's ingredients. Get it? Got it. Good.

Who Is the Audience?

The audience, also referred to as the *demographic*, defines who will be motivated by your animation. We're not talking about a list of names here. We're talking about types of people—*profiles*, to be precise. How about that? For once, you get to do something that a policeman can't do. Your client should be able to define her audience in terms of age (say, 18 to 35 years), gender, economic scale, geographic region, sexual proclivity, political persuasion, and so on. Obviously, so as not to offend anyone, the trade has concocted an unofficial, unwritten vocabulary of politically correct terminology (well, to a minimum standard of correctness). Because these terms change frequently and are different from city to city, I won't risk giving you a complete glossary of current New York examples here. If you are in doubt about any term, it never hurts to ask, because, after all, who wants to risk a possible misunderstanding when the launch is next month?

You can learn more about these labels by attending lots of bid meetings at advertising agencies and asking some "dumb" questions. I say "dumb" because even the most sophisticated commercial producers get frustrated with these labels, and they seem to take turns being made fun of and making fun of each other in such environments. Another great way to learn the current buzzwords and sociologically accurate trends in demographics is to read *American Demographics*, a publication of *Advertising Age* (www.adage.com).

The practical application of "audience" in an animation will affect the way you interpret the design. An animated character for urban children, for instance, would look completely different than the same character designed for Republican retirees in Phoenix. How do you design for one or the other? That takes research. You might have to find out what movies kids watch in Harlem, and find fashion expressions, such as a baseball hat turned sideways, or verbalizations, such as the ubiquitous "Nomesayin'?" If you can interpret the audience's expectations, apply them to your animation, and explain them to your client, you'll win proposals.

When Is the Deadline?

This is a simple thing. The client says, "I gotta have your master tape by July 1." The wise animator cuts a week off that date and writes down "June 23" without even thinking. Already, she has created a proposal that guarantees a deadline-happy client.

Animators, like many artists, are reputed by clients to be "deadline-challenged." That means we are simply sloppy when it comes to turning in our work on time. Don't let yourself be grouped in with the stereotypes of our business. When a client says "July 1," you say, "You mean June 23, right?", and smile. The client will get the message and begin to regard you in a light of higher respect.

What Is the Budget?

Like getting the message, getting the budget is also difficult. Clients don't want to give away their "magic number," knowing that each bidder is going to submit an estimate really close to it. They may want to interject a wide range in order to see if some idiot is going to come in 110% lower than another bidder. It happens, because there are a million variables in animation. By simply eliminating ray tracing, for instance, a bid can be reduced by as much as 20%. And how many clients know what ray tracing is? Are you going to waste your time educating the client and risking that glazed-eyeballs look that says you just lost the bid? Not me. That's why you simply have to get at least a ballpark range of budget expectation. If the client says, "Well, between $30-40,000," at least you know you're not going to make a kung-fu army using motion capture.

Often, clients will even think this question is somewhat rude or inappropriate. If you see a strange expression cross your client's face when you ask, "How much do you expect this to cost?", or "What is your ballpark budget for this project?", you can counter with, "Well, from your description so far, this project could cost between [X] and [Y]." Use a really broad range of costs—say, from $10,000 to $100,000. That will usually shake out a more specific target. The client will say, "Well, I definitely don't want to spend over $50,000!" Now you have a target. And from that target, you can backtrack to a line-item budget that will produce the required total of, say, $49,999.

Keep in mind that no client is going to have her specs ready for you in the order or breakdown I have suggested here (unless she is an avid reader of my books). Consequently, you may have to use a mental or written checklist to make sure you get what you need to do a full proposal. When I go to a bid meeting, I like to tell the client that I need only ask four questions to fulfill the bid request, and then I rattle them off. This sometimes gets a laugh, but the client is always aware that I come to the meeting with a lot of experience, and I can boil down an often unpleasant experience to a minimum amount of time.

At the end of a verbal bid meeting, you should have all of the information you need to make a proposal. Don't worry too much if you've missed something, or if you need to ask the client a question during the proposal-writing stage. However, be sure to write down all your questions in one place and try to ask them all at one time. It's a good idea to ask these questions as late in the process as you can. Often, a client will feel compelled to share your questions, and her answers, with all of the bidders. If you ask these questions early in the game, you could give away your strategy or allow your competitors to use your questions and the client's answers to their benefit.

Written RFPs

Written RFPs come in many forms, but their purpose is to describe the scope of work more carefully than can be done in an informal verbal meeting. While verbal RFPs tend to be generated and delivered by creative people or prime contractors, written RFPs tend to be generated by purchasing agents and lawyers. These individuals pride themselves on being very specific and detailed. For example, written RFPs for animation projects commonly employ a video engineer's definition of "broadcast quality," specifically define the pixel dimensions and resolution of the frames you will create, and describe the penalties that will be levied against you if you fail to produce satisfactory work. Formal RFPs are scary things!

In order to function properly, a written RFP must have six basic elements:

1. Scope
2. Specifications
3. Timeline
4. Management
5. Contractual obligations
6. Location

On occasion, a budgetary expectation might be included in the document, usually expressed as a "not to exceed" limit.

Scope

The scope of an RFP is simply a list of all the things you must do. In a construction job, for instance, the scope might be digging a hole, pouring a cement floor, building cinderblock walls, and so on. With animation RFPs, the contracting agency might not be familiar with all the steps required. Your scope, therefore, might only be "supply a 30-second high-definition animation on D-5 videotape." Then it's up to you to break down the elements into "create a storyboard, approve storyboard with client, design 3D landscape, design characters," and so on. Regardless of the specificity of the RFP's scope, you must know the steps. And if you want to educate your client, you must include these steps in your proposal.

Specifications

Specifications or *specs* are the technical requirements of the project. Here, the client may define the dimensions and resolution of each frame in the sequence, and the picture format to be employed. Again, very little may be provided here by the client, but the client's ignorance is no excuse for you to disregard specifications. If they aren't in the RFP, you must acquire them. This may necessitate a formal request to the client in writing. Never assume specifications that are not given, because even though the client may not have thought the specs were important at bidding, at delivery, suddenly they become practically contractual.

For instance, let's say a client gives you an RFP for a standard-definition animation delivered on 10,000 VHS videotapes that will be distributed in France and Brazil. Her specifications don't have any details regarding videotape formats. You neglect to ask about formats. You make the video in the common U.S. standard, NTSC, duplicate it, and deliver the tapes as requested in the RFP.

Then you get a call from the client, complaining that the tapes don't play in France or Brazil. The client, having educated herself before calling you, says that you neglected to transfer the tapes into PAL format for France and PAL-M format for Brazil. Does the client expect you to eat the costs of shipping the cassettes back home, transferring two new master tapes, reduplicating the dubs, and reshipping the release copies?

Well, you could argue that the client never specified the formats in the RFP. But the client could argue that you were the expert, and you should have realized that France uses PAL and Brazil uses PAL-M. Now, at best, you are at a 50-50 split-the-bill resolution, but you've probably lost a client. Maybe you eat the whole deal. The point is this: If there are insufficient or missing specs, get the specs and be sure the client agrees to them in writing.

Timeline

The *timeline* refers to one of the four most important questions, "When is the deadline?", but in more detail. Often, on a long project, a client will impose *milestones*. These are dates when the client expects certain portions of your work to be done, such as the design of all characters. The client may expect you to prove the work is done by submitting it for approval. When you're breaking down an RFP, compare the client's expectations to what you know you or your shop can deliver. Don't just look at the deadline, seven months away, and assume you can squeeze the entire job into the sixth month and everything will be cool. *You* might work well under such pressure, but *clients* rarely do.

Management

This is the part of an RFP that tells you who the key people are on the client side (and often requests that you list who the key people are on your side). There are usually three people who are important on the client side: the purchasing agent, the receiving agent, and the client who is contracting for the work.

The purchasing agent is an internal police officer in the client's organization. He keeps clients from making secret deals, taking kickbacks, and making other grievous mistakes, like sending out RFPs without specifications. Usually a purchasing agent is familiar with the technology and practices of animation, but sometimes not. If not, you might have to invest some time in very delicately educating the agent. A good relationship with a purchasing agent can often lead to tons more work from the company than you could ever get from the contracting client alone. Although it is not often useful to make sales calls to purchasing agents (because most of them don't return the calls), once you've got a job working through them, the purchasing agent can be a really good source of work. And you almost never have to pitch them—they call you.

The receiving agent is usually a warehouse person, if your deliverables are bulk items like boxes of videocassettes or DVDs, or an engineer if your deliverables are frame sequences or master tapes. Of the two, the engineer is the most critical. This person will be testing your work against the published specifications, and if they are not up to par, your work will be rejected and you won't be paid. The warehouse guy only wants to see boxes coming into the right door with the right labels, printed exactly as described in the RFP's delivery orders.

The contracting client is the main contact to whom you originally sold the job, manages the job during your production, and uses the results of your job when you're done. This person's happiness is your master goal, but don't forget the important role played by the purchasing and receiving agents before, during, and after your assignment.

Contractual Obligations

This is one of the most critical portions of an RFP, and you are encouraged to run a lengthy RFP past your attorney at least once to have each clause explained. Here, you will find all the things the client's lawyers wanted in the contract. These things include what happens if you don't deliver the job and the client loses money as a result (this is called "consequential damages"), and what happens if you use copyrighted material in your project and the owner of the material sues the client (this is called "third-party damages," and the protection is a "hold harmless" clause).

I cannot go into all the complexities of the possible contractual obligations you may encounter in an RFP, but be aware that if they are in the RFP, they (and per-haps more) will be in the final contract if you win the bid. Certain contractual obligations entail expenses that would not be, but for their inclusion, part of your bid total. For instance, the contract might call for you to be "bonded," meaning you must provide insurance that you will not screw up the job. This insurance is expensive. If you have to pay for it and don't figure its cost into your bid, you could lose money—even if you don't screw up the job.

You can find more information on legal issues in production contracts by reading Chapter 7 of my book *Desktop Video Studio Bible: Producing Video, DVD, and Websites for Profit*. But by all means, if you don't completely understand every paragraph of the contractual obligations, either abandon the bid or hire an attor-ney. If your project is the least bit artistic, low- or no-cost volunteer attorneys can be hired through Volunteer Lawyers for the Arts (www.vlany.org). Even a full-cost attorney, at between $100 to $300 per hour, is a good investment, because one or two hours can save you hundreds of thousands of tear-stained dollars.

Location

Sometimes an RFP will specify where the work must be done and where it must be delivered. Because animations are often incorporated into other works, clients are sometimes concerned with where you will produce the work, how they will come and see the work in progress, and how you will fit your work in with others in various locations.

In this Internet age, however, it is not uncommon for location to play no important role whatsoever in an RFP or contract. Many animators use "back office" labor in India or Russia without their clients even knowing. Why should they know? If the RFP makes no mention of location, you can safely ignore the need to specify where you will produce the work.

Breaking Down the RFP

In breaking down an RFP, your entire job is dedicated to figuring out how much time it's going to take you to do the job and, to a lesser extent, how much you are going to spend on materials. When you obtain these figures, you will have your *direct cost*. The easiest way to do this is to use one of the popular spreadsheet programs like Lotus or Excel. Of course, you cannot use this as your bid price, because you would not make any profit and would not get any money to pay the *indirect costs* of your business.

Direct costs include the labor required to execute the job—both your own labor and that of your employees—as well as the labor of subcontractors, rental of equipment, such as a mo-cap system, and costs of materials, like videotape, blank DVDs, and even pencils and paper. You can estimate these costs by listing all the procedures of the job in one column and then adding columns for the hourly rate of each line item, the number of hours required, and the multiplied result.

Indirect costs, also called *overhead*, include the costs of running your business during the time you are completing the job, such as your office rent, electricity, insurance, advertising, and the most expensive category of all: taxes. Don't forget to add in the time you and your administrators spend managing the company and getting clients. This cost of time is often neglected by young professionals, yielding a big negative cash-flow crisis. To determine your indirect costs, you must create a separate spreadsheet that lists all of these expenses. Your accountant can give you this list, or you can simply go through a year's worth of operation invoices to get a good annual total. Next, you divide the annual total by the number of working days in a year. (Not calendar days—I use 250, which is 50 working weeks—only two weeks off for vacations!—multiplied by five working days per week.) This gives you your operating costs per day. You will be surprised at the amount.

For a good estimate of your indirect costs, figure out how many days it will take to produce the project, and then multiply this number by your cost per days.

Once you've added your direct and indirect costs, you will know the least amount of money you should charge for the project—the amount that would result in a break-even. If you don't think the client will cough up this amount, abandon the bid.

Finally, it comes time to add your profit, the amount of money you will "take home." When you choose this amount, either in terms of dollars or a percentage of the total costs, also consider the effect of income and corporate taxes that will be levied against that cash. If you are working under a Chapter-C corporation, you will pay twice the taxes, once for the corporation and once for your personal tax. Don't charge $30,000 and think you're going to go *home* with $30,000. In some cases, it will be more like $10,000!

As a general rule, you can figure that your indirect costs and profit should be at least twice the direct costs of your project. This may sound like a lot, charging $50,000 for an animation that cost you $25,000 to produce, but once you've done the numbers, you may even be tempted to charge more.

If you are smart, you will attempt to add as much profit as you can without losing the bid. Your principal task in breaking down an RFP is to figure out how much time and materials you are going to put into the job. With the exception of printing, which usually breaks out to 50% time and 50% materials, most media production projects are labor-intensive. More than 80% is going to be spent on labor.

The Length of an RFP

The ideal RFP will be short, boiled down to the essential information you need, and easy to understand. This is not often the case, especially with government RFPs. They tend to be about 10 times longer than they need to be, usually because they are composed of *boilerplate* paragraphs. These are paragraphs that were created by a government lawyer and stored in a database from which purchasing agents cobble their RFPs. These RFPs obviously contain tons of text that's only tangentially related to your work, such as the requirement to dispose of hazardous chemicals in an environmentally acceptable manner. This one always seems to get included in anything regarding motion pictures, because some lawyer realized that film developing labs create waste chemicals. Because the relevance of these clauses most often do not apply to your work, often the RFP becomes too laborious to deal with. In some cases, it might be more economical to trash the RFP and move on to another, more profitable opportunity.

One popular misconception among artists is that the creative proposal must be as long and complicated as the RFP. This is not so. I have used a one-page proposal to respond to a 66-page RFP. I even won the job! As long as you can fulfill all the requirements of the RFP, the proposal can be any length you wish, but it should always be easy and quick to read. Avoid the common legal mumbo-jumbo of the RFP and tell your story in simple, exciting prose.

So let's assume you've done your homework and counted the hours, and you know how many man-hours it takes to do every job in your category. You know it like a Portsmouth lobsterman with a blown knee knows when it's going to rain. Where do you go from there?

Spreadsheets to Build a Budget

One of the most important elements of your proposal will be a line-item budget. This is, as far as I can determine, a somewhat rare thing to include in a creative proposal. Funny as it may seem, the majority of RFP respondents, your competitors to be exact, favor very simple budgets. Some might have only three lines—"pre-production, production, post-production," or "digitizing, animating, rendering." Some only have the bottom-line total!

Many animators think this is a good idea. They argue that their clients are not sophisticated in the technical aspects of animation and don't want the details. They say the clients are offended because all the lines of numbers and totals make them feel dumb, and that they just look at the bottom line anyway.

Yes, these statements are somewhat true. Nobody likes to read numbers for a living. Nobody *I* want to get hammered with, anyway. But if you design your spreadsheet so that the bottom-line numbers are right there at the top in bold text, you can't lose. The simple stuff is there for simple-minded clients, and the complex stuff is down below for clients who like to nitpick. If you offer the best of both worlds, you can't go wrong.

What's a Spreadsheet?

I'm an old-timer, so I like to use Lotus 123 because the complex keystrokes required to build a spreadsheet rattle out of my fingers without a thought. Most of you will be using Excel. Fine, no matter. If you don't know what a spreadsheet is and might not ever touch one but for my advice, here's why it's good to learn Excel.

A spreadsheet program allows you to easily create tables, the contents of which follow simple arithmetic rules. Here is a real-life example:

Generic Animation Budget

Task Categories	Total Estimate
1. PRE-PRODUCTION	$2,050
2. AUDIO PRODUCTION	6,650
3. ANIMATION PRODUCTION	16,145
4. POST-PRODUCTION	$1,250
Grand Total	$26,095

Tasks

1. PRE-PRODUCTION	Rate	Period	Amount	Total
Logistics				
Consultation with clients	450	Half day	1	$450
Research				
Research method of action of product	450	Half day	1	$450
Graphics Preparation				
Storyboards	15	Per panel	30	450
Casting				
Casting Narrators—3 Sample Tapes	150	Per sample	3	450
Misc. Office Expense	250	Flat	N/A	250
Pre-Production SUB-TOTAL (1.)				$2,050

2. AUDIO PRODUCTION	Rate	Period	Amount	Total
Director—Supervising	150	Per hour	4	$600
Narrator	1,000	Per session	1	1,000

	Rate	Period	Amount	Total
Stock Music Search	300	Per hour	2	600
Recording Studio—Narration	750	"	2	1,500
Recording Engineer	150	"	2	300
Audio Effects Search	100	"	2	200
Effects and Music License Fees	1,000	Flat	N/A	1,000
Audio Editing and Mixing	300	Per hour	2	600
Audio Editing Engineer	150	"	4	600
Stock Tape, CD master	250	Flat	N/A	250
Audio Production SUB-TOTAL (2.)				$6,650

3. ANIMATION PRODUCTION	Rate	Period	Amount	Total
Director—Supervising	1,200	Per day	6	$7,200
Create Models of Elements	1,000	"	2	2,000
Create Setting for Animation	1,000	"	2	2,000
Create Motions and Interactions	1,000	"	2	2,000
Test Rendering—SD	100	Per hour	4	400
Copies for Client Review	15	Each	3	45
Final Rendering	100	Per hour	16	1,600
Frame Sequence to D-5 Tape	350	"	2	700
D-5 Tape Stock (Orig. & Protection)	100	Each	2	200
Animation Production SUB-TOTAL (3.)				$16,14

4. POST-PRODUCTION	Rate	Period	Amount	Total
Director—Supervising	150	Per hour	2	$300
D-5 High Definition Editing	350	"	2	700
Backup Master Tape (D-5)	250	"	1	250
Post-Production TOTAL (4.)				$1,250

This spreadsheet is for a real animation project I completed a few years back. As you can see, the task categories (or the "bottom line") are grouped at the top, where the client can see them first. If the client isn't interested in the rest of the lines, they are easy to ignore. Usually, I put the budget at the end of my proposals, just before *my* contractual terms, such terms being really the most boring part of the proposal.

Notice that to the right of every task or task category is a text field that acts as a heading. In the task categories, this heading is the total price for that category. In the tasks, there are four headings: *Rate*, which is the cost per unit of each task, such as dollars-per-hour; *Period*, which defines what unit I am using, such as "per hour"; *Amount*, which is the number of units for each specific task, such as "6 hours"; and *Total*, which is the multiplication of *Amount* and *Rate*, unless the task is a "flat fee" task, in which the *Total* duplicates the *Rate*.

These categories and the table grid that holds them are easy to create in Lotus, Excel, or any spreadsheet program. Once you have all the task categories and tasks listed (which come from the scope and specifications of your RFP), you can start filling in the numbers.

Spreadsheets are capable of storing formulas in each of the cells. For instance, in the cell that holds the total at the end of each horizontal line, there is a formula that multiplies the *Rate* times the *Amount*. So, if I decide that I need 3 hours to search for stock music, instead of 2, I can simply type a 3 over the 2 and the number in the *Total* cell will change from 600 to 900.

At the bottom of the *Total* column for each task category, I have another formula in the last cell that says, "Total all the contents of the cells above this one in this category." The formula is actually something like sum(E7.E40), but these formulae are easy to learn and let you create boilerplate budget templates that you can use over and over again. So, when I change the amount of stock music search from 2 hours to 3, this total changes as well, automatically.

At the top of the spreadsheet, where I've summarized the contents of each subtotal in the lines below, each cell has a formula that captures the content of each task category *Total* at the bottom of each task category column. So when I change any number in the spreadsheet, these numbers change as a result. As long as all the numbers and formulae are correct, I can change the spreadsheet a million times and the Grand Total will always be accurate. In fact, this is how I "tune" a spreadsheet to come out with the exact total price I think my client will accept.

What's a Fixed-Price Budget?

Keep in mind that this spreadsheet is for a *fixed-price* budget. This means that I am making the best determination of the time and materials needed to complete the job. If I overestimate and win the bid, I get to keep the surplus. No one needs to know how much surplus I acquire, or how much loss, if I underbid. Animations with fixed, firm specifications are easily handled with fixed-price budgets, because both the client and the animator have a fixed amount of money to work with. Unless the client drastically changes the parameters of the job after it has begun, both parties know how much the project will cost.

Incidentally, if the client changes the project such that the original budget no longer applies, the animator is required to submit a "change order" or "overage request" to the client in writing, prior to beginning any extra work. Once signed, the overage request serves as a legal amendment to the contract, authorizing the animator to collect extra money when the job is done.

So, learning how to make a spreadsheet and designing one is really almost a one-time thing. In fact, you can use my sample above as your working model, because it has many of the categories and line items that a beginning animator will need. Obviously, each project is going to be a little different from the next, and my sample might not fit every RFP you get, but I think there is enough here to get you started. The prices, by the way, are not all accurate. I have done this purposely to encourage you to establish your own competitive rates.

What's a Cost-Plus Budget?

Incidentally, I have found that 95% of the clients out there accept the practice of including your overhead and profits within each line item—that is, they prefer fixed-price budgets. That's why you do not see them broken out individually above. In other words, when I select an amount for the Rate cell, I choose a figure that includes my direct and indirect costs as well as my profit. Consequently, if a client wants to adjust a budget by, say, taking out the audio production or switching from stock music to composed music, the resultant changes reflect all my costs and profit as well.

The alternative to this method is called a *cost-plus* budget. It's also referred to as a *time and materials* or *T&M budget*. This budget's rates are your direct rates as determined by the charges you get from your vendors (which, in some cases, may be audited by your client), and the rates you set based on your labor and materials costs.

In the summary portion of the cost-plus budget, two additional lines are added to the total: the *Overhead*, which is usually a simple percentage (calculated from your annualized direct costs divided by your annualized indirect costs), and the *Profit*, also a simple percentage, usually from 10 to 18%.

Most animators don't like cost-plus bids because they reveal too much about the animator's business. After all, how much profit you are making and the cost of running your shop are your private business. However, a cost-plus bid carries a major bonus: It is based on the actual time and materials you spend.

Governments, advertising agencies, and very large corporations with frequent animation needs, like movie studios, prefer cost-plus budgeting. They have the power to determine every aspect of your bid, from the direct costs, which they monitor carefully, to the profit, which they sometimes dictate.

The good thing about a cost-plus budget is that it is not fixed. If you end up actually taking 10 hours to find the right piece of stock music, you submit an invoice for that amount, based upon the rate you stated in the budget. Consequently, the cost-plus budget provides the animator with a final fee based upon the actual time and materials spent. This is particularly good when the client is fussy about quality and demands more hours, or when the client is not too sure what she wants—and requires a lot of exploratory time finding out.

You might insist on a cost-plus budget whenever you sense that a client is vague in the scope or specifications. Simply make sure that your rate is adequate, and then keep very careful records of every hour and every expenditure. Also extend the courtesy of keeping your client up to date on a regular basis, say weekly, about all costs incurred and the current total job cost.

Less Formal Bids

Often, you will get an informal bid request from a client, sometimes over the phone, that would seem to require a less formal response than I've demonstrated above. Often a client may just want a ballpark bid to use in his own internal budgeting. In such cases, you can offer a response that is equally informal, but always be aware of one important fact: It is easier to come down on a price you have given than to go up.

Therefore, it's necessary for you to maintain the discipline of making a spreadsheet for every price you give, even a ballpark figure, because someday that client will come back and want to put the ball right there in the park. On such occasions, if you have prepared a spreadsheet, saved it on your HDD, and made a copy and filed it conveniently under "Ball Park Bids" or some other file that is easy to locate, you will never be caught wondering what you bid or having bid too low.

Even on such ballpark bids, I make the spreadsheet, print it out as an Adobe Acrobat (.pdf) file, and email it to the client. The result might look too formal for the request, but the client is always impressed with my discipline and "open book" attitude that shows every element of my pricing decision.

Sell the Sizzle, Not the Steak

Once you have created a budget that establishes the limits of your time and materials, you can concentrate on the other half of your proposal, the text. You can consider the budget half to be like a piece of tasty steak, just what your client is looking for to satisfy his hunger. But a wise salesman once said, "Sell the sizzle, not the steak." In other words, excite your customer's appetite and he'll enjoy the steak.

The text part of your proposal is the sizzle. This is the part of the proposal where you must kindle the reader's imagination and entice him to enter your world with his needs.

As a creative person, you may exercise whatever style, technique, and fireworks you wish as you craft your text. Try your best to match your style to the style of the company, and yet create something unique. If the company is a creative firestarter, toss some linguistic gasoline on the flame. If the company is stodgy and conservative, tread carefully and gently push the envelope.

One idea you might employ is to explore the company's Web site and see how the webmaster expresses the company's profile. While the style of a company's site sometimes varies from the company's true nature, and outdated contents and styles proliferate, this source of style and content is often your best bet for a hint of where to begin. Often, just the effort of researching a company's site before writing a proposal can provide you with valuable insights. At the very least, you can find a copy of the company's logo and swipe it for your cover page!

The Elements of a Proposal

In addition to the budget, which we've covered, all good proposals have three additional basic elements:

1. Description
2. Schedule of Performance
3. Qualifications
4. Contractual Terms

Every RFP implies a challenge. If the client did not have a need, there would be no RFP.

As you read an RFP, try to understand the challenge that is expressed. What bottom-line result is the client requesting? Why is the client venturing to produce this media? How does the RFP address the four most important questions (message, audience, deadline, and budget), especially in terms of audience and message?

Description

You could call this part of the proposal the "description of the challenge and your approach to the solution." The "description of the challenge" is your recapitulation of the client's RFP. You include this description to prove to the client that you understand the mission. This may sound simplistic, but many RFPs are so convoluted that the challenge is not clearly apparent. Consequently, many bidders write responses to RFPs without a clue as to what the client most desires. Not wishing to blame themselves or the people who are entrusted with the task of writing the RFP, clients often find it very beneficial to interpret their challenges with intelligence and sensitivity. If you open your proposal with a quick summation of the task at hand, it tends to rank your response with immediate favor.

Obviously, if you simply rewrite the RFP in different words, you will bore, disappoint, and perhaps insult your client. Your description must be filtered through and amplified by your own creative and analytical sensibilities.

What if I came to you and said, "My foot hurts. Can you help me?" You would not reply, "Your foot hurts. I can help you." No. This would not inspire my trust in you, nor would I think you were very sympathetic. If, instead, you said, "Foot pain can be caused by stress, disease, or injury. Let me examine your foot and try to determine which of these possibilities could be the cause," then I might take off my shoe and let you have a look.

The same goes for the description of the challenge and your approach to the solution. The deeper you can understand the client's challenge and propose a logical, efficient solution, the better chance you have of winning the client's confidence and getting the contract.

As you formulate your answer, keep the budget you prepared earlier close at hand. I prefer to keep the spreadsheet open on the same computer. Often, as I formulate the solution to the challenge, I find that the solution differs from what I had assumed to be necessary in the budget. For instance, I may devise a plan that takes two days of shooting instead of the one day I had quoted in the budget. Consequently, I may work back and forth between text and numbers, attempting to solve the challenge while remaining within the target budget. This struggle sometimes becomes the core of creative thought itself, and often leads to revelations that, when carefully explained in the text, win the bid.

One recent RFP from an out-of-state client, for instance, requested that I travel to the client's headquarters to meet the client and then return later to shoot a minor video element. However, the target budget only allowed enough money for one trip. Realizing that the video was generic, with content that would remain the same regardless of the project's creative development, I proposed to shoot the video during the same trip as the initial meeting. The suggestion was a bit radical, since it meant that in the morning I would meet the client for the first time and then in the afternoon shoot their video, but the solution saved $2,000. In the end, the client passed on the suggestion, but complimented me on my effort in their behalf.

After describing the challenge and your solution, your labors are nearly done. The budget you've already completed, and the rest of the proposal may be composed of boilerplate text that can be used over and over again with minor revisions.

Schedule of Performance

The production schedule may be created with a number of computer programs like Microsoft Project, Sure Trak, and Fast Tracker, which offer elaborate methods of building complex schedules, linking tasks, and assigning personnel. A much simpler program is Project Kickstart (www.projectkickstart.com), which is perfectly designed for doing small schedules that are ideal for media production proposals. Project Kickstart is highly intuitive and guides you through creating your schedule in eight easy steps. Using this software, it will take you less than an hour to build an elegant schedule and print it out, either as a task list or as a Gantt chart. A Gantt chart is a horizontal timeline with "begin" and "end" times for each task, indicated by ends of colored lines whose length is proportionate to the task's time. When you've completed the schedule in Project Kickstart, you can select any one of 16 word processors, spreadsheets, or project management software products, and link your work to it instantly if it is installed on your computer.

Of course, you can simply type a schedule into your word processor. Be sure the schedule includes the items that the *client* should deliver to the project, along with the dates they are due. Such deliverables might include product samples, graphics, script approvals, spokespersons and of course, your payments.

Qualifications

This piece of text is like your showreel. You will write it once and then revise it frequently as your qualifications and experience grow and improve. Your qualifications "chapter" should be in three parts. Each part may be as short as a paragraph or as long as a full page. Part one should state the general philosophy of your company, its history, reputation, size, location(s), and equipment.

The next part describes the people in your company, with brief biographies of the people who will work on the project. This portion may be a lot larger if the RFP actually requests full biographies. In such a case, the qualifications chapter may require a full page and even a photograph of each individual.

The final part should list your company's significant credits and any awards or honors your company has received. In listing the credits, try to select clients who are known to be in a similar business category as your client. Don't worry too much about quoting credits from one of your client's direct competitors. Only agencies and vendors who work on *retainer* need concern themselves with *client conflicts*, and such conflicts only apply if there is a current relationship in force. So if you are not currently on retainer or working for a competitor under a long-term contract, you might just as well list the credits from such a competitor. If your clients have any problem with such a listing, they can offer to hire you exclusively.

Over the course of your career, you will create various versions of your qualifications chapter for different types of clients. If you are smart, you will keep them all in one subdirectory on your computer, labeled according to date and business category. For instance, if you are doing a lot of sports work, you might create a qualifications chapter titled QualSports.doc for proposals that highlight your sports credits, and reuse that chapter for all RFPs dealing with sports subjects. Other documents might be composed of credits with an emphasis on each of your specialties as you develop them, and a QualGeneral.doc should always be at hand for use in proposals for which you require no specific category.

Contractual Terms

When submitting a proposal, it is your hope that the client will choose to contract with you to execute the terms of your proposal. Therefore, it makes good sense to consider your proposal to be a contract, and to include whatever terms you will expect in a forthcoming agreement with the client.

These terms are best placed at the end of your proposal, kept to a minimum, and written in plain text. The terms should conclude with your company's authorized signature under the statement "Written and prepared by," followed by your company's name. Below your signature, add the phrase "Agreed and accepted to proceed by," with a line for the client to sign, a line for the date, and a final line under which is printed, "Please print name and title above."

Often, a client will accept your proposal and the contractual terms, sign the proposal, and pass a copy to the purchasing department to issue a purchase order. Other times, the client may submit your proposal to in-house legal counsel who will review your terms. Sometimes the client may request additions, deletions, or changes to your terms. Other times, the client may issue you a completely new contract. It depends on the client, but my experience has shown that most often, a well-prepared proposal with contractual terms is simply accepted as-is and the project begins.

In the next chapter, you will find more details on contracts and legal issues, but for now, know that a proposal should end with contractual terms and a place for the client to sign on the "bottom line." I can't think of a more compelling way to conclude a document that is directed to contracting work, can you?

Ideas vs. Production

In some forms of media production, such as meetings and events, the success of a proposal is based almost entirely on the creative idea or ideas presented. Each bidder spends thousands of dollars, on *spec*, to hire writers and graphic designers to create elaborate presentations of fresh new ideas. The contractor then awards the bid, presumably to the bidder with the best idea. This is an asinine way of working, and the one reason I won't work in the meeting business or submit proposals based on ideas.

Ideas are property. You don't give away property. While the custom in *idea bidding* is that the best idea wins, contractors have often been known to steal an idea from one bidder and give it to another bidder to produce. And why not? If you don't have enough pride in your ideas to demand their value prior to disclosure, why shouldn't someone value them even less and steal them?

Occasionally, a contractor of great integrity will offer to pay for proposals based on ideas. This is the only ethical way to work. The implication here is that the ideas are worth money, and the client is willing to underwrite at least a portion of that cost to get good ideas. And the contractor is very wise, because if she likes the idea of a bidder, but not the production capability, she has already established a purchase price for the idea, and can acquire it and kiss the idea's creator a guilt-free goodbye.

If you're in the business of producing meetings and events, your goose is already cooked. Your industry's client base has already devalued your most valuable asset. But if you are in the video, CD, DVD, Internet, or print trades, you still have an opportunity and even a duty to guard your industry's jewels. Don't give away your ideas!

Protecting your ideas is a principle you can uphold or reject. If you stand by this principle, you may lose a bid to someone who does not. That's what makes good character. Long ago, I chose not to give away my ideas for free. On every proposal I submit, the first page has the following notice:

"This document is essential to the business of the parties named above. It may not be copied in any form or distributed in any way to any party not named above. This document is the property of Avekta Productions Inc. Copyright [date], Avekta Productions Inc. All rights reserved, worldwide."

And whenever a potential client has violated that notice, I have pursued the case to the fullest extent of my ability.

What's Next?

You now move on to the final chapter, Chapter 12, which again brings you back to the happy struggle of learning Softimage, hands-on. In this chapter, you'll learn how to render your projects to frame sequences and thence to video or film. Tony has some terrific tutorials here and some inside tips on how to get the most from your renders in the shortest time. After all, time is money.

Chapter 12

Rendering

Okay, now that most of the hard work is done, it's finally time to output your creation. For the sake of convenience, I will use the Flying Logo project that we worked on in Chapters 4 and 6. You have many options as to how you render your final project. Some of these choices will be made for you based on the format that was determined by your client, but you still have many choices to make that will affect the speed of the render and final quality of the frames. In general, anything that improves the look of your images is likely to increase the time it takes to render them. It is impossible in one short chapter to go over all of the rendering techniques available in XSI, but I will attempt to cover some of the biggest traps and alert you to a few tips that will make your life easier.

Many concepts relating to rendering have already been covered in earlier chapters, video formats, aspect ratios and compression, and so on. Also, some of the tutorials have asked you to turn up a certain setting, with promises of further explanation later. Well, here my later explanation. As we work through the various options and tabs in the Render Settings PPG, hopefully you will begin to understand that most difficult of concepts: satisfying your artistic vision while meeting the client's deadline!

Using the Render Region

One of the most important rendering tools that XSI provides is the Render Region (shortcut key: Q). We have already used this tool to preview the look of the shaders in Chapter 6, and to examine the lighting in Chapter 10. What you perhaps didn't know is that you can copy any settings that you create in the Render Region preview to the Render Options PPG that controls the final frame rendering. In addition, the anti-aliasing quality can be adjusted with the small slider at the side of the yellow box surrounding the Render Region (see Figure 12.1). As a reminder, both the Region PPG and the Render PPG are located in the Render Module (press 3 on the keyboard), under the Render menu. For many adjustments, you will find it much more efficient to tweak the settings while watching the results update interactively in the region. Then click the Copy Options from the Region button in the Render Options PPG.

Figure 12.1 *Adjusting anti-aliasing.*

Let's start by opening a scene, drawing a render region, and opening both the Region Options PPG and the Render Options PPG. Click the lock icon in the upper-left corner of each PPG as you open them, so they don't recycle. You can double-click on the blue bar at the top of whichever window you are not using, to roll it up like a window shade. The first three tabs in the Render Options PPG don't exist in the Region Options. They have to do with render location, format, and style. We will start here.

Figure 12.2 shows the output tab. Here you specify a name and a location for your rendered frames. There are good descriptions of the various file formats in the manuals and in the help menu (click the ? button on any PPG to access context-sensitive help), so we will focus on the stuff that you will need to guarantee a good first render.

XSI must always render a sequence of images. As you will see later, you can opt to have a movie generated automatically from these frames, or you can leave the frame sequence as-is.

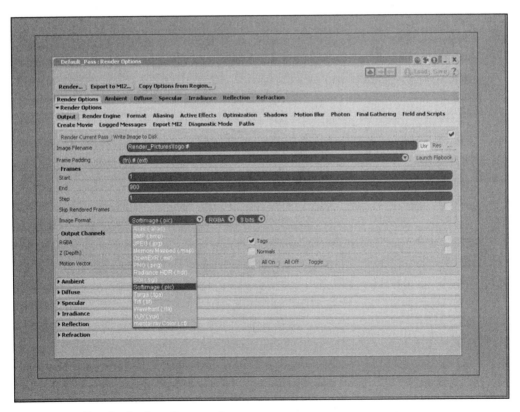

Figure 12.2 *Render Options Output tab.*

The Softimage file format uses a lossless compression codec, so that you get a high-quality image that is somewhat smaller than the standard Tiff or Targa images that you might otherwise choose for a lossless sequence.

What is *critical* is that you choose a valid path for your frame location. If the button labeled Usr is down, you can type in any path that you want. However, if the location is wrong, the render will fail. Click the Res button to show the resolved path. If XSI cannot find the location that you specify, the path will turn red. It is my suggestion that you use the "…" button to choose your render location from a browser window.

(In releases prior to XSI version 5, the Usr and Res buttons were, "Rel" and "Abs," which stand for relative and absolute, respectively.)

The "Frame Padding" option is important if you are outputting to another device that expects a specific numbering system. It is important to note that the Softimage format includes an extra period between the filename and the number, which might cause problems if you try to upload these sequences to some compositing and nonlinear editor (NLE) programs. Most compositing and editing systems will recognize the XSI format without incident if they handle Softimage still image files. Once you settle the issue of frame padding, specify the start and end frames, and click the next tab.

Choosing a Render Engine

The render engine that you choose will determine the options that are available. Mental Ray is the default engine in XSI. It is an extremely powerful raytracing engine that, with the correct settings, is capable of photorealism and distributed rendering. Most of the settings that we will be discussing later in this chapter assume that you are using this engine to render your frames. Mental Ray is available as an additional, third party rendering engine in other software packages, as well, but due to the long partnership between Mental Images and Softimage, Mental Ray is completely integrated into XSI. In fact, when you draw a render region, you are automatically using Mental Ray. See Figure 12.3.

Most of the other engines in the list allow you to output the various display modes that are available in the view windows. Choosing OpenGL or DirectX will allow you to render these realtime shader modes, assuming that you can see them correctly displayed in your interface. The sub-tabs for Ambient, Diffuse, Specular, and so on, allow you to create separate passes (image file sequences) for the various components of your shaders. (Separating and compositing passes is a vast topic that's best left for the next book.) Leave the render engine set to Mental Ray and proceed to the next tab.

The Format tab (see Figure 12.4) is somewhat self-explanatory. A good deal of discussion in this book has already been given to the topic of resolution and aspect ratio. And as I said earlier, more than likely you have been instructed to deliver in a specific format. However, if you need to make adjustments to one of the standard formats in the drop-down menu, click the Inspect Output Format button. Also, make sure you have selected the correct camera from the list, if you have created more than one. There is nothing worse than leaving a render chugging away all night long, only to discover the next morning that you rendered the whole thing from the wrong angle!

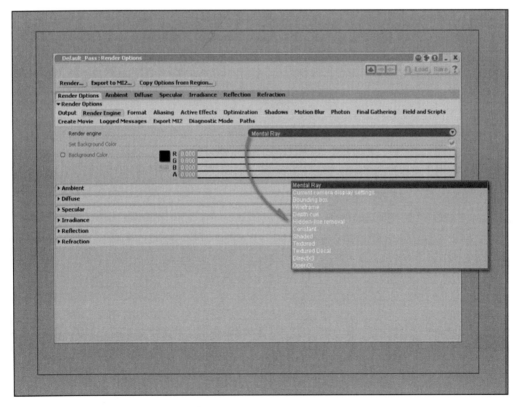

Figure 12.3 *Choosing a render engine.*

The next tab is Aliasing. This is the first tab in the Render Region page, and one that you will definitely want to adjust while watching the region window. Therefore, make the changes first in the Render Region PPG and then click the Copy Settings button in the Render Options PPG. You will notice that if you slide the little slider up and down on the edge of your render region window, the anti-aliasing values (Min and Max Sampling) will change in the Render Region PPG. Aliasing is the stair-stepping effect that you see at the boundary of dissimilar colors, especially in the diagonal borders or on the edges of objects against a transparent background when working at low resolutions. And like it or not, most video and animation is rendered at pretty low resolution compared to print files. Therefore, it is necessary to anti-alias these edges by blending in-between color values at the seams, or feathering at the edges.

The number of times this process is applied, with what precision and at what threshold level anti-aliasing begins, are the things that these mysterious sliders

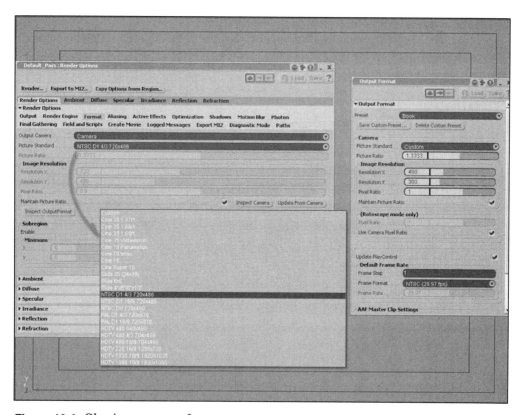

Figure 12.4 *Choosing an output format.*

control. As you can see by sliding the Min and Max sample sliders (or the window slider), the higher the values, the better the edges look. However, there is a great increase in the refresh time as you push these values higher. Part of the problem in previewing and assigning values for anti-aliasing is that the effect is not even applied unless the threshold is exceeded, and then all of a sudden the great calculations begin. A much better balance can be achieved by lowering the threshold setting thereby allowing the filtering to occur more frequently but at a lower setting.

So, before you start cranking up the Max Value past 1 or 2, try lowering the Threshold from .2 to something between .05 and .1. This will give you a gentler anti-aliasing that is applied all the time, and a much faster overall render than a high anti-aliasing that occurs only on certain frames. You should also consider that the Threshold setting allows you to anti-alias only in certain colors or only at the edge of the Alpha (transparency). See Figure 12.5.

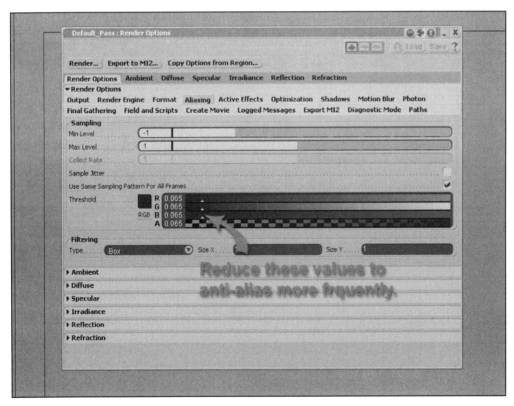

Figure 12.5 *Determining anti-aliasing frequency.*

On to the next tab. Active Effects (see Figure 12.6) is just what it sounds like. This is where you specify which effects XSI should render. It is completely reasonable to leave everything at the default settings, but if you are trying to optimize the speed of your render, uncheck anything that you are sure is not present in your scene. For example, if you aren't using lens flares or a fish-eye effect, chances are you can uncheck the Lens box. No smoke or fog? Uncheck Volume. This way, Mental Ray doesn't have to waste rendering time to check the scene and determine whether it needs to render these effects. When in doubt, try unchecking the various options in the Render Region PPG while observing the results. When you know what can be turned off, copy the settings to the Render Options.

Along with the Alias settings, the controls in the Optimization tab provide the most dramatic control over the render time of your scene. Before you start adjusting the raytracing depth, perhaps a word is in order about what raytracing is.

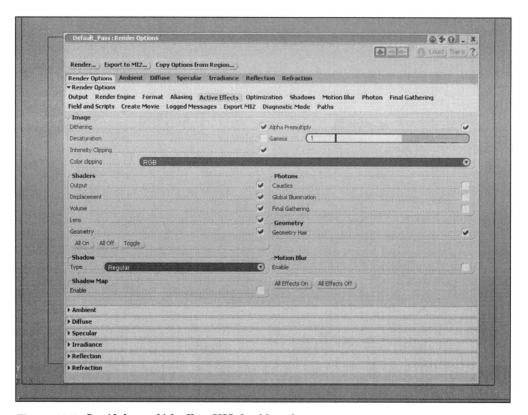

Figure 12.6 *Specify here which effects XSI should render.*

Figure 12.7 shows a simplified diagram of your eye tracing a ray of light back through a scene as the ray reflects off or is refracted through various objects. Refraction occurs each time a ray passes through the surface of an object. Depending on the index of refraction of a given material, the ray either passes straight through (index of 1.0), or is angled inward or outward (values greater than or less than 1.0) until it comes in contact with the next surface. This value is set in the Transparency tab of a material's PPG. If the material has a value greater than 0 in the Reflection tab, the ray is bounced off the surface at a given strength.

In addition to the material value, the Raytracing Depth setting in the Optimization tab defines the number of times a ray can pass through surfaces in your scene, the number of bounces it can make, and a sum total of events that will stop the calculations after that number is reached, even if there are still reflections or refractions left. This is an extremely powerful tool (see Figure 12.8). If you have no reflective or transparent surfaces in your scene, turning the values down can give you a tremendous increase in speed. By the same token, if you don't have a high enough refraction setting, you may not be able to see through a glass object to what's behind it. Glass is a material that can really slow down your renders if it is applied to many objects. For example, consider a mad scientist's laboratory with many beakers and test tubes, all transparent and reflective. You may need a high number of both reflective and refractive rays before it begins to look real.

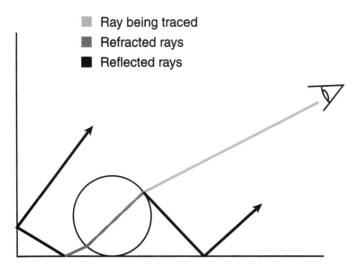

Figure 12.7 *How the human eye traces a ray of light back through a scene.*

An explanation of BSP and tile settings should be left for another book, but in essence, they control how your scene is chopped up prior to rendering. Mental Ray cuts your scene into cubes, and then checks the number of triangles in each cube before beginning the rendering process. Memory limit is important if you are worried about how memory is being allotted to rendering.

The purchase RAM capacity is not the place to scrimp when it comes to 3D rendering. If you have to micromanage your memory resources during renders, you will end up in trouble. If too little memory is allotted, you will find yourself paging to the hard drive. On the other hand, if you don't have the available RAM, you will probably have trouble with your system resources. The default setting of 768MB assumes you have about 1GB of RAM installed on your computer.

Finally, perhaps one of the most overlooked optimization settings is the Face mode. If you have no transparent materials and no holes cut into any of your surfaces, why should you waste time rendering the insides of your objects? That may sound obvious, but this is a simple step that is frequently ignored. Take the case of

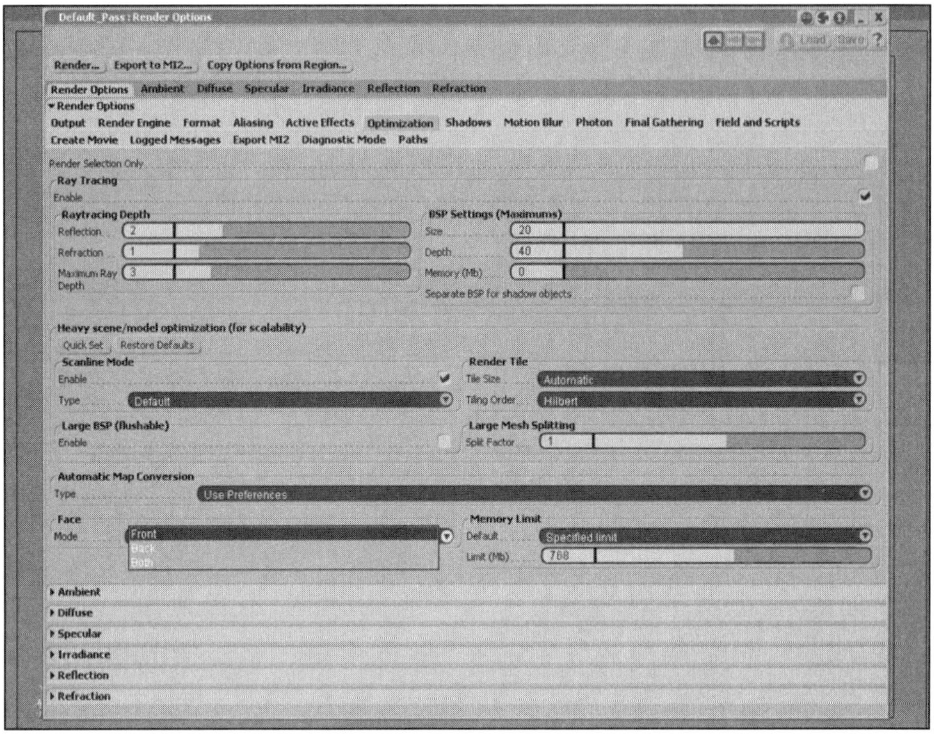

Figure 12.8 *Using the Optimization tab.*

our shield logo from Chapters 4 and 6. The logo includes text objects, and the shield. They all spin around, but we never see inside any of these objects. By specifying, "front faces only," you will cut the math in half.

We will skip over the Shadow, Motion Blur, and Photon tabs. If you are using shadow maps on any of your lights, enable the checkbox on the Shadow page before rendering your scene. If you wish to render with motion blur, check the tab on that page. We looked at Final Gathering in Chapter 10, so that brings us to the Create Movie page. If you wish to generate a QuickTime movie automatically, check the Create Movie box and select a location for the creation of your movie file.

The other movie format is an Avid Media file format. If you are outputting media for one of the Avid editing programs, you can use this format. You may also use the Avid QuickTime or Meridian codec (downloadable from the Avid site) to output media that is compatible. The QuickTime codecs that are available to you will depend on the other software that you have installed on your computer. If you

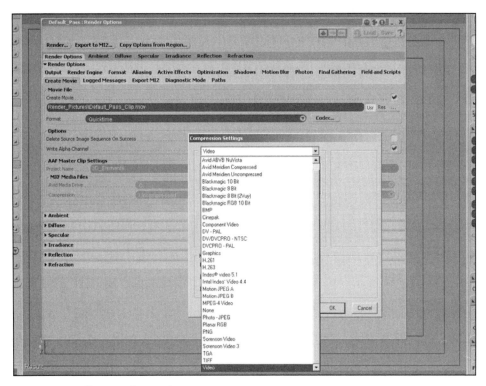

Figure 12.9 *Compression settings.*

want an uncompressed, lossless movie, I would recommend setting the Animation codec to Best Quality. Save your scene.

The last rendering topic that I would like to address is that of logged messages. You can render your frames from either inside or outside XSI. In either case, the Logged Messages tab, as shown in Figure 12.10, allows you to determine the type of feedback that you get during the render process. You can specify a destination for saved log files by accessing File > Preferences > Scripting. If you render from the render PPG or by choosing Render > Render > Current Pass, the messages appear in the information bar at the bottom of the XSI interface.

When rendering with Mental Ray, XSI automatically accesses all processors in your current machine (up to four with the Advanced License). If you wish to use additional processors on other computers on your local network, make sure that you have installed the Render Only version of the software on each machine. Also, you must edit the .ray3hosts file. Simply open the file and add the names of all machines other than the server. This is documented well in the "Distributed Rendering" section of the XSI Help files.

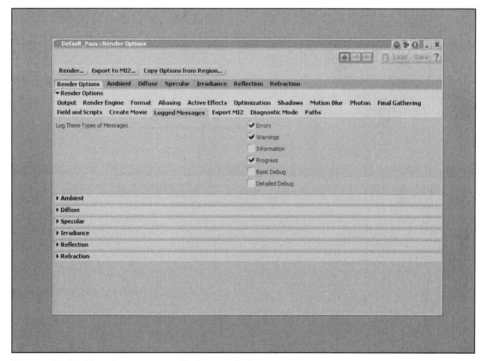

Figure 12.10 *Logging messages during rendering.*

EXERCISE 12.1: Distributed Rendering

Professional animation facilities employ more than one computer in the process of rendering large sequences for commercials, feature films, or television programs. The computers comprise what is called a "render farm." If you have more than one computer, you can build your own render farm, by networking the computers and installing the appropriate software. Rendering externally produces an overall faster output and a conservation of RAM on your host machine.

1. If you choose to save some RAM by rendering externally, save your scene file after setting all of the desired render options.
2. Make sure you have transferred any settings you were experimenting with from the render region PPG.
3. Close SOFTIMAGE|XSI.
4. Use My_Computer or Windows Explorer to navigate to the Scenes folder in your XSI database. You should have an XSI Batch Render Icon on your desktop from the installation.

   If not, create one from C:\Softimage\XSI_5.0\Application\bin \scriptxsi.bat.
5. Simply drag and drop the scene file (see Figure 12.11) on top of the XSI Batch Render icon. A command prompt window opens and the batch render script executes.

   Depending on the level of feedback you requested in the Logged Messages tab, you may see a list of completed frames or actual progress reports on each frame (see Figure 12.12).

   View any sequence of images using the Flipbook utility, which you can access from the Start menu, if XSI is not running, or from the Playback button in the XSI interface (see Figure 12.13).

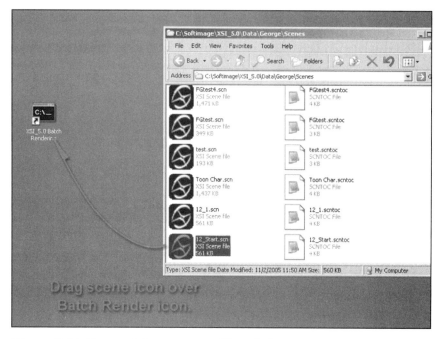

Figure 12.11 *Drag and drop your scene file to the icon.*

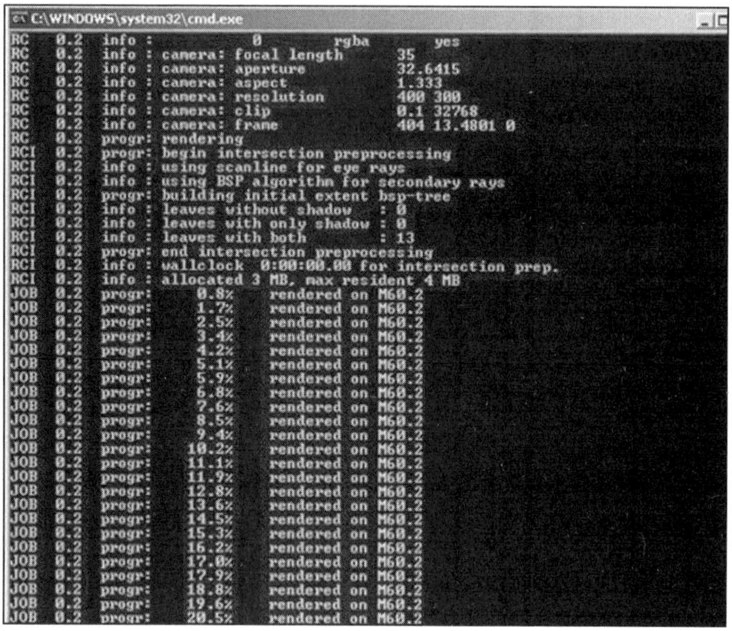

Figure 12.12 *Viewing the logged messages.*

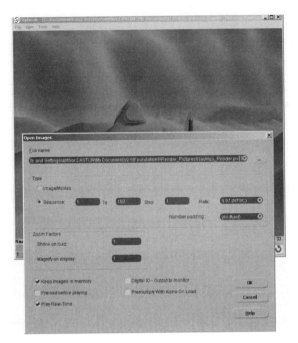

Figure 12.13 *You can use Flipbook to play frame sequences.*

It's a Wrap!

Finally, you have come to the end of everything I have to offer you in this book. You have learned how to obtain an entry level learning position or internship, and to use that position to learn the professional expectations of your craft. While interning, you started building your show reel, using tutorials from this book to customize examples of your skills.

Using your showreel, you learned how to convert your internship to a full-time job and how to establish an ethical method of working and serving your employer. Hopefully, you spent some of the extra cash you made in that full-time job to buy your own computer and Softimage software. If so, perhaps you moved from a salaried job to the independent role of a business owner.

As a business owner, you might have employed the skills demonstrated in this book to identify and pitch a growing list of clients that come back to your shop again and again. That would certainly have provided you with enough income to grow your business in obtaining more workstations and to have provided opportunities to other young artists moving up their own ladders of success.

And then again, maybe you've just bought this book, skipped to the last pages to see how it all ends, and you haven't done any of these things, yet. If so, please don't be afraid to take that first step. Too many people buy books like this and never follow the lessons or do the work. You have here, in your hands, the key to your future. All you have to do is put it into the lock of your ambition and turn it a minimum of effort. I hope you will.

And if you do, perhaps you too, will be lucky, like me, to enjoy more than two decades of work where you honestly enjoyed every day.

 You can say that again, my son!

My poor dad worked the last 15 years of his career hating every day of it. Imagine—because if you're the kind of person who reads this book, it is likely you are the farthest thing from a person who would endure 15 years of labor you hated—imagine what it must be like to wake up Monday morning and have to drag yourself through a 40-hour work week, hating every hour of it.

Know this, dear reader; if most men (and women) lead lives of quiet desperation, we, professional artists, are the very rare few who lead lives of joyous celebration. True, we have to pay the price — long hours, sometimes low pay, sometimes difficult clients, but ah, the pure fun of creating reality like minor gods. Pay your dues, try to be the best, always keep your mind open to new ideas, and never forget to spare a little time every day to sell yourself.

If you follow this advice, you might even be lucky enough to find a few other people of like mind, with whom you can work and play. These people will become your team. Over the years, as team members come and go, you will hone all your skills together, and share both your triumphs and failures. I'm sure I speak for all the members of my team for this book (XSI animation instructor, Tony Johnson, cover artist Bryan Eppeheimer, the staffs of Avid and Course Publishing) when I say that we all want you to get right to work this very minute and make the most of what we have created for you.

And if you ever see us around the industry, working or lecturing or just hanging out, come on up and introduce yourself. Tell us how far up the ladder you climbed and how much enjoyment you get from your work. Make our day!

Index